The Politics of Thatcherism

edited by
Stuart Hall
and
Martin Jacques

LAWRENCE AND WISHART
in association with Marxism Today
LONDON

Lawrence and Wishart Limited
39 Museum Street
London WC1A 1LQ

This edition first published May 1983
Reprinted June 1983

Photoset in North Wales by
Derek Doyle & Associates, Mold, Clwyd
Printed and bound in Great Britain by
The Camelot Press Ltd, Southampton

Contents

Preface

This book is based on a series of articles that have appeared in *Marxism Today*, the theoretical and discussion journal of the Communist Party, from 1979 onwards, on the causes, nature and consequences of Thatcherism. The contributions fall into three main categories. Firstly, there are those which were originally published in *Marxism Today* and have been only slightly modified for the book: the original date of publication is given in brackets. These are: Martin Jacques, 'Thatcherism: Breaking out of the Impasse' (October 1979); Ian Gough, 'Thatcherism and the Welfare State' (July 1980); Stuart Hall, 'The "Little Caesars" of Social Democracy' (April 1981); Martin Kettle, 'The Drift to Law and Order' (October 1981); Bob Rowthorn, 'The Past Strikes Back' (January 1982); Tom Nairn, 'Britain's Living Legacy' (July 1982); Robert Gray, 'The Falklands Factor' (July 1982); Lynne Segal, 'The Heat in the Kitchen' (January 1983) and Eric Hobsbawm, 'Falklands Fallout' (January 1983). Secondly, there are those which have been more substantially re-written, though still being based, to a greater or lesser extent, on the original article in *Marxism Today*. These are: Stuart Hall, 'The Great Moving Right Show' (January 1979); David Currie, 'World Capitalism in Recession' (April 1980); Steve Iliffe, 'Dismantling the Health Service' (July 1980); Jon Bloomfield, 'Labour's Long Haul' (December 1980); Jean Gardiner, 'Women, Recession and the Tories' (March 1981) and Andrew Gamble, 'The Impact of the SDP' (March 1982). Finally, there are those which are almost entirely new. These are: Andrew Gamble, 'Thatcherism and Conservative Politics'; Tony Lane, 'The Tories and the Trade Unions: Rhetoric and Reality' and Michael Bleaney, 'Conservative Economic Strategy'.

The index was prepared by Sally Townsend.

Introduction

The essays in this volume cover the first two phases of 'Thatcherism': from the conquest of the Tory Party in 1974 and the period of intense political propaganda and preparation for power, to the electoral success of 1979 and the disastrous first period in government. 'Thatcherism' appeared at a historic conjuncture, where three trends converged: first, the point where the long-term structural decline of the British economy synchronized with the deepening into recession of the world capitalist economy; second, in the wake of the collapse of the third post-war Labour government and the disintegration of the whole social democratic consensus which had provided the framework of British politics since 1945; third, at the resumption of the 'new Cold War', renewed at a frighteningly advanced point in the stockpiling of nuclear weaponry, and with Britain sliding, under Thatcherite inspiration, into a mood of intense, bellicose, patriotic fervour.

'Thatcherism' has often been regarded by the left as simply the old Conservative enemy in suburban disguise. Its rise – it is assumed – can be attributed to the natural swing of the electoral pendulum. As soon as the failures of monetarist policies became apparent, it was assumed that the working classes would come running back to the shelter of the tried and tested ways of post-war Labour governments: incomes policies, corporate wage bargaining, neo-Keynesian economic management, etc. These assumptions almost certainly underestimate the novelty of 'Thatcherism' as a political force, the 'radicalism' of its political strategy, the long-term shifts and reversals which it regards as its historic mission, and the degree to which the 'natural' swings and roundabouts of the electoral pendulum, along with many of the other regular rhythms of post-war politics, have been deeply interrupted. Two episodes – one at the beginning, the other towards the end of Thatcher's first administration – provide evidence enough. The 1979 election marked the penetration of Thatcherite appeal deep into the very heartlands of traditional Labour support. The Falklands crisis demonstrated Thatcherism's capacity to exploit the appeal of 'Nation' and to manipulate the symbols of an imperialist nostalgia in a patriotic mobilization which cut across traditional political allegiences. Both indicated that the Thatcherism which emerged from the 1970s was a novel and exceptional political force.

Of course, political formations do not arise out of thin air. Thatcherism has deep roots in the political traditions of the right. For example, there were the free marketeers who rejoiced with Churchill in 1951 at the 'bonfire' of wartime egalitarian controls; and the backwoods of the Party who, in the era of permissiveness, regularly turned out at Party conferences to embarass the front-bench modernizers by their faithful support for hanging, law-and-order, censorship, the virtues of competition and racist programmes. 'Powellism' in the late 1960s, the Selsdon Man policies with which Mr Heath went to the country in 1970, the gospel of Sir Keith Joseph, which – John the Baptist like – prepared the way for the advent of Mrs Thatcher in the mid-1970s – were all anticipations of Thatcherism. They all addressed populist elements and recidivist instincts inside and outside the party. They attempted to construct them into a moral-political force. They rallied this constituency against the neo-Keynesians, creeping collectivists and fellow-travelling social democrats *everywhere* – installed, as they saw it, in positions of influence within the state apparatuses, inside the power bloc and lurking in the Tory Party itself. Thatcherism was grafted onto this resentment of the 'little non-political person in the street' against the big, corporate battalions – 'big government' *and* 'big unions' – which characterized the *statism* of the social democratic era. It managed, by the end of the 1970s, to identify itself with 'the people' when they could be defined in this way. Its novelty lies, in part, in the success with which this 'populist' appeal was then orchestrated with the imposition of authority and order. It managed to marry the gospel of free market liberalism with organic patriotic Toryism. 'Free market, strong state, iron times': an authoritarian populism.

The historic mission of Thatcherism has not been to win this or that election – astute as it has been at mastering the ebb and flow of the opinion polls. It is much more ambitious than that. Its project has been to reverse the whole postwar drift of British society, to roll back the historic gains of the labour movement and other progressive forces, and to force-march the society, vigorously, into the past. These aims give some indication of the *radicalism* of its project. It opened a struggle on all fronts, the like of which has not been seen – from left or right – since the War.

The exceptional character and consequent disasters of the years of Mrs Thatcher's administration are documented in the essays which follow. In ideological and political terms, Thatcherism has gone some way towards substituting a new, reactionary kind of 'common sense'. It has made a series of damaging raids on the social democratic consensus. The main reference points of the postwar political settlement – already weakened and eroded in fact under successive Labour governments – have been contested *in principle*. One after another the old landmarks – full employment, welfare state support, equality of opportunity, the 'caring' society, neo-Keynesian economic management, corporatist incomes policies – have been reversed. In their place a new public philosophy has been constructed, rooted in the open affirmation of 'free market values' – the market as the measure of everything – and reactionary 'Victorian' social values – patriarchalism, racism and imperialist nostalgia. The whole shift towards a more authoritarian type of regime has been grounded in the search for 'Order' and the cry for 'Law' which arises among many ordinary people in times of crisis and upheaval – and which has been dovetailed into the imposition of authority from above. There seems little doubt that, in the absence of a credible alternative, this reactionary common sense has made significant headway.

In the management of capitalism, the outstanding achievement of Thatcherism has been to disorganize the opposition. It has weakened and undermined the defensive organizations of the labour movement, exploited the unpopularity of the trade unions, threatened its strongest centres of resistance (for example in the shop stewards movements), used the 'dull compulsion' of unemployment to compel workers to accept the 'realism' of low wage settlements and the dole queue. It has apparently withdrawn the state from frontal

engagement with different sectors of, especially, public sector
workers, whilst supporting the struggle by management to
regain control and restore profitability from a position just
beyond the line of fire. It has, in these and other ways, altered
the whole post-war balance of social forces.

On the economic front, it has savaged public expenditure and
the welfare state, put the economy into the monetarist strait
jacket and come close to putting the 'fight against inflation'
above 'unemployment' in the list of public priorities. Lower rates
of inflation have been achieved at the cost of the destruction of
Britain's industrial productive capacity and a level of economic
activity which stubbornly refuses to rise a point or two from the
sea-floor. The opening of the gates to unrestricted foreign
competition and investment and the concentration of currency
questions and the manipulation of interest rates is what now
stands in the place of a general economic strategy. The laws of
the market have taken their savage toll in the reappearance of
mass unemployment. For much of the postwar period the left
assumed that, whoever was in power, modern capitalism
inevitably required a 'corporatist' style of management.
Advanced capitalism, it was assumed, could not survive without
a large public sector, a welfare state, sensible bargaining
arrangements between capital and labour, full employment, etc.
And this, it was assumed, tended to make Labour-style
governments the 'natural' managers of capitalism – give or take
the odd swing of the electoral pendulum – and some sort of state
management of economic policy inevitable. Mrs Thatcher, no
doubt with the US rather than European capitalism in mind, set
her face resolutely against the whole inevitable corporatist drift –
and has attempted to stabilize the management of a modern
capitalism on the basis of a new relationship between capital,
labour and the state.

It is difficult to call an economic strategy which results in
some four million unemployed and the shutting down of
substantial sectors of the economy, a 'success'. In fact,
Thatcherism's success – in general – is difficult to estimate. In
the later stages of its first administration it was far from
commanding a numerical electoral majority – though the
divisions within the left and between the left and centre-right
formations rendered them incapable of maximizing on this. With
the exception of the Falklands euphoria, there was no later

popular groundswell: though Thatcherism retained its stubborn popularity amongst some sectors of the population who could expect no material gain from it, and its populist themes continued to have a deep resonance even amongst anti-Thatcher supporters.

In fact, it may be that Thatcherism is not finally to be judged in electoral terms – important as these moments of mobilization are in the political process. Rather, it should be judged in terms of its success or failure in disorganizing the labour movement and progressive forces, in shifting the terms of political debate, in reorganizing the political terrain and in changing the balance of political forces in favour of capital and the right. In that sense, Thatcherism has already achieved a great deal. On the other hand, it has shifted the terrain without solving the problems. It has provoked a rupture – but failed to resolve it. As a result, regeneration will continue to be a long, contested and painful process. There is, indeed, no guarantee that this will have exhausted the repertoire of the radical right. Alternatively, at some point something worse, something more authoritarian could follow. On the other hand, Thatcherism with its simple moral pieties, its reactionary world-view, its money supply simplifications, could well give way to more centre-right corporatist strategies for capitalism. But such developments would take place on altered political territory, with the left in disarray, the defences of the labour movement weakened, the progressive social movements demoralized and the overall balance of political forces tilted much more favourably towards a hegemony of the right. In that sense, Thatcherism could 'lose' – and still succeed in fulfilling its political mission.

The gaps, limits and internal contradictions of Thatcherism as a political formation are constantly exposed by its very commitment to full-frontal contestation. The question is whether a credible, alternative political force can be constructed equal to the historic tasks which confront the country at this juncture and capable of matching Thatcherism on the many fronts on which it has engaged. In that context, Thatcherism is a problem, not just 'for' the left, but *of* the left. Its rise was predicated on Labourism's decline. It seized on precisely those points of popular consciousness which Labourism had abandoned. It exploited the internal contradictions which the social democratic corporatist strategy of successive Labour governments had generated. In the face of industrial struggles which fail to generalize themselves for society as a whole, which are as much for the low-paid, the unskilled, the black or women workers as they are for the advanced sectors of skilled, white, male labour, it is possible to represent the trade unions as a sectional interest. In circumstances where the commitment to 'welfare' fails to redistribute wealth or to increase real changes in the balance of power, it is possible to make the return to possessive individualism and competitiveness look like 'common sense'. In conditions where benefits are administered by a gigantic state bureaucracy and the content and forms of decision-making remain deeply undemocratic, individualism and 'freedom' can be made to appear attractive. Thatcherism did not advance into an empty space. It invaded and seized territory from a Labourism which had lost its popular-democratic connections and which appeared increasingly as, simply, a less and less efficient or convincing manager of capitalist crisis.

But it is not only in short-term ways that Thatcherism capitalized on Labour's failures. It has been working on long-term trends affecting the labour movement, some aspects of which were discussed in *The Forward March of Labour Halted?* (E.J. Hobsbawm et al, London 1981). The changing composition of the working class — a process much acclerated by the crisis itself — with the decline of those sections on which the labour movement has historically rested and by which it has been moulded; the failure of the labour movement to 'change with the times' in terms of communication and culture; Thatcherism has coincided with and exploited these longer-term tendencies which themselves necessitate a major political, social, cultural and ideological renewal of the labour movement. The new social forces and movements, which have put a set of profound new questions on the political agenda, have not been adequately combined with an older style of class politics. Nor, for the most part, have they been allowed to have a sufficiently transformatory impact on the traditional organizations and programmes of the left. This is the kind of mistake which Thatcherism, with its attention to the centrality of women's domestic role, the policing of black communities and the frontal engagement with the peace movement, has not committed. In destroying the old political mould, Thatcherism has unwittingly allowed many of these contradictory forces and pressures to play more freely into the political backyard of the left and the labour movement, precipitating its own fracturing and internal crisis.

Paradoxically, these longer term problems make Thatcherism not only a grave threat for the left, but also a considerable opportunity. The transformation of the left could not take place so long as its traditional elements and relationships remained credible and in place. But now transformation is the only real and practical alternative for the left. It will, of course, be prolonged and painful. The unity of skilled and unskilled, of employed and unemployed, of whites and blacks, of men and women, of the new public sectors with the traditional private sector struggles will not be 'given' by circumstances. And such alliances cannot occur without painful readjustments and without a profound reshaping of the traditional demands and programmes of the left. There is no guarantee that, because these opportunities exist, they will be seized or successful. But this is in fact the real nature of the 'struggle against Thatcherism': a struggle *against* the danger posed by the radical right which is at the same moment a struggle for the renewal of the politics of the left, the labour movement and its allies.

It is necessary to confront, soberly and without false illusions, the nature of the reversals which Thatcherism has already imposed on the left. But it is also necessary to understand its weaknesses. Its 'popularity' is as much due to the lack of an alternative as the product of its own achievements. After all, monetarism's most outstanding success is to get the figures for the unemployed up to the four million mark – and unemployment *is*, once again, regarded as the principal issue facing the country. That cannot automatically produce a popular surge for Thatcherism – unless there is no other available rallying point. Thatcherism's strength reflects the labour movement's weaknesses. But the weaknesses of Thatcherism can also be the labour movement's strengths. And it is highly vulnerable to attack – as the campaign against Cruise missiles, for one, has clearly demonstrated.

In addition, as we have pointed out, though Thatcherism has proved to be an effective, populist force, it continues to be a minority one. The divisions of the left enhance its appearance of popularity, unity and coherence. The task of the left, in these circumstances, is not simply to pose the alternative – but to concert the anti-Thatcher forces. This is our most crucial task. But this does not consist simply of a defensive gathering of forces around the old strategies, but the construction of a new political force, the building of a new network of alliances. Specifically, this requires two things, which must be seen as interconnected. Firstly, it means the kind of *transformation* of the labour movement we referred to above. Secondly, it requires the construction by the labour movement of the broadest possible set of alliances against Thatcherism, involving, in the initial instance, possibly quite modest objectives.

I   The Background

Stuart Hall

The Great Moving Right Show

No one seriously concerned with the development of left political strategies in the present situation can afford to ignore the 'swing to the right' which is taking place. We may not yet fully understand its extent, specific character, causes or effects. There is still some debate as to whether it is likely to be short-lived or long-term, a movement of the surface or something more deeply lodged in the body politic. But the tendency is hard to deny. It no longer looks like a temporary swing of the pendulum in political fortunes. Indeed, it would be wrong to identify the rise of the radical right solely with the success in the political party stakes of Mrs Thatcher and the hard-edged cronies she has borne with her into high office inside the Conservative Party. Mrs Thatcher has given the 'swing to the right' a powerful impetus and a distinctive personal stamp, but the deeper movement which finds in her its personification has — when properly analysed — a much longer trajectory. It has been well installed — a going concern — since the late 1960s. It has developed through a number of different phases. First, the 'backlash' against the revolutionary ferment of '1968' and all that. Then, the bold, populist bid by Mr Powell — speaking over the heads of the party factions to 'the people', helping to construct 'the people' in their most patriotic, racist, constitutional disguise. Then — borrowing the clothes of his opponent, in the best Tory tradition — Mr Heath: a politician instinctively of the soft centre, but not averse, in the anxiety-ridden days of the early 1970s to going to the country with a programme to restore 'Selsdon Man' — a close cousin of Neanderthal Man — at the centre of British politics. It was this Heath version of the backlash — a chillingly reactionary spectre in its own way — which the miners and others stopped in its tracks. But they did not cut short the underlying movement.

There now seems little doubt that, as we moved through the 1970s, the popular mood shifted decisively against the left. This fact was mirrored in the decline of Mr Callaghan's government. As Labour lost parliamentary strength, so it has drifted deep into the ideological territory of the right, occupying with panache many of the positions only just evacuated by the right. It was Labour, not the Conservatives, which applied the surgical cut to the welfare state. And there was Mr Healey's not wholly unexpected conversion to orthodox monetarism and fiscal restraint – tutored by the IMF and the oil price. In this climate of austerity, Keynes has been decently buried; the right has re-established its monopoly over 'good ideas'; 'capitalism' and 'the free market' have come back into common usage as terms of positive approval.

And yet the full dimensions of this precipitation to the right still lacks a proper analysis on the left. The crisis continues to be read by the left from within certain well-entrenched, largely unquestioned assumptions. Our illusions remain intact, even when they clearly no longer provide an adequate analytic framework. Certainly, there is no simple, one-to-one correspondence between a 'correct' analysis and an 'effective' politics. Nevertheless, the failure of analysis cannot be totally unrelated to the obvious lack of political perspective which now confronts the left.

In spite of this there are still some who welcome the crisis, arguing that 'worse means better'. The 'sharpening of contradictions', comrades, together with the rising tempo of the class struggle, will eventually guarantee the victory of progressive forces everywhere. Those who hold such a position may enjoy untroubled nights; but they have short political memories. They forget how frequently in recent history the 'sharpening of contradictions' has led to settlements and solutions which favoured capital and the right rather than the reverse.

Then there are those who dismiss the advance of the right as 'mere ideology'. Ideology, as we know, is not 'real' and so cannot become a material factor, let alone a political force. We have only to wait until the *real* economic forces exert their absolute determinacy, and then all this ideological vapour will be blown away ... Yet another common response is an extension of this last position. It argues that the current 'swing to the right' is only the simple and general expression of every economic recession. On this view, there are no significant differences between the present and any other variant of Tory philosophy. 'Thatcherism', 'Baldwinism', etc – each is only a name for the same phenomenon: the permanent, unchanging shape of reactionary ideas. What is the point of drawing fine distinctions?

Such arguments are especially characteristic of a certain hard-headed response from the 'hard' left. All this analysis, it is implied, is unnecessary. The committed will not waste time on such speculations, but get on with the job of 'engaging in the real struggle'. In fact, this last is a position which neglects everything that is specific and particular to this historical conjuncture. It is predicated on the view that a social formation is a simple structure, in which economic conditions will be immediately, transparently and indifferently translated on to the political and ideological stage. If you operate on the 'determining level', then all the other pieces of the puzzle will fall into place. The idea that we should define a conjuncture as the coming together of often distinct though related contradictions, moving according to different tempos, but condensed in the same historical moment, is foreign to this approach. The name of Lenin is frequently and reverently invoked in these circles. Yet it precisely neglects Lenin's graphic reminder that 1917 was 'an extremely unique historical situation', in which 'absolutely dissimilar currents, absolutely heterogeneous class interests, absolutely contrary political and social strivings have merged ... in a strikingly "harmonious" manner' (*Letters From Afar*, No. 1). Above all, it takes for granted what needs to be explained – and is in no sense simple or obvious: namely, how a capitalist economic recession (economic), presided over by a social democratic party with mass working-class support and organized depth in the trade unions (politically) is 'lived' by increasing numbers of people through the themes and representations (ideologically) of a virulent, emergent 'petty-bourgeois' ideology. These contradictory features of the present crisis are absorbed into some orthodox analysis only at considerable cost. The ideology of the radical right is less an 'expression' of economic recession than the recession's condition of existence. Ideological factors have effects on and for the social formation as a whole – including effects *on* the economic crisis itself and how it is likely to be resolved, politically.

We also encounter variants of 'revolutionary optimism' as a counter to what is considered to be exaggerated 'revolutionary pessimism'. The left, it is said, will rise again, as it has done before. We should look for the points of resistance — the class struggle continues! Of course, in one sense, they are right. We must not underestimate the possibilities of struggle and resistance. We must look behind the surface phenomena. We must find the points of intervention. But, on the other hand, if we are to be effective, politically, it can only be on the basis of a serious analysis of things as they are, not as we would wish them to be. Gramsci once enjoined those who would be politically effective to turn their thoughts 'violently' towards the present *as it is*. Whistling in the dark is an occupational hazard not altogether unknown on the British left. Gramsci's slogan is old, but it contains the essence of the matter none the less: 'Pessimism of the intelligence, optimism of the will.'

Finally, there is the long-awaited threat of 'fascism'. There is a sense in which the appearance of organized fascism on the political stage seems to solve everything for the left. It confirms our best-worst suspicions, awakening familiar ghosts and spectres. Fascism and economic recession together seem to render transparent those connections which most of the time are opaque, hidden and displaced. Away with all those time-wasting theoretical speculations! The Marxist guarantees are all in place after all, standing to attention. Let us take to the streets. This is *not* an argument against taking to the streets. Indeed, the direct interventions against the rising fortunes of the National Front — local campaigns, anti-fascist work in the unions, trades councils, women's groups, the mobilization behind the Anti-Nazi League, the counter-demonstrations, above all Rock Against Racism (one of the timeliest and best constructed of cultural interventions, repaying serious and extended analysis) — constitute one of the few success stories of the conjuncture. But it *is* an argument against the satisfactions which sometimes flow from applying simplifying analytic schemes to complex events. What we have to explain is a move toward 'authoritarian populism' — an exceptional form of the capitalist state which, unlike classical fascism, has retained most (though not all) of the formal representative institutions in place, and which at the same time has been able to construct around itself an active popular consent. This undoubtedly represents a decisive shift in the balance of forces, and the National Front has played a 'walk-on' part in this drama. It has entailed a striking weakening of democratic forms and initiatives; but not their suspension. We miss precisely what is specific to *this* exceptional form of the crisis of the capitalist state by mere name-calling.

An Organic Crisis?

The swing to the right is part of what Gramsci called an 'organic' phenomenon:

> A crisis occurs, sometimes lasting for decades. This exceptional duration means that uncurable structural contradictions have revealed themselves ... and that, despite this, the political forces which are struggling to conserve and defend the existing structure itself are making efforts to cure them within certain limits, and to overcome them. These incessant and persistent efforts ... form the terrain of the conjunctural and it is upon this terrain that the forces of opposition organize (Gramsci, *Prison Notebooks*, p. 179).

Gramsci insisted that we must get the 'organic' and 'conjunctural' aspects of the crisis into a proper relationship. What defines the 'conjunctural' – the immediate terrain of struggle – is not simply the given economic conditions, but precisely the 'incessant and persistent' efforts which are being made to defend and conserve the *status quo*. If the crisis is deep – 'organic' – these efforts cannot be merely defensive. They will be *formative*: aiming at a new balance of forces, the emergence of new elements, the attempt to put together a new 'historic bloc', new political configurations and 'philosophies', a profound restructuring of the state and the ideological discourses which construct the crisis and represent it as it is 'lived' as a practical reality: new programmes and policies, pointing to a new result, a new sort of 'settlement' – 'within certain limits'. These new elements do not 'emerge': they have to be constructed. Political and ideological work is required to disarticulate old formations, and to rework their elements into new ones. The 'swing to the right' is not a reflection of the crisis: it is itself a *response* to the crisis. In what follows I consider some aspects of that response, concentrating particularly on the neglected political and ideological dimensions.

Economic Crisis

We must examine first the precipitating conditions. These are the result of a set of discontinuous but related histories. In economic terms, Britain's structural industrial and economic weakness emerged in the immediate aftermath of the postwar boom. The 1960s were marked by the oscillations between recession and recovery, with a steady underlying deterioration. These effectively destroyed the last remnants of the 'radical programme' on the basis of which Wilson won power in 1964, and to which he tried to harness a new social bloc. By the end of the 1960s, the economy had dipped into full-scale recession – slumpflation – which sustained the exceptional 'Heath course' of 1971-4, and its head-on collisions with organized labour. By the mid-1970s, the economic parameters were dictated by a synchronization between capitalist recession on a global scale, and the crisis of capital accumulation specific to Britain – the weak link in the chain. Domestic politics has thus been dominated by crisis management and containment strategies: dovetailed through an increasingly interventionist state, intervening to secure the conditions of capitalist production and reproduction. The dominant strategy had a distinctively corporatist character – incorporating sections of the working class and unions into the bargain between state, capital and labour, the three 'interests'. Crisis management has drawn successively on different variants of the same basic *repertoire*: incomes policy, first by consent, then by imposition; wage restraint; social contracting. The 'natural' governor of this crisis has been the party of social democracy in power: Labour. This last factor has had profound effects in disorganizing and fragmenting working class responses to the crisis itself.

At the ideological level, however, things have moved at a rather different tempo; in certain respects they predate the economic aspects. Many of the key themes of the radical right – law and order, the need for social discipline and authority in the face of a conspiracy by the enemies of the state, the onset of social anarchy, the 'enemy within', the dilution of British stock by alien black elements – had been well articulated before the full dimensions of the economic recession were revealed. They emerged in relation to the radical movements and political polarizations of the 1960s, for which '1968' must stand as a convenient, though inadequate, notation. Some of these themes got progressively translated to other fronts as the confrontation with organized labour, and military resistance developed during the Heath interregnum. For the constitution of the principle thematics of the radical right, this must be seen as a formative moment. (We have attempted a fuller analysis of this moment elsewhere: the chapters on the 'Exhaustion of Consent' and 'Towards the Exceptional State' in *Policing the Crisis*, Hall, Clarke, Critcher, Jefferson and Roberts, London 1978).

The Radical Right

The radical right does not therefore appear out of thin air. It has to be understood in direct relation to alternative political formations attempting to occupy and command the same space. It is engaged in a struggle for hegemony, within the dominant bloc, against both social democracy and the moderate wing of its own party. Not only is it operating in the same space: it is working directly on the contradictions within those competing positions. The strength of its intervention lies partly in the radicalism of its commitment to break the mould, not simply to rework the elements of the prevailing 'philosophies'. In doing so, it nevertheless takes the elements which are already constructed into place, dismantles them, reconstitutes them into a new logic, and articulates the space in a new way, polarizing it to the right.

This can be seen with respect to both the earlier competing positions. The Heath position was destroyed in the confrontation with organized labour. But it was also undermined by its internal contradictions. It failed to win the showdown with labour; it could not enlist popular support for this decisive encounter; in defeat, it returned to its 'natural' position in the political spectrum, engaging in its own version of corporatist bargaining. 'Thatcherism' therefore succeeds in this space by directly engaging the 'creeping socialism' and apologetic 'state collectivism' of the Heath wing. It thus centres on the very nerve of consensus politics, which dominated and stabilized the political scene for over a decade. To sustain its credibility as a party of government in a crisis of capital, 'Thatcherism' retains some lingering and ambivalent connections to this centre territory: Mr Prior is its voice – but *sotto voce*. On other grounds, it has won considerable space by the active destruction of consensus politics from the right. Of course, it aims for the construction of a national consensus of its own. What it destroys is that form of consensus in which social democracy was the principal tendency. This evacuation of centrist territory has unleashed political forces on the right which have been kept in rein for most of the postwar period.

The Contradictions Within Social Democracy

But the contradictions within social democracy are the key to the whole rightward shift of the political spectrum. For if the destruction of the Heath 'party' secures hegemony for 'Thatcherism' over the right, it is the contradictory form of social democracy which has effectively disorganized the left and the working class response to the crisis, and provided the terrain on which Thatcherism is working.

This contradiction can be put in simple terms: to win electoral power, social democracy must maximize its claims to be *the* political representative of the interests of the working class and organized labour. It is the party capable of (a) mastering the crises, while (b) defending – within the constraints imposed by capitalist recession – working class interests. It is important here to remember that this version of social democracy – 'Labourism' – is not a homogeneous political entity but a complex political formation. It is not *the* expression of *the* working class 'in government', but the principal means of the political representation of the class. Representation here has to be understood as an active and formative relationship. It organizes the class, constituting it as a political force of a particular kind – a social democratic political force – in the same moment as it is constituted. Everything depends on the means – the practices, the apparatuses and the 'philosophies' – by which the often dispersed and contradictory interests of a class are welded together into a coherent position which can be articulated and represented in the political and ideological theatres of struggle.

The expression of this representative relationship of class-to-party, in the present period, has depended decisively on the extensive set of corporatist bargains negotiated between Labour and the trade union representatives of the class. This 'indissoluble link' is the practical basis for Labour's claim to be the natural governing party of the crisis. This is the contract it delivers. But, once *in* government, social democracy is committed to finding solutions to the crisis which are capable of winning support from key sections of capital, since its solutions are framed within the limits of capitalist survival. But this requires that the indissoluble link between party and class be used not to advance but to *discipline* the class and the organizations it represents. This is only possible if the class-to-party link can somehow be redefined or dismantled and if there can be substituted for it an alternative articulation: people-to-government. The rhetoric of 'national interest', which is the principal ideological form in which a succession of defeats has been imposed on the working class by social democracy in power, are exactly the sites where this contradiction shows through and is being constantly reworked. But people-to-government dissects the field of struggle differently from class-to-party. It sets Labour, at key moments of struggle – from the strikes of 1966 right through to the 1979 5% pay norm – by definition 'on the side of the nation' *against* 'sectional interests', 'irresponsible trade union power', etc., i.e. against the class.

This is the terrain on which Mr Heath played such destructive games in the lead-through to the Industrial Relations Act and its aftermath, with his invocation of 'the great trade union of the nation' and the spectre of the greedy working class 'holding the nation to ransom'. 'Thatcherism', deploying the discourses of 'nation' and 'people' against 'class' and 'unions' with far greater vigour and populist appeal, has homed in on the same objective contradiction. Within this space is being constructed an assault, not on this or that piece of 'irresponsible bargaining' by a particular union, but on the very foundation of organized labour. Considerable numbers of people – including many trade unionists – find themselves reflected and set in place through this interpellation of 'nation' and 'people' at the centre of this mounting attack on the defensive organizations of the working class.

Anti-Collectivism

A closely related strand in the new philosophy of the radical right are the themes of anti-collectivism and anti-statism.

'Thatcherism' has given these elements of neo-liberal doctrine within conservative 'philosophy' an extensive rejuvenation. At the level of theoretical ideologies, anti-statism has been refurbished by the advance of monetarism as the most fashionable economic credo. Keynesianism was the lynch-pin of the theoretical ideologies of corporatist state intervention throughout the postwar period, assuming almost the status of a sacred orthodoxy or *doxa*. To have replaced it in some of the most powerful and influential apparatuses of government, in research and the universities, and restored in its place the possessive individualist and free-market nostrums of Hayek and Friedman is, in itself a remarkable reversal. Ideological transformations, however, do not take place by magic. For years bodies like the Institute for Economic Affairs have been plugging away in the margins of the Conservative Party and the informed public debate on economic policy, refurbishing the gospel of Adam Smith and the free market, undermining the assumptions of neo-Keynesianism, planning and projecting how the 'competitive stimulus' could be applied again to one area after another of those sectors which, as they see it, have fallen into the corporatist abyss.

Gradually, in the more hospitable climate of the 1970s, these seeds began to bear fruit. First in the learned journals, then in the senior common rooms, finally in informal exchanges between the 'new academics' and the more 'sensitive' senior civil servants, a monetarist version of neo-classical economics came to provide the accepted frame of reference for economic debate. The economic journalists helped to make this revolution in ideas acceptable in the media and the serious financial press – and thus, not long after, in the boardrooms of enterprises which everyone imagined had long since abandoned open competition for the safer waters of state capitalism.

Neither Keynesianism nor monetarism, however, win votes as such in the electoral marketplace. But, in the discourse of 'social market values', Thatcherism discovered a powerful means of translating economic doctrine into the language of experience, moral imperative and common sense, thus providing a 'philosophy' in the broader sense – an alternative *ethic* to that of the 'caring society'. This translation of a theoretical *ideology* into a populist *idiom* was a major political achievement: and the conversion of hard-faced economics into the language of compulsive *moralism* was, in many ways, the centrepiece of this transformation. 'Being British' became once again identified with the restoration of competition and profitability; with tight money and sound finance ('You can't pay yourself more than you earn!!') – the national economy debated on the model of the household budget. The essence of the British people was identified with self-reliance and personal responsibility, as against the image of the over-taxed individual, enervated by welfare state 'coddling', his or her moral fibre irrevocably sapped by 'state handouts'. This assault, not just on welfare over-spending, but on the very principle and essence of collective social welfare – the centrepiece of consensus politics from the Butskell period onwards – was mounted, not through an analysis of which class of the deserving made most out of the welfare state, but through the emotive image of the 'scrounger': the new folk-devil.

To the elaboration of this populist language and the reconstruction of a 'free-market' ethic both the excessively high-minded Sir Keith Joseph and the excessively broad-bottomed Rhodes Boyson, both the 'disinterested' leader writers of *The Times, Telegraph* and *The Economist* and the ventriloquists of populist opinion in the *Mail*, the *Express*, the *Star* and the *Sun* lent their undivided attention. The colonization of the popular press was a critical victory in this struggle to define the common sense of the times. Here was undertaken the critical ideological work of constructing around 'Thatcherism' a populist common sense.

Thatcherite populism is a particularly rich mix. It combines the resonant themes of organic Toryism – nation, family, duty, authority, standards, traditionalism – with the aggressive themes of a revived neo-liberalism – self-interest, competitive individualism, anti-statism. Some of these elements had been secured in earlier times through the grand themes of one-Nation popular Conservatism: the means by which Toryism circumnavigated democracy, lodged itself in the hearts of the people and lived to form many another popular government. Other elements derived from the anachronistic vocabulary of political economy and possessive individualism. The latter had been absorbed into Conservative rhetoric only when the old Liberalism ceased to provide the Conservatives with a viable political base. The idea that 'freedom of the people equals the free market' has never been wholly banished from the Tory universe; but, despite Powellism, and Mr Heath of the 'Selsdon Man' phase, it has failed to achieve full ascendancy within the party in the postwar period, until recently. But now, in the wake of an era dominated by the social-democratic consensus, and a Conservatism tainted with distinct corporatist tendencies, 'Freedom/free market' is once again in the foreground of the conservative ideological repertoire. 'Free market – strong state': around this contradictory point, where neo-liberal political economy fused with organic Toryism, the authentic language of 'Thatcherism' has condensed. It began to be spoken in the mid-1970s – and, in its turn, to 'speak' – to define – the crisis: what it was and how to get out of it. The crisis has begun to be 'lived' in *its* terms. This is a new kind of taken-for-grantedness; a reactionary common sense, harnessed to the practices and solutions of the radical right and the class forces it now aspires to represent.

The Repertoire of Thatcherism

Two aspects of this rich repertoire of anti-collectivism, only, can be remarked on in the space available here. First, there is the way these discourses operated directly on popular elements in the traditional philosophies and practical ideologies of the *dominated* classes. These elements – as Ernesto Laclau and others have argued (see *Politics and Ideology in Marxist Theory*, Ernesto Laclau, London 1977) often express a contradiction between popular interests and the power bloc. But since the terms in which this contradiction is expressed have no intrinsic, necessary or fixed class meaning, they can be effectively recomposed as elements within very different discourses, positioning the popular classes in relation to the power bloc in different ways. When, in a crisis the traditional alignments are disrupted, it is possible, on the very ground of this break, to construct the people into a populist political subject: *with*, not against, the power bloc; in alliance with new political forces in a great national crusade to 'make Britain "Great" once more'. The language of 'the people' unified behind a reforming drive to turn the tide of 'creeping collectivism', banish Keynesean illusions from the state apparatus and renovate the power bloc is a powerful one. Its radicalism connects with radical-popular sentiments; but it effectively turns them round, absorbs and neutralizes their popular thrust, and creates, in the place of a popular rupture, a *populist unity*. It brings into existence a new 'historic bloc' between certain sections of the dominant and dominated classes. We can see this construction of ideological cross-alliances between 'Thatcherism' and 'the people' actually going on in the very structure of Mrs Thatcher's own rhetoric: 'Don't talk to me about "them" and "us" in a company,' she once told the readers of *Woman's Own*: 'You're all "we" in a company. You survive as the company survives, prosper as the company prospers — everyone together. The future lies in cooperation and not confrontation.' This displaces an existing structure of oppositions — 'them' *vs.* 'us'. It sets in its place an alternative set of equivalents: 'Them *and* us equals *we*'. Then it positions we — 'the people' — in a particular relation to capital: behind it, dominated by its imperatives (profitability, accumulation); yet at the same time, yoked to it, identified with it. 'You survive as the company survives'; presumably also, you collapse as it collapses ... Cooperation not confrontation! The process we are looking at here is very similar to that which Gramsci once described as *transformism*: the neutralization of some elements in an ideological formation, their absorption and passive appropriation into a new political configuration.

The second aspect is closely related to this process of transformism. For what we have so far described could well appear — and has often been described by the traditional left — as mere illusion, pure 'false consciousness': just a set of ideological con-tricks whose cover will be blown as soon as they are put to the stern test of material circumstances. But this reading greatly underestimates both the rational core on which these populist constructions are situated, *and* their real, not false, material basis. Specifically, such a reading neglects the materiality of the contradictions between 'the people' — popular needs, interests, feelings and aspirations — on the one hand, and the actual, imposed structures of the interventionist state — the state of the monopoly phase of capitalist development — on the other. 'Thatcherism', far from simply conjuring demons out of the deep, operated directly on the real and manifestly contradictory experience of the popular classes under social-democratic corporatism.

It is important to understand why Labourist social democracy was vulnerable to the charge of 'statism' — and
therefore why 'anti-statism' has proved so powerful a populist
slogan: otherwise, we may confuse ourselves into believing that
the headway which 'Thatcherism' is undoubtedly making among
working people, committed Labour voters and some sectors of
skilled labour, can be wholly attributed to 'false consciousness'.
As we have seen, the project which social democratic
corporatism set itself was the containment and reform, not the
transformation, of the crisis of British capitalism. What capital
manifestly could no longer accomplish on its own, 'reformism'
would have to do by harnessing capital to the state, using the
state as representative of the 'general interest' to create the
conditions for the effective resumption of capitalist
accumulation and profitability. Social democracy had no other
viable strategy, especially for 'big' capital (and 'big' capital had
no viable alternative strategy for itself) which did not involve
massive state regulation and support. Hence the state has
become a massive presence, inscribed over every feature of
social and economic life. But, as the recession bit more deeply,
so the management of the crisis required Labour to discipline,
limit and police the very classes it claimed to represent — again,
through the mediation of the state.

The best index of this problem was the incomes policy
strategy, especially in its last and most confusing manifestation,
the Social Contract. The Social Contract was one of those open-
ended or double-sided ideological mechanisms into which each
side could read quite contradictory meanings. To the left, it
represented an attempt to use the corporatist bargaining of the
state to graft certain powerful social and economic objectives on
to the 'price' of limiting wage demands. To the Labour
Government, it clearly represented the only form in which social
and economic discipline could be 'sold' to the trade union
movement. The glaring discrepancies between the redistributive
language of the Social Contract and its actual disciplinary
character was the best index of how 'the state' under corporatist
management came to be experienced as 'the enemy of the
people'. This contradiction bit deeper and deeper into the
Labour/trade union alliance until, with the revolt against
incomes policies and in favour of 'collective bargaining', it
undermined the credibility and *raison d'être* of Mr Callaghan's

government itself. The radical right welcomed this trade union revolt against 'state interference in free collective bargaining' much in the manner of the Prodigal Son.

It would be easy to believe that Labourism has been trapped by the statist dilemma only recently and inadvertently. In fact, 'Labourism' or Labour socialism has been marked from its origins by its Fabian-collectivist inheritance. The expansion of the state machine, under the management of state servants and experts, has often been defined in this tradition as synonymous with socialism itself. Labour has been willing to use this state to reform conditions for working people, provided this did not bite too deeply into the 'logic' of capitalist accumulation. But it has refused like the plague the mobilization of democratic power at the popular level. This has always been the site on which Labour has been brought back from the brink into its deep reverence for 'constitutionalism'. Nothing, indeed, so rattles the equanimity of Labour leaders as the spectacle of the popular classes on the move under their own steam, outside the range of 'responsible' guidance and leadership. The fact is that 'statism' is not foreign to the trajectory of Labour socialism: it is intrinsic to it. Corporatism is only the latest form in which this deep commitment to using the state on behalf of the people, but without popular mobilization, has manifested itself.

The radical right has capitalized on this fatal hesitancy, this deep weakness in Labour socialism. Mrs Thatcher is therefore guilty of exaggeration — but of no more than that — when she identifies state bureaucracy and creeping collectivism with 'socialism', and 'socialism' with the spectre of 'actual-existing socialism' under the East European regimes: and then counterposes to this fatal syllogism the sweet sound of 'Freedom' which, of course, she and her New Model Conservative Party represent.

It is also the case that the actual experience which working people have had of the corporatist state has not been a powerful incentive to further support for increases in its scope. Whether in the growing dole queues or in the waiting-rooms of an over-burdened National Health Service, or suffering the indignities of the Social Security, the corporatist state is increasingly experienced by them not as a benefice but as a powerful bureaucratic imposition *on* 'the people'. The state has been present to them, less as a welfare or redistributive agency, and more as the 'state of monopoly capital'. And since Labour has foregrounded the requirements of monopoly capital above all others, what is it that can be said to be 'false' in this consciousness?

Instead of confronting this contradiction at the heart of its strategy, Labourism has typically fallen back on reaffirming the neutral-benevolent definition of the state, as incarnator of the National Interest, above the struggle between the contending classes. It is precisely this abstract state which now appears transformed in the discourses of Thatcherism as the enemy. It is 'the State' which has over-borrowed and overspent; fuelled inflation; fooled the people into thinking that there would always be more where the last handout came from; tried to assume the regulation of things like wages and prices which are best left to the hidden hand of market forces; above all, interfered, meddled, intervened, instructed, directed — against the essence, the Genius, of The British People. It is time, as she says, with conviction, 'to put people's destinies again in their own hands'.

Thus in any polarization along the fissure between state and people, it is *Labour* which can be represented as undividedly part of the power bloc, enmeshed in the state apparatus, riddled with bureaucracy, in short, 'with' the state; and Mrs Thatcher, grasping the torch of Freedom with one hand, who is undividedly out there, 'with the people'. It is the Labour Party which is committed to things as they are — and Mrs Thatcher who means to tear society up by the roots and radically reconstruct it! This is the process by which — as they say — the radical right has 'become popular'.

Education

We might turn to another area of successful colonization by the radical right: the sphere of education. Until very recently, the social democratic goals of 'equality of opportunity' and 'remedying educational advantage' were dominant throughout the world of secondary education. The struggle over comprehensivization was its political signature. Contestation in this areas has only gradually developed, through a series of strategic interventions. The 'Black Paper' group — at first no more than an elitist, education rump — has moved from very modest beginnings to the point where it could justly be claimed (and was) that its preoccupations set the agenda for the 'Great Debate' which the Labour Government initiated in 1978. In the 1960s 'progressive' and 'community' education made considerable advances within state schools. Today, 'progressivism' is throughly discredited: the bodies of a whole series of well-publicized schools – William Tyndale and after, so to speak – lie strewn in its path. The panic over falling standards and working class illiteracy, the fears concerning politically-motivated teachers in the classroom, the scare stories about the 'violent' urban school, about the adulteration of standards through the immigrant intake, and so on have successfully turned the tide in the education sphere towards themes and goals established by the forces of the right. The press – especially those three popular ventriloquist voices of the radical right, the *Mail*, the *Sun* and the *Express* – have played here a quite pivotal role. They have publicized the 'examples' in a highly sensational form – and they have drawn the connections.

These connections and couplings are the key mechanisms of the process by which education as a field of struggle has been articulated to the right. There are long, deep-seated resistances within the philosophy of state education to any attempt to measure schooling directly in terms of the needs and requirements of industry. That these were resistances often shot through with ambiguity is not so important for our purposes. However it arose, the reluctance to cash schooling in terms of its immediate value to capital was one on which campaigns could be mounted with some hope of professional administrative support. These defences have now been dismantled. Clear evidence is supposed to exist that standards are falling: the principal witnesses to this alarming trend are employers who complain about the quality of job applicants: this, in turn, must be having an effect on the efficiency and productivity of the nation – at a time when recession puts a premium on improving both. Once the often ill-founded elements can be stitched together into this chain of reasoning, policies can begin to be changed by leading educationists of the political right, indirectly, even before they took charge at the DES. And why?

First, because the terrain on which the debate is being conducted has been so thoroughly reconstructed around this new 'logic' that the groundswell for change is proving hard to resist. Second, because Labour itself has always been caught between competing goals in schooling: to improve the chances of working class children and the worse-off in education, and to harness education to the economic and efficiency needs of the productive system. We can see now that this contradiction, even within the social democratic educational programme, is another variant of what earlier we called the principal contradiction of social democracy in this period. The educational experts and spokesmen, the educational press, sections of the profession, the media, many educational interest groups and organizations have been operating exactly on the site of this dilemma and – in conditions of recession – carried the argument with the Labour Government which in turn took the lead in promoting debates and policies designed to make this equation – success in education = meeting the needs of industry – come true!

The 'Great Debate'

Thus the agenda for the 'Great Debate' was indeed set for social democracy by the social forces of the radical right. And the language of comprehensive education has been effectively displaced by the language of educational excellence. The Labour Government, which initiated this 'Great Debate' was almost certainly still convinced that this is largely a non-political debate, as debates about education ought to be. 'Education should not be a political football,' Labour ministers solemnly declared – a slogan they should try selling to the public school Headmasters' Conference! And, lest it be thought that this is, after all, only a debate, we should be aware that a major restructuring of the educational state apparatuses is taking place. The Department of Education and Science (DES) is to be set somewhat to one side, and new apparatuses capable of realizing the equation in more immediate and practical forms have moved into a central position in the field: the Manpower Services Commission, the new TSA and 'Tops' retraining programmes, directly geared to the demands and movements of industry and to the silent reskilling and deskilling of the unemployed.

The restructuring of the state apparatus from above is one thing. But the active and positive support from parents – including many working-class ones – is another. As unemployment grows, working-class parents are obliged to take the competitive side of education more seriously: being skilled – even if it is only for particular places in dead-end, low-skill, routine labour – is better than being on the dole. If comprehensivization in the form in which it was offered is not going to deliver the goods, then working-class children may have to be content to be 'skilled' and 'classed' in any way they can. This is what Marx meant by the 'dull compulsion' of economic existence.

But it is also the case that, as the failure of social democratic initiatives to turn the tide of educational disadvantage becomes more manifest, so the positive aspirations of working people for the education of their children can be rearticulated towards the support for a more conventional and traditional approach to the educational marketplace. This great exodus back to known and familiar territory, to tried pathways, to the traditional and the orthodox, to the safe territory of *what is*, is one of the strongest and deepest of common-sense sentiments: and, for that reason, one of the most resonant themes in the discourse of the radical right. In the 1960s, 'parent power' belonged with the radical movements, with Ivan Illych and 'deschooling'. In the 1970s and 1980s it was one of the strongest cards in the educational pack shuffled by Tory education spokespersons.

Law and Order

If education is an area where the right has won territory without having to win power, two other areas in the repertoire of the radical right – race and law and order – are ones where the right has traditionally assumed a leading role. We can be brief about them since they have gained considerable attention on the left in the recent period. They are chosen as examples here only to make a general point. On law and order, the themes – more policing, tougher sentencing, better family discipline, the rising crime rate as an index of social disintegration, the threat to 'ordinary people going about their private business' from thieves, muggers, etc., the wave of lawlessness and the loss of law-abidingness – are perennials of Conservative Party Conferences, and the sources of many a populist campaign by moral entrepreneur groups and quoting editors. But if the work of the right in some areas has won support over into its camp, the law and order issues have scared people over. The language of law and order is sustained by a populist moralism. It is where the great syntax of 'good' versus 'evil', of civilized and uncivilized standards, of the choice between anarchy and order, constantly divides the world up and classifies it into its appointed stations. The play on 'values' and on moral issues in this area is what gives to the law and order crusade much of its grasp on popular morality and common sense conscience. But it also touches concretely the experience of crime and theft, of loss of scarce property and fears of unexpected attack in working class areas and neighbourhoods; and, since it promulgates no other remedies for their underlying causes, it welds people to that 'need for authority' which has been so significant for the right in the construction of consent to its authoritarian programme.

Race constitutes another variant of the same process. In recent months questions of race, racism and relations between the races, as well as immigration, have been dominated by the dialectic between the radical-respectable and the radical-rough forces of the right. It was said about the 1960s and early 70s that, after all, Mr Powell lost. This is true only if the shape of a whole conjuncture is to be measured by the career of a single individual. In another sense, there is an argument that 'Powellism' won: not only because his official eclipse was followed by legislating into effect much of what he proposed, but because of the magical connections and short-circuits which Powellism was able to establish between the themes of race and immigration control and the images of the nation, the British people and the destruction of 'our culture, our way of life'.

I have looked exclusively at some political-ideological dimensions of the emergence of the radical right, not to evoke wonder at its extent, but to try to identify what is specific to it, what marks its difference from other variants which have flourished since the War. The first is the complex but interlocked relationship of the right to the fortunes and fate of social democracy when the latter takes power in a period of economic recession, and tries to provide a solution 'within certain limits'. It is always the case that the right is what it is partly because of what the left is. The second is its popular success in neutralizing the contradiction between people and the state/power bloc and winning popular interpellations so decisively for the right. In short, the nature of its *populism*. But now it must be added that this is no rhetorical device or trick, for this populism is operating on genuine contradictions, it has a rational and material core. Its success and effectivity does not lie in its capacity to dupe unsuspecting folk but in the way it addresses real problems, real and lived experiences, real contradictions – and yet is able to represent them within a logic of discourse which pulls them systematically into line with policies and class strategies of the right. Finally – and this is not limited to this analysis, though it seems especially relevant – there is the evidence of just how ideological transformations and political restructuring of this order is actually accomplished. It works on the ground of already constituted social practices and lived ideologies. It wins space there by constantly drawing on these elements which have secured over time a traditional resonance and left their traces in popular inventories. At the same time, it changes the field of struggle by changing the place, the position, the relative weight of the condensations within any one discourse and constructing them according to an alternative logic. What shifts them is not 'thoughts' but a particular practice of class struggle: ideological and political class struggle. What makes these representations popular is that they have a purchase on practice, they shape it, they are written into its materiality. What constitutes them as a danger is that they change the nature of the terrain itself on which struggles of different kinds are taking place; they have pertinent effects on these struggles. their effect is to constitute a new balance of political forces. This is exactly the terrain on which the forces of opposition must organize, if we are to transform it.

Martin Jacques

Thatcherism — Breaking Out of the Impasse

Thatcherism has changed the face of British politics. In 1979, many on the left, and elsewhere, did not believe it would happen. It has happened. And, by and large, it has taken the left by surprise and left it in a state of shock. That is now beginning to change. But if we are to come to terms with this new phenomenon we need to understand it much better — and its place in post-war history. If we do not, the left will find itself in steady and continuous retreat.

The Evolving Crisis

Britain's decline is, of course, no new phenomenon. It dates back at least a century. But it has asserted itself with a new force — after an apparent lull — since the early sixties, and with profound consequences. Indeed, these years provide us with a new and critical point of departure in British politics.

The 1945 Labour Government, under the impact of war and the radicalisation of the working class, carried through a series of major structural changes including nationalisation, the welfare state and full employment. At the same time, it sought to restore Britain's international position in the context of the new post-war situation. This involved the maintenance of the Empire and its legacy together with a major international military and financial role for Britain. The key here was the relationship with the United States, which, given the weakness of other western powers and the onset of the cold war, was seeking a special relationship with Britain.

Already, well before their return in 1951, the political centre of gravity in the country was shifting to the Tories. Once in office, they continued with aspects of Labour's domestic policies, for example the welfare state, and almost wholly with its external strategy. Given the relatively favourable international environment – including the preoccupation of key competitors like Japan and West Germany with post-war recovery – this strategy was both viable and allowed relatively rapid economic growth (albeit lethargic by European standards). Indeed, the fifties saw rising living standards, full employment and a relative social stability (which was aided by the cold war). An unusual consensus characterized British society – presided over by the Tories – in which conflict appeared relatively marginal or at least thoroughly contained.

By the late fifties, early sixties, this apparent picture of social harmony was being undermined. The first cracks in the cold war, the rise of CND, growing concern about the economy, together with other events, combined to create a new situation which served to undermine Conservative dominance and eventually enabled the return of Labour in 1964.

At the centre of this changing situation was Britain's economic position though this was by no means the only factor. By the early sixties, it was becoming increasingly evident that the 'new dawn' of the fifties had only been a temporary interregnum: Britain's relative decline had continued unchecked. The rapid growth of Britain's competitors exposed its underlying weakness. A strategy based on traditional imperial markets, sterling as a reserve currency and Britain as a major military power became increasingly difficult to sustain. As a consequence, during the sixties, there was a growing recognition, not least within ruling circles, that some kind of new response was required.

The Labour Governments 1964-1970

The return of Labour in 1964 occupies a central position in this changing context.[1] Labour's victory stemmed partly from an increasing recognition of the seriousness of Britain's situation, and partly from a growing conviction of the need to modernise the economy and society. Here, Wilson's theme of the 'white hot technological revolution' and his attacks on the social archaism of the Tories struck a popular chord. Labour – in 1964 and even more in 1966 – succeeded in uniting large sections of the working class together with an important section of the middle strata around its appeal.

Four elements, broadly speaking characterized the 'modernist' approach of the 1964-70 Labour Governments. Firstly, industrial capital was to be made more competitive, partly through increased investment to be achieved by boosting profits and restricting wages through incomes policies (and later trade union legislation). Secondly, the state itself was seen as a key agency for restructuring important areas of industry (for example, the creation of British Leyland and GEC-AEI through the IRC), and rationalising the labour-process (through productivity agreements etc). At the same time, the state itself was identified as a major area for reform – including the civil service (the Fulton Report 1966), higher education, and local government. Thirdly, the Wilson approach rested on tripartite collaboration between the state, big business and the unions, a development which had been initiated in the early sixties by the Tories with Neddy etc, but which now assumed a more central role. Fourthly and lastly, following the effective collapse of sterling as a reserve currency in 1967, the government increasingly looked to the EEC as the new international framework for British capitalism.

The modernism of the Wilson governments, however, proved quite inadequate to the problems. The attempt to reorganise industrial capital was half-hearted, given the profound weakness of Britain's productive base. In this context the central problem was the failure of Labour to tackle the alliance that had underpinned Britain's post-war course and which was responsible for its economic decline; namely, the externally orientated interests of sections of big industrial capital together with the City. Indeed, Labour, between 1964 and 1967, still gave priority to the defence of sterling and only abandoned the latter's reserve role when it was forced to do so. In the process, economic growth was sacrificed. By the late sixties, indeed, little remained of the 'grand design'. Faced with continuing economic difficulties, the government increasingly resorted to one aspect of its modernist strategy, an attack on the economic position of the working class, through bouts of deflation, wage restraint, and then *In Place of Strife*. This led to growing trade union opposition which further undermined Labour's strategy. The failure of modernisation – together with growing tension in its relationship with the working class – eroded Labour's 1966 bloc of support and paved the way for the Tory victory in 1970.

These developments, however, must be placed in a broader context. By the late sixties, a much wider crisis of society was becoming apparent. The student movement, the events of 1968, the beginnings of the nationalist upsurge, the growth of racialism – each was both a symptom and an expression of this wider crisis. The Labour governments had been a *response* to this process, but in the event proved quite incapable of dealing with it.

The period of the fifties was not just one of consensus: it was also a phase in which, allied to this national consensus, the ruling bloc (i.e. big capital, the City, the upper echelons of Whitehall, etc.) exercised a comprehensive dominance over British society. By the early sixties, the basis of this dominance, this leadership – or hegemony – was being eroded. Critically, one of its crucial supports, the external imperial strategy, was no longer viable. This had deep and long-term implications. An immediate effect was the defeat of the Tories, the political embodiment of the previous stability and success, and the return of Labour.

But we must see the problem in a wider context than this. The previous ruling strategy was increasingly seen to have failed. This was not just an 'economic question': it concerned Britain's international orientation, its 'standing' in the world, its domestic standard of life, etc. Its failure therefore impinged on all aspects of society: on the prestige of the ruling bloc, on the respect for Britain's political system and institutions, on the identity and definition of Britain as a nation, and on the established pattern of alliances. What was involved, then, was a crisis in the authority of the traditional ruling bloc, a crisis of its leadership, of its hegemony over British society. This did not mean a crisis of hegemony in the sense that the ruling bloc's position has been under open and explicit challenge from the working class. Far from it, indeed. Rather it has been a crisis of the established forms of hegemony, a situation where the old forms of rule, previous ideological assumptions and the established pattern of alliances became increasingly difficult to sustain.

The failure of the old imperial strategy meant that the ruling bloc was obliged to undertake a strategic shift in response. This shift was, in the early sixties, broadly along the lines of Labour's modernism. And it further exacerbated the crisis of hegemony in three key senses. Firstly, a popular support had to be won for policies which often involved a major readjustment of attitudes and outlook: that is the modernist strategy itself required a major reorganization in the forms of hegemony. Entry into the EEC, the growing role of the state and the reform of such institutions as higher education and local government are obvious examples. Secondly, the success of the modernist response in solving the problems it was designed to tackle was crucial if the crisis of hegemony was to be resolved. If, on the contrary, it proved unsuccessful, then that crisis could only grow more acute (which, of course, is what has happened). Finally, the modernist approach – in its diverse Labour and Tory variants – involved new burdens and new costs for working people. This, obviously, greatly increased the delicacy – and vulnerability – of the operation.

The weakening of the established forms of hegemony has been accompanied by, over the period since the mid-sixties, a transformation in the terms of British politics, as different class forces and social groups have been sensitised to new problems and acquired new aspirations. The future of Scotland and Wales, the Irish question, the position of women, morality, the role of trade unionism – the examples are legion. Old conflicts have reappeared in new forms, new contradictions have surfaced for the first time – with their origins lying in a complex interaction between Britain's specific crisis and more general features associated with the development of advanced capitalism. These various developments have posed a profound challenge to the previous pattern of alliances and assumptions and, consequently therefore, also the positions of the various political parties.

The Tory Goverment 1970-1974

The return of the Heath government in 1970 marked a distinct shift in the new phase of British politics ushered in from the mid-sixties. Its character and the nature of its strategy requires some prior consideration of changes in the Tory Party.

The fifties saw the Conservative Party resume what had been its traditional mantle in post-1918 politics – as the main governing party, inextricably linked with the establishment and the national tradition, albeit on the basis of a tacit acceptance of many of Labour's post-war reforms. Such a role was no longer possible in the same way in the new phase; the old assumptions no longer worked and Labour's modernism had to some extent deprived the Tories of the centre ground. In response to this situation the Tory Party began to shift to the right.

In the consensus tradition of the fifties – and long before – the Party had rested on a unique relationship between its high-Tory leadership, characterised by such figures as Macmillan, Eden and Home and enjoying close connections with the City, big capital, and the traditional 'upper classes', and a cadre force drawn from the middle classes, the professional groups, the self-employed, foremen and such like, and sections of the working class. In 1965 an important component and expression of this arrangement was removed: the leader was no longer to 'emerge' in the time-honoured patronage style of the establishment, but was to be elected by the parliamentary party. The outgoing incumbent, Home, admirably caricatured the high-Tory leadership model and its imperial tradition: Heath was, up to a point, a more accurate reflection, both in ideology and style, of the cadre force of the Tory Party, in particular its middle classes.

These internal changes were closely linked to the strategy evolved under Heath. This was, like the Labour governments before, a response to the new phase, but it was no simple continuation of Labour's particular modernist approach. On the contrary, in one crucial respect, it marked a sharp break with Labour's strategy. In place of interventionism in industry and tripartite planning, for example, the Tories at first leaned heavily on a more laissez-faire conception of economic and industrial policy, laying stress on the function of market forces and a reduced role for the state. At the same time they adopted a more administrative and coercive approach towards working class resistance, as exemplified by the Industrial Relations Act. Indeed, a key theme of the Heath government, more widely, was the need to reassert authority and law and order – in relation to working class militancy, crime, student unrest, etc. – with the state, including the law, playing a growing role. Finally, the Heath strategy involved a determined and unambiguous attempt to enter the EEC and adopt a fully-fledged 'European' orientation.

The more aggressive attack on the position of the working class, however, led to trade union militancy unparalleled since the 1920s. The Industrial Relations Act, for example, almost resulted in the first General Strike since 1926 with the imprisonment of the Pentonville 5. Indeed, it was the success of this resistance – notably the UCS work-in and the first miners' strike against the policy of 'lame ducks' and incomes policy[2] respectively – which finally forced the Tories to abandon their 'market' policies. Heath moved from a 'pre-Thatcherite' position to a comprehensive corporatist approach, which more closely resembled Labour's Modernism. This, too, however, met bitter resistance.

A situation, in a sense, of impasse was created. The modernist strategy – in its Heath variant – provoked such working class resistance that key elements of it were either defeated or effectively immobilised. The climax, of course, was the miners' strike, leading to the three day week, a General Election, and the return of a minority Labour Government.

The Nature of the Working Class Response and What It Meant

The modernist strategy – in its various forms – involved a new kind of attack on the position of the working class. The working class resisted important elements of this offensive – in the period of Labour Government and then, more dramatically, with the Tories. A new factor entered the political scene: a level of working class militancy not witnessed since the war. But what was the nature of these struggles?

Certainly they went beyond the narrowly 'economic', raising wider issues. The UCS struggle, though admittedly exceptional, posed the question of who is competent to run industry, while the struggles against *In Place of Strife* and the Industrial Relations Act had, given the nature of the modernist attempt to contain the working class, a wider democratic aspect. These struggles were also more than simply defensive. The fight to defeat wage restraint, for example, acquired, for the more powerful bargaining groups, the character of a wage offensive. At the same time, some of the battles began to take on a distinctly anti-Tory dimension, particularly the second miners' strike.

Nonetheless, the primary characteristic of these struggles was a *trade union* response to the offensive of the Labour and particularly the Conservative governments. They represented a limited and predominantly defensive response to aspects of the modernist strategy. Their hallmark was resistance to wage restraint, 'lame ducks' and trade union legislation. In coming to terms with the significance of this resistance, it is important to grasp the breadth of the modernist strategy. The more dramatic features were trade union legislation, wage restraint, etc. – because of the working class response. But the attempt to modernise went well beyond this, embracing higher education, reform of the judiciary, entry into the EEC, new immigration laws, police reform, restructuring of the health service, reform of the civil service, local government, and so forth.[3] It is obviously difficult to generalise across such a wide area, particularly as there were also important differences between the approaches of the Wilson and Heath governments; there was, however, a general tendency towards more centralized and less democratic forms. Now while the 'industrial relations' aspect of the strategy was in large measure successfully resisted, the great majority of the others were not, and some, for example reform of local government, encountered relatively little opposition. This is important for two reasons: firstly, the modernist strategy involved a much wider attempt to rationalize British society and change the balance of class relationships than the left fully grasped; secondly, it tells us something about the limitations of working class consciousness.

This second point needs taking further. One of the key indications of the nature of working class resistance was the fact that it did not gravitate in any mass way towards political organisation or new kinds of political solutions. There was, of course, a powerful and widespread anti-Toryism, but not much beyond. Indeed, in this context, other problems were revealed in the 1974 elections which we will look at shortly. In some ways, this picture is not surprising. We are, after all, confronted with a quite central political problem, namely, that the mass party of the working class, the Labour Party, was itself – in government – one of the main vehicles for the modernist strategy. The fact that it adopted a more militant rhetoric during the Heath period does not change the issue. At the same time, although left militants and Communists emerged as key rank-and-file leaders in the Heath phase, political support for the alternative positions of the Communist Party and Labour left remained, in popular grassroots terms, marginal, though these positions made some progress within the labour movement itself. It should be added

here, also, that the left, including the Communist Party, itself
tended to exaggerate greatly the impact of the industrial
militancy of the period on the political consciousness of the
working class and to underestimate the relative importance of
independent political activity on the shopfloor and elsewhere.

The argument, then, is that working class resistance
successfully prevented the implementation of important aspects
of the modernist strategy of both the Labour and Tory
governments. This resistance, however, was both limited in
scope and primarily defensive. British politics was – until the
Thatcher government – therefore characterised by a certain
impasse: the ruling bloc has been unable to secure the working
class acquiescence it required in key areas, the working class
itself was unable to unite around an alternative political solution.
Like all impasses of this character, however, it cannot last
forever: it is resolved, ultimately, either by a decisive shift to the
left or right based on a major realignment of class and social
forces.

This situation of impasse, however, must be placed in its
broader context. The crisis of hegemony, far from being resolved
by the turn towards a modernist strategy, was actually
exacerbated by it. Labour's particular modernist response failed
ignominiously. The popular resistance of the working class, in
helping to undermine the Heath strategy, and ultimately the
Heath government as well, further aggravated this more general
crisis of hegemony. The most dramatic illustration was working
class militancy, but this should not blind us to a wider process of
fragmentation, erosion and realignment that was taking place.
This found expression in the widening range of issues and
conflicts that developed including around immigration and race
relations, law and order, morality, the national question, and
women. Moreover, these issues were not somehow fenced off
from those sections involved in the industrial militancy of the
1970-74 period: on the contrary, these groups were as intimately
affected as others by this broad panorama of issues.

In the 1974 election, this widening crisis of hegemony found
clear political expression – it surfaced, with a new twist, at the
level of party politics. Labour was returned, but with its lowest
share of the vote since 1935. It got in simply because the Tories
did even worse. The real electoral beneficiaries were political
forces outside the two main parties. The resurgence of

nationalist politics in Scotland and Wales around the SNP and Plaid Cymru, the growing polarisation within Northern Ireland, and the dramatic rise of the Liberals within England led to the most hybrid parliament since the twenties. The threat to the two-party system, as it had operated more or less since 1931, was because new political forces came to tap – however temporarily – some of the new currents in British society.

Two points merit particular emphasis here. Firstly, the crisis of hegemony increasingly threatened the established position of the Labour Party and the Conservative Party. This was revealed, above all, by the two elections in 1974. Secondly, the industrial militancy of these years, whilst producing a minority Labour government, did not result in any serious shift to the left in British society as a whole. Indeed, we can detect in this period a continuing process in which the bonds between the labour movement as a political force, and the people, were weakened.

The Labour Governments 1974-1979

Labour's return in 1974 took place in the context of heightened working class militancy and a significant shift to the left in the Party as illustrated by the 1974 Manifesto. For the first year or so this was reflected in the Government's policies, notably the dismantling of the more offensive aspects of the Tories' industrial relations policies and the legislating of a new deal for the unions.

This did not imply any major change of direction. Rather it must be seen as part of the Government's attempt to ensure working class acquiescence in the central tenets of its strategy. As opposed to the 'coercion' of the Tories, which had ultimately been shipwrecked, the Wilson-Callaghan axis claimed it could achieve trade union cooperation through consent – based on the social contract.

The fundamental contours of Labour's approach became much clearer from mid-1975, following the defeat of the left in the EEC referendum campaign. Formally speaking, the modernist project remained, but, as Britain's own economic crisis grew increasingly acute with the onset of the international capitalist recession, the Government's approach consisted of little more than pragmatic crisis-management in which the central element was securing working class acquiescence to cuts in real wages and public expenditure together with rising unemployment. Indeed, it paved the way for the more doctrinaire attack of Thatcherism on the post-1945 gains. At the same time it did virtually nothing to undo the Tory measures in such areas as local government and immigration, though its minority status must be seen as a factor, albeit a secondary one, in this.

Two wider themes need to be explored in this context. The first concerns a hitherto singular feature of the new phase: working class resistance to aspects of the modernist strategy. The return of Labour in 1974 inevitably cast this in a more complex mould. Resistance in a situation of Tory government could spontaneously associate with popular anti-Toryism, with Labour as the alternative. This option did not exist for the labour movement in a situation of Labour government. This undoubtedly was a key factor in the support won throughout the labour movement and amongst the working class for the social contract. But the deepening recession was also a very important factor here. It affected working class resistance in two ways: it acted as a disciplining factor, making, for example, conventional forms of wage-militancy, for sections threatened by unemployment, less viable. It also greatly intensified the level and feeling of 'national crisis'.

Working class quiescence finally broke with the 'winter of discontent' in 1978-9. It followed major struggles in the trade union movement and was a renewed, if belated, demonstration of working class resistance to the harshest yet attacks on its living standards. But this, too, bore the imprint of the new context of recession and Labour government. On the one hand, the militancy of these months tended to be more sectionalised and fragmented than that of the Heath period and, on the other hand, it contained within it a new, understandable, but nonetheless disturbingly anti-Labour current (for example, in the Ford strike,[4] in the 'winter of discontent' and, on a different note, in the election result itself).

The second theme concerns our wider context of the underlying erosion of established social alliances and political patterns. In the latter years of Labour's tenure, there was growing evidence of a shift to the right in the country. This, of course, was partly related to the traditional mechanics of the two-party system – with the Conservatives being the 'natural' alternative during a period of Labour government. But it was much more than that. The deepening crisis of hegemony – the failure of this Labour government and the previous Heath government – led to new tensions and realignments. In response, a new kind of popular rightism began to gain ground. Already by 1966 (and indeed earlier), the contours of such an approach were evident with the rise of Powellism. The diverse progressive expressions of the late sixties and beyond – the student movement, the 'underground', the women's movement – contributed towards the emergence and definition of a conservative backlash. The development of working class militancy in the Heath period provided a new, powerful and more political focus. The increasing gravity of Britain's situation from 1974, including the assertion of the politics of recession, together with Labour's failure, gave it further momentum.

A number of its characteristics merit particular stress here. It was a populist development in that it had a powerful presence at the grass-roots and was not confined to the organisational structures of the political right. This found reflection in the character of some of its leaders, such as Powell and Whitehouse, who were essentially 'charismatic' figures whose support did not depend simply on their formal positions within established organisations.

It was also an increasingly global movement. Its dominant philosophical characteristic was essentially backward-looking, the desire to assert traditional ideological themes such as the family, the nation, patriotism, free enterprise and authority. It embraced a multitude of responses including the Black Papers on education, Chicago monetarism, the Festival of Light, SPUC, the National Viewers' and Listeners' Association, the Institute of Economic Affairs, the National Front and racialism. Finally, this broad right trend – at once economic, social, cultural and ideological – increasingly, and especially after the fall of the Heath government, became linked, through figures such as Keith Joseph and Rhodes Boyson, to political developments in the Tory Party as expressed in 'Thatcherism'. This link was a moment of great significance in the evolution of the rightist response to the crisis of hegemony.

Political Forces and the New Phase

A central theme of our argument is that the established framework of British politics has, since the mid-sixties, been steadily eroded. The expressions are numerous: the precipitous decline of Britain as an international power including the collapse of the Empire and imperial role together with consequent realignments, the emergence of new national tensions within Britain, powerful working class militancy, persistent and chronic economic crisis, a new social challenge from women and now a growing threat to the post-1945 achievements of full employment, the welfare state and the nationalised sector. These developments have weakened previous class and social alignments, provoked a growing crisis of hegemony and challenged the established structures, assumptions and ideologies of the right and left in British politics.

The Tory Party

The Tory Party has come under profound challenge in the new context of British politics. In the period 1964-79, it has been in government for only four out of a total of fourteen years — compared, for example, with 37 out of 46 between 1918 and 1964 (including the coalition governments from 1931 to 1945 in which the Tories were generally the dominant force). The Tory Party can thus no longer be regarded as the dominant national party in the way it was prior to the mid-sixties. In the period from 1964 until the 1979 election, indeed, it has faced a serious if erratic electoral decline and important fissures in its bloc of support. The Tory Party, as a consequence, has been posed with the growing need to recoup and reorganise its social base.

Tory Share (%) of Vote at General Elections 1945-1979[5]

1945	39.8	1966	41.9
1950	43.5	1970	46.4
1951	48.0	1974 (Feb)	37.9
1955	49.7	1974 (Oct)	35.8
1959	49.4	1979	43.9
1964	43.4		

The dominant response within the Tory Party since the mid-sixties to its own problems on the one hand and Britain's crisis on the other has been of a rightist complexion. It found its first expression – within the mainstream of Tory politics – in Heath, especially the Heath of 'Selsdon' and the 1970-72 period, and then, more clearly in the rise of Thatcherism.[6]

The precise character of Thatcherism is complex. Two clear elements, however, can be pinpointed. Firstly, there is a strong emphasis on a more traditional arguably petty-bourgeois ideology – the virtues of the market, competition, elitism, individual initiative, the iniquities of state intervention and bureaucracy. In a sense, this represents a return to the pre-Butskellism, pre-1950s style of Tory politics: it is also quite explicitly an attempt to roll back the collectivist notion associated with the post-war advances of the labour movement. In a period of recession (perhaps particularly in its earlier phases), these individualist values strike – indeed have struck – a real chord amongst people well beyond even the traditional areas of Tory support. Secondly, Thatcherism has successfully attempted to organise the diverse forces of the 'backlash' – reacting against trade union militancy, national aspirations, permissiveness, women's liberation – in favour of an essentially regressive and conservative solution embracing such themes as authority, law and order, patriotism, national unity, the family and individual freedom.

Thatcherism, in this context, must be seen as a rejection of major aspects of the modernist approach as it has evolved since the mid-sixties. Indeed, this has been a key source of its appeal – the need for change, a break with the unsuccessful past. Instead, Thatcherism seeks to restructure industry through the operation of market forces and to curtail drastically the economic activities of the state. In contrast with the previous Labour governments and the second phase of the Heath government, it is deeply and ideologically opposed to state intervention. It seeks to reverse the structural achievements of the labour and democratic movements and, at the same time, coupled with a comprehensive, popularly-based ideological and political offensive, undermine working class resistance to this process of rationalisation. Thatcherism thus combines a neo-liberal economic strategy with reactionary and authoritarian populism.

This assertion of popular *and* authoritarian rightism in the context of a more divided and polarised society is *new*. It is a rejection of the notion of the Tory Party as the party of consensus, as the national party in the old sense. It is a *new* response by the right to the underlying crisis of hegemony. It seeks to resolve that crisis and the accompanying impasse by mobilising a reorganised, expanded and sensitised social base embracing sections of the middle classes, the self-employed and the working class together with key elements of big capital.

The Crisis of Social Democracy

There has recently been considerable discussion of the fortunes of the labour movement over the last three decades. That controversy is readily understandable. On the surface, at least, we have been presented with something of a paradox – at least until 1979: on the one hand, the unparalleled success of the Labour Party as a governmental force, the growing power of the trade unions, on the other hand a declining Labour share of the vote and falling membership of the Labour Party and, indeed, also of the Communist Party. How do we sort out this paradox?

The new phase of British politics posed the labour movement with a new situation. The erosion of Tory-dominated consensus politics from the late fifties gave the Labour Party a new opportunity: its response was to pose as the champion of modernism, an appeal that enabled it to hold office from 1964-70 (and, in degenerate form, again later). Here we are confronted with an important characteristic of the new phase. Labour now became the predominant party of government. But the strategy of modernisation it sought to carry through – aimed at a major transformation of the economy and society – proved not only completely inadequate relative to the nature and scope of the problem but, crucially, it also involved an attack on the unions, in other words, on its own social base.

This is crucial to understanding a key facet of the new phase of British politics – the decline of the Labour Party as a popular political organisation. Labour's share of the vote at General Elections has declined from 44.1% and 47.9% in 1964 and 1966 respectively, to 43% in 1970, 37% and 29.2% in the two 1974 elections and 36.9% in 1979. The fact that it was nonetheless able to form minority governments in 1974 was because the Tories experienced an even bigger decline. In addition, the

Labour Party's individual membership – a crucial barometer of its effectiveness as a party – has declined from 830,000 in 1964 to 680,000 in 1970 and 676,000 in 1978 (according to the official figures which themselves are gross overestimate). It is clear these trends represent a very serious erosion of the Labour Party's position in British society.

Labour Share (%) of Vote at General Elections 1945-1979[7]

1945	47.8	1966	47.9
1950	46.1	1970	43.0
1951	48.8	1974 (Feb)	37.1
1955	46.4	1974 (Oct)	39.2
1959	43.8	1979	36.9
1964	44.1		

Labour Party Individual Membership 1945-1978[8]

1945	487,000	1966	776,000
1950	908,000	1970	690,000
1955	843,000	1974	692,000
1961	751,000	1978	676,000
1964	830,000		

Explaining this is obviously not easy: many factors are involved. Moreover, as is clear from the table, it is not simply a post 64/66 problem. For the decline in the new phase is also part of a longer-run tendency which was briefly reversed in the early mid-sixties. This longer-run tendency is, amongst other things, related to Labour's inability to respond adequately to underlying trends in society, such as changes in the class and occupational structure. But here we are concerned specifically with the new phase of British politics. Clearly, a crucial factor in this period has been the role of Labour governments as the central vehicle for the modernist strategy. This has meant that the Labour Party has become increasingly identified with an attempt to restructure the economy and society in a manner which did not seriously challenge the key pillars of power (the big firms, the City, the character of Whitehall, the public schools etc.) and which brought it into conflict with its own social base, the organised working class. And, moreover, if it needs adding, that strategy has been patently unsuccessful.

This attempt to modernise without disturbing the underlying structure of power meant that far from being able to champion those broad democratic movements that developed, partly as a response to this strategy, Labour governments have been in direct opposition to many of them. Far from, for example, being able to pose as the champion of new democratic aspirations, Labour became identified with the increasing use of the state in an administrative, impersonal, bureaucratic and even authoritarian manner; or, to put it another way, a growing trend towards statism. This, of course, is not the whole picture. There were important countervailing pressures, related to the character of the Labour Party and its social base. And these found expression in, amongst other things, sex equality legislation and belatedly, devolution. The dominant tendency, however, is apparent.

The implications of this have been profound. The Labour Party for many people, *especially* young people, was no longer seen as an effective oppositional, anti-establishment force: on the contrary, for many it became an establishment party, partially incorporated into the state structures. This degeneration is well illustrated by comparing the social ambition of the 1945 government and even the modernising appeal of the 1964 campaign with the retreat into managerial pragmatism evident in 1979. Inevitably, this has undermined the position of the Labour Party as a *party*, rooted in society, enjoying a popular activist base, and committed to reforming society.

Of course, there can be no simple return to the past – 1945 or whatever. Indeed, Labour's victory then was the product of a specific post-war situation and its strategy depended upon Britain's continuing international strength. That material base and the space it provided has gone. Moreover, the social reforms that Labour pioneered then, such as the welfare state and a nationalised sector, were, up to a point, consolidated: increasingly, indeed, attention was focused on the problems they gave rise to – for example, accountability and bureaucracy. Where next? Apart from the brief upsurge of modernism in the sixties, right social democracy had little to offer. Yet there is no simple process of linear advance. Unless new directions are charted and popularised, then existing positions will be undermined and past gains threatened. We are faced, thus, with a very deep and wide-ranging crisis – indeed, exhaustion – of right social democracy from which no section of the left is completely immune. That has become abundantly clear since 1979.

The Rise of Trade Unionism

An historic feature of the British working class has been the strength of its trade union organisation and consciousness. This was clearly revealed in the new phase of British politics. Indeed, the latter was accompanied by a strengthening of trade unionism – the unionisation of new sections including women and white-collar groups, the consolidation of shop-floor organisation, the encompassing of new issues. Specifically, the attack on the economic position of the working class involved in the modernist strategy produced a powerful trade union response: it was that response, that resistance, which was a primary factor in foiling the various modernist solutions and ensuring the continuing impasse at the centre of British politics.

This response was primarily economic and defensive in character – although, of course, it had wide political implications. Militant trade union activity, however, does not automatically transform working class consciousness in a leftward direction or produce a general political advance. Indeed, while trade union resistance helped prevent the ruling bloc solve the crisis on its terms at least until 1979, it was accompanied by a decline in the established forms of Labour and socialist consciousness. The most striking example of this was 1970-4. Trade unionism, thus, cannot act as a substitute for political forms of consciousness, organisation and practice. Any illusions about this can only serve – indeed *have* served – to weaken the left's independent political identity and intervention.

The role played by the unions has been bound up with important political changes in the trade union movement. In this context, the shift to the left over the period from the early sixties to the late seventies (though ambiguous and uneven) was very significant. It was crucial in enabling the kind of resistance we have discussed to happen: further, although it took place primarily around forms of opposition to the economic attacks on the working class, it also helped to generate within the trade union movement – and the Labour Party – pressures for a more radical change, as the growing support for alternative economic policies indicates.

Consciousness and the Left

When it comes to wider developments on the left, the new phase
of British politics presents us with a complex picture. The last
period since the early sixties has seen the development of a
diverse and rich range of democratic movements: on the one
hand, the strengthening of the trade union movement with the
emergence of new forms of organisation and action (e.g.
combine committees, Lucas Aerospace Plan) and, on the other
hand, the development of new movements, such as the peace
movement, nationalist forces, women's movement, abortion
campaign, black movement and community organisations. But
these were and are accompanied by a decline in the established
forms of Labour and socialist consciousness and organisation.

Right-wing Labourism, indeed, has been quite unable to
assimilate these aspirations and thereby renew the labour
movement as a political force. Indeed, it has found itself in
opposition to many of them. And ultimately this has led to deep
inroads being made into Labour's established social bloc. The
question posed now is how can the labour movement, under the
impulse of the left, begin to construct a new and enlarged system
of alliances.

This is clearly a critical problem for the labour movement.
But it has also acquired a new urgency for other democratic movements. Thatcherism represents a new kind of
global rightism. Its offensive impinges on most areas of society.
This has meant that a certain space which existed previously has
for the most part been closed down, with most of these
movements being forced onto the defensive (e.g., devolution,
immigration, abortion, trade union rights). In other words, for
them too, the ability of the labour movement to demonstrate a
wider political and social leadership has become of more central
importance.

In this context, it should be noted that social alliances can
only acquire permanence, stability and strategic perspective
through *political* organisation and intervention. That, ironically,
is one of the lessons of Thatcherism. This does not mean that
political organisation — be it the Labour Party or the
Communist Party (in their different ways, of course) — can in
any way substitute for such democratic forces. Rather, it is to
argue that part of their unique contribution is to enable these

various forces to act in concert, to acquire coherence as a social bloc with a political identity and direction. The new context of Thatcherism — and recession — has elevated the problem of political organisation in a quite new way. Its role will be critical in enabling a coming together — in a new way — of the labour and democratic movements.

But the response, here, of the political organisations of the working class will be crucial. And ultimately, the position of the political left will be vital — in helping to bring about the necessary profound transformation of the labour movement (not *just* in policies but also style of work, priorities and practice) that is required. That political left — by which is meant here the Labour Party (in particular the Labour left), the Communist Party, and others — remains, in numerical terms, very weak and fragmented. Under the impact of the crisis of hegemony, it too has been forced to undertake a process of change and renewal. That process is incomplete. In general, it remains too narrowly oppositional in its outlook; it tends to be stronger on economic than political questions; its influence within the labour movement is far greater than its wider base in society (and its own style of work reflects this). Nonetheless, in key ways, it has acquired a new strength and potential as a result of this renewal.

The Labour Left

One of the most important responses to the crisis of social democracy has been on the one hand a strengthening of the left within the Labour Party and on the other hand a limited shift in the politics of that left.

The Labour left is now a stronger force in the Labour Party than at any stage since the war notwithstanding recent setbacks. This has, in recent years, found some expression at all levels within the Labour Party — including the Annual Conference, the National Executive Committee, Parliamentary Labour Party and constituency parties. The reasons for this are manifold: the recognised failure of Labour governments, the tendency towards schisms in the traditionally close relationship between the unions and the right-wing Labour leadership, the decline of the Labour Party and the specific role played by the EEC issue.

The rise of the left has also been a product of significant changes in its own character, largely centred around Benn's position. Traditionally, the Labour left has tended to act as the conscience of the Party, more concerned with long-term objectives and moral questions than the immediate problems of tactics and policies. In a sense, therefore, it has tended to complement rather than contradict the right which has been of the opposite orientation. During the seventies, however, the left – including the Tribune Group – became increasingly concerned, in the context of the failure of Labour in office, with the elaboration of alternative policies, notably in the economic and industrial fields, but also more widely, which provide the kernel of a different kind of democratic modernist solution. As a result, it has entered battle with the right in a way which represents a real threat to the latter's position of domination within the Party.

This is clearly of great importance occurring as it does within the major working class party. We need to add, however, a number of other points, partly by way of qualification. Firstly, the left itself, despite this progression, remains very diverse, with a number of different strands. Apart from the Benn tendency, it includes, for example, moral-liberalism, fundamentalism and Trotskyism. Secondly, the left, for the most part, remains tied to an essentially electoralist-parliamentary view of politics, not only in theory but also in its practice. In this context, it tends to give, at best, only a secondary, supportive role to social and economic forces outside the Labour Party (and more unevenly, the trade union movement). This is evident, for example, in its attitude towards industrial movements, broad nationalist forces, the women's movement and CND. But this is a wider problem than simply the left: it is bound up with the nature of the Labour Party itself as a political organisation. Finally, while there are many points of renewal within the Labour left, by and large it continues to underestimate the extent of the crisis faced by the Labour Party and the labour movement. This crisis is not simply reducible to 'policies' and 'leadership'. It is the result not just of Thatcherism, but, for example, of long term changes in the composition of the working class and therefore the very structure, traditions, ideologies and culture of the movement and its social constituencies.

Finally, we must be realistic about the extent to which the left – in its diversity – has developed an overall alternative to that of the right: devolution, sexism, the social contract and reform of local government provide good examples here.

The development of a more powerful and refined Labour left is of critical importance for the transformation of the Labour Party. There is still, of course, a long way to go. And some of its limitations must be seen as wider limitations of the Labour Party itself as a vehicle for transforming popular consciousness. Nonetheless, the advances of the past period are an indication of certain possibilities.

The Communist Party

Of all the forces on the left, the Communist Party has probably been the most influenced by and responsive to the questions raised and forces unleashed by the crisis of hegemony. The CP has been deeply affected, for example, by industrial militancy, feminism, the nationalist resurgence and the student movement. In the process it has been forced to re-evaluate some of its own positions. The 1977 edition of its programme, *The British Road to Socialism* — and specifically such concepts as the broad democratic alliance, the mode of rule and the revolutionary process — evolved as responses, above all, to this crisis of hegemony. Indeed, it represents by far the most advanced *strategic* response to have come from the left. At the same time, its response to Thatcherism and the crisis of the labour movement has been more serious and coherent than anything else in the organised left. The CP has thus gone through a profound process of change over the last decade which was both essential and involved a major reorientation of its politics.

In practice, that reorientation is not yet complete. In particular, it has yet adequately to renew and clarify its role and practice. This is crucial if it is to develop a clear, popular identity. That is no easy problem — but it is a most urgent task. The biggest single weakness of the CP's practice in the new phase of British politics — and in contrast to its programme (which, in part, was a response) — was a tendency to underestimate the extent of the crisis and the range of issues around which popular support can be mobilised. Since 1979, that weakness has, in some measure, been remedied.

Postscript

The foregoing article was written in the summer of 1979, just after Thatcher's election. In this version, I have restricted myself to little more than cosmetic changes. Doubtless, if I started again from scratch, it would look a little different, not least because much has happened since then, including an interesting and stimulating debate on the left about Thatcherism. Nonetheless, such changes would not, I feel, change much of my basic argument. Events since, indeed, have reinforced much of it. Originally, the article finished with a section entitled 'Prospects'. This is obviously now inappropriate. On re-reading it, however, I am struck by one thing in particular. When it was first written, I think the majority (the great majority?) of those on the left would probably have regarded it as an exaggeration of both Thatcherism and the crisis of the labour movement. Today, unfortunately, it reads like an underestimation of the problem.

Notes

[1] For an excellent account of contemporary British politics, see Stuart Hall et al, *Policing the Crisis*, 1978.

[2] This was what might be described as the Government's informal incomes policy.

[3] See, for instance, Hall et al, op. cit.; Paul Corrigan, 'The Local State', *Marxism Today*, July 1979; Martin Jacques, 'Universities and Capitalism', *Marxism Today*, July 1975.

[4] For the Ford strike, see the interview with Dan Connor, *Marxism Today*, February 1979.

[5] D. Butler and Anne Sloman, *British Political Facts 1900-1975*, pp. 184-6; *The Times Guide to the House of Commons May 1979*.

[6] T. Russel, *The Tory Party*, 1978.

[7] Butler and Sloman, op. cit.

[8] Labour Party Annual Conference Reports.

Bob Rowthorn

The Past Strikes Back

It is a commonplace to point out that Britain's present crisis is the culmination of more than a hundred years of economic decline, during which her position as the world's leading industrial power has been destroyed, and that her economy is now one of the weakest in Western Europe. The prospect of such a decline, and its consequences for the British people, were already clear to such writers as J.A. Hobson at the end of the last century, and have been a familiar theme of commentators ever since. Despite such warnings, however, governments have been unwilling to confront the problem of decline or to act decisively so as to halt it.

The British state has displayed an extraordinary passivity and incapacity in the face of growing economic difficulties, and has never seriously pursued a concerted modernising strategy of the kind implemented, on occasion, in countries such as France or Japan. This is true even in the post war period when, apart from a brief flirtation with the idea of planning, governments have not even tried to develop a coherent and positive programme for the regeneration of British industry, nor to create the kind of civil service and state apparatus required to implement such a programme.

The hesitant and ineffectual character of government policy since the war is the outcome of a particular balance of class forces in Britain during this period. Capital has in general been opposed to a policy of vigorous planning and detailed state intervention in industry, whilst the working class has lacked the consciousness or unity of purpose to impose such a policy. The reasons for capitalist 'opposition' are both economic and political. On a political level, most capitalists are frightened of any really determined and coherent policy to modernise industry and plan its development. They believe that such a policy is the thin end of the wedge and, if successful, would legitimise socialist ideas in popular consciousness, and give rise to pressure for more radical forms of state intervention, or even for outright expropriation. Such a belief is well-founded and reflects a sound appreciation of the way in which capital maintains its hegemony in British society. Britain is a highly proletarianised country. It has a small petty bourgeoisie, the peasantry disappeared long ago, and the bulk of the population consists of wage and salary earners and their dependents. There is a strong trade union movement and, until recently, a substantial proportion of the working class supported the Labour Party. Ever since 1918 this party has been formally committed to the establishment of a socialist society, based on the 'common ownership of the means of production, distribution and exchange', and there has always been a significant element in the trade unions and Labour Party who take this commitment seriously. Given the numerical importance of the working class, the very existence of such a strong and potentially radical labour movement has posed a permanent threat to the continued survival of capitalism in Britain.

One of the main political objectives of the capitalist class has always been to contain this movement and to isolate its more radical elements. To achieve this objective, capital has been forced to forgo the economic advantages of certain kinds of state intervention because their success would legitimise socialist ideas and strengthen the left within the labour movement and society at large. Planning and nationalisation, for example, are widely associated with socialism in the public mind, and they have either been opposed outright by capital – or else, where such measures have been unavoidable, efforts have been made to give them a form which minimises the political dangers involved. In conformity with capitalist opinion, planning agencies such as the National Economic Development Council and the ill-fated Department of Economic Affairs were denied the powers they required to function effectively; there has been a persistent emphasis on the voluntary character of relations between capital and the state; and the National Enterprise Board, the Industrial Reorganisation Corporation, and many other government agencies, have been set up as semi-autonomous bodies – which are explicitly not part of a coherent central planning framework. Capital has also sought to prevent detailed intervention into the day to day workings of industry by forcing the government to deal with trade associations and similar bodies, rather than with individual companies. In these and in many other ways, capital has kept the state at arm's length and prevented the establishment of a strong and integrated planning system, whose very existence might have been politically dangerous.

Quite apart from any political motives, capital has also had strong economic reasons for opposing the establishment of an effective central planning system in Britain. Much of this capital has extensive international connections and is worried that detailed state intervention in its affairs will inhibit its global freedom of manoeuvre. This is most obvious in the case of the City of London whose role as a world banking and commercial centre requires great flexibility and involves the perpetual transfer of funds across national boundaries. It is less obvious in the case of industrial firms, but over the past thirty years they, too, have become increasingly international in character. British industry is now dominated by great multinational companies, which own productive facilities in many different countries and organise a complex international division of labour within their own enterprise. Most of these firms are British, some are American and some are Continental; but no matter what their legal nationality, all of them think in international terms and wish to minimise detailed state intervention in their operations. Thus, although there have certainly been conflicts between industry and the City during the postwar period, they have shared a common interest in opposing state policies which might disrupt their international operations. This is even true as far back as the 1950s when, although still mainly national in operation, big British industrial firms were already thinking in international terms and beginning to invest heavily overseas. Given the excellent long term prospects for such investment, these firms were quite unwilling to sacrifice their freedom of action in the interests of national economic growth. Even when British firms later became worried about economic decline and began to support planning in the early sixties, the kind of planning they had in mind was so weak as to be almost useless.

So, there are both economic and political reasons to explain why, throughout the postwar period, capital has opposed the kind of planning and state intervention required to halt Britain's economic decline. By legitimising socialist ideas such measures could have been politically dangerous and undermined the hegemony of capital; and by controlling the international operations of industry and the City these measures could have jeopardised the profits they derived or hoped to derive from such operations. This opposition from capital has been remarkably successful both in preventing the emergence of an effective planning system and in discrediting the whole idea of systematic planning in popular consciousness. It is, perhaps, the main reason why government attempts to halt Britain's economic decline have been so ineffectual.

Britain's Decline

At this point it will be useful to consider briefly Britain's postwar decline whose various phases illustrate clearly the factors we have just described. When the Labour government took office in 1945 it inherited a crude but effective planning apparatus, which it used to organise the conversion of the economy from war production to peacetime operation. Once this task was complete, the planning apparatus was dismantled and, from then on, no serious attempt was made to organise postwar economic development. Economic surveys were produced outlining future requirements, but these documents were unimpressive and there was no effective system to ensure the various targets were actually met. Because of Treasury hostility and in deference to capitalist opinion, those responsible for planning were denied any real power; the surveys soon degenerated into little more than a public relations exercise in market forecasting and were finally abandoned when the Tories took office in 1951. So ended the first exercise in planning.

The new Tory government explicitly rejected planning and systematic state intervention in the economy, arguing that the allocation of resources and the direction of economic activity should be decided by market forces. At first, this policy was successful, living standards rose and British capital prospered. However, Britain was living in a fool's paradise and success was based on a special combination of factors which could not last. After the Korean War, food and raw material prices fell dramatically and military expenditure was drastically reduced. Up to the mid-1950s this had provided considerable resources with which to increase living standards without harming the profits of British capital. However, it was a once and for all gain, and from then on any further increase in popular living standards had to come from increased productivity or at the expense of profits. Internationally British capital also came under pressure as Britain's formal and informal empire began to crumble at the end of the 1950s. For some years after the Second World War British firms had enjoyed captive markets in the Empire, from which most foreign rivals were excluded; moreover, many of their potentially dangerous rivals in continental Europe and Japan took some years to recover from the effects of the war. Later during the 1950s however, as the empire disintegrated, British firms began to experience increasing competition in formerly captive markets from both the Americans and the newly recovered Continental and Japanese rivals. Imperial decline also created difficulties for the City of London. In the 1950s the prosperity of banking and commercial capital was still based on the use of sterling as an international currency, and this in turn depended on Britain's continued domination of her formal and informal empire (i.e., the so-called 'sterling area'). As this domination was undermined, the position of sterling became even more vulnerable, and the long term future of London as a world financial centre became increasingly uncertain.

Thus, on almost all fronts, British capitalism was in difficulties by the end of the 1950s. With the loss of imperial power and increasing competition from abroad, the balance of payments became weaker, sterling crises became endemic, and the prospects for sustained growth seemed gloomy. There was a widespread feeling, especially amongst industrial capitalists, that something had to change, and in 1961 the Federation of British Industries floated the idea of national planning as a way out of the difficulty. Such planning, they hoped, would give big firms the security they needed to undertake long term investment projects and might also persuade the trade unions to accept wage restraint. However, for the reasons described at the beginning of the article (fear of the working class, international connections etc.), the kind of planning envisaged by industrial capitalists was extremely weak, and they were never willing to surrender any real power to the authorities. In 1964 Labour won the election and, after denouncing Tory planning as a fraud, set up their own planning agency called the Department of Economic Affairs. Amidst a fanfare of publicity, they unveiled the National Plan in 1965. This looked impressive, but was really little more than a set of pious hopes. In deference to capitalist opinion, the planning authorities were once again denied the powers required to operate effectively, and the plan was already a dead letter by the time it was published. It was formally buried in July 1966 when, in response to a severe sterling crisis, the Labour government abandoned its commitment to growth and full employment, and implemented an emergency package of deflationary measures designed to save the pound against speculative attack.

The implementation of this deflationary package is often portrayed as a victory of the City over industry, but such an argument is misleading. It implies that there existed at the time a viable alternative strategy for growth which industrial capital would have been willing to support. There was certainly some support in 1966 amongst industrial capital for devaluation as an alternative to deflation, but this was by no means universal. Moreover, as later experience demonstrates, devaluation by itself would not have saved either the economy or the pound, and was not in the long run a viable alternative to deflation. The only real alternative was either a *dirigiste* policy involving state control of investment and foreign trade — which industrial capital did not want — or else a full socialist programme involving the wholesale takeover of private firms — which industrial capital wanted even less. Thus, the abandonment of growth and full employment by the Labour government did not occur, as many believe, because the City triumphed over industry. It occurred because no significant section of capital was willing to support the kind of state intervention required to avoid deflation and maintain economic growth, and because the Labour government lacked both the will and the popular support to implement such a programme against the opposition of capital and its allies at home and abroad.

Labour's burial of the National Plan in July 1966 marks the beginning of a prolonged economic and political crisis which has lasted to this day. During this crisis, Britain's decline has decelerated and all pretence at national planning has been abandoned. As economic difficulties have multiplied, government policy has gone from one desperate experiment to another and, until the advent of the Thatcher government in 1979, there has been nothing which can really be described as a long term strategy for the economy. The nearest approach to such a strategy was, perhaps, the Barber 'dash for growth' in 1972-73, when the Tories sought to encourage investment through a combination of selective state intervention, financial incentives and an expansionary demand policy. However, this was not a well-articulated programme and it disintegrated as the world economic crisis built up towards the end of 1973.

In 1974 the Tories were replaced by a Labour government which promised to plan the economy and implement a vigorous programme of industrial regeneration. However, because of their radical thrust, these proposals were bitterly opposed by capital and were never implemented in anything like their original form. What finally emerged was a minor set of piecemeal reforms bearing only superficial resemblance to the ambitious industrial strategy contained the Labour Party's 1973 manifesto and advocated by left wingers such as Tony Benn. Having abandoned this part of its programme, the Labour government lost all sense of direction and its economic policy became even less coherent than that of its predecessors. Buffeted by inflation and balance of payments crises, it lurched from one emergency to another, pursuing a highly restrictive combination of deflation and wage restraint, and the result was almost complete industrial stagnation.

Table 1   Percentage change in industrial production
(excluding oil and gas)

	1951 to 1966	1966 to 1974	1974 to 1979	1979 to mid 1981*
Belgium	51	46	5	−1
France	127	56	10	−8
Italy	227	53	10	6
Spain	238	123	7	0
Sweden	103	44	−2	−1
West Germany	185	43	10	−1
UK	57	18	−1	−14

Source: NIESR, B. Mitchell, European Historical Statistics.
* 2nd quarter 1981 compared to average for 1979.

Table 2   Changes in employment in the UK 1966-81 (thousands)

	June 66 to June 74	June 74 to June 79	June 79 to March 81
Manufacturing	−713	−695	−1000
Non-manufacturing	+250	+825	−596
Total	−463	+130	−1596

Thatcherism

Looking back at postwar history up to 1979, Britain's economic decline is evident. Up to 1966 industrial production grew reasonably fast – more slowly than in other countries, but quite fast by historical standards (see Table 1). Over this period manufacturing employment rose somewhat and, apart from a few regional blackspots, there was little unemployment by current standards. From 1966 onwards however, the situation changes. Economic growth slows down and the first signs of 'deindustrialisation' appear as manufacturing employment begins to fall (see Table 2). Even so, there is some growth – by 1974 industrial production is 18% higher than in 1966 – and economic decline is relative rather than absolute. After 1974, however, even this modest expansion comes to a stand-still. Unlike other capitalist countries, Britain fails to recover from the world slump in 1974, and over the next five years output and productivity stagnate. The contrast with other countries is most striking in the case of productivity. Over the period 1974-79 output per person hour in manufacturing rose by 5% in Britain, as compared to anything between 14 and 29% elsewhere (see Table 3).

By the late 1970s the British economy was clearly in a bad way and things could not go on as they were. Something had to give. The Labour government tried to save the situation by turning on the working class. Under the guise of the social contract it administered a real wage reduction of around 8% in 1976-77. This was bitterly resented by workers and was followed by a wages explosion as they sought to recoup their losses, and finally in 1979 the Labour Government fell amongst a welter of recrimination. There was a large swing to the right, particularly amongst skilled manual workers, and a new Tory government was elected on a platform of extreme economic liberalism. Under such slogans as 'roll back the frontiers of the

Table 3   Output per person-hour in manufacturing
(percentage change)

	1974 to 1979	*1979 mid 1981*
USA	+15	+4
Canada	+14	+1
Japan	+29	+7
France	+25	+2
W Germany	+23	+2
Italy	+15	0
UK	+5	+3

Source: NIESR.

state' and 'set the people free', the Tories preached a virulent free market ideology and began a frontal assault on the institutions and practices which had grown up in postwar Britain. The approach of the Thatcher government to economic affairs marks a radical break with what has gone before and, contrary to what many people believe, is by no means stupid or ill-considered. Politically, its driving force is the widespread hostility amongst the petty bourgeoisie and the middle class towards trade unions and the welfare state, and for this reason its rhetoric is often highly demagogic in character. But beneath this demagogy the Thatcherites have a fairly coherent idea of what is wrong with British capitalism and how it can be put right. This theory has extremely unpleasant consequences for the working class and it may be completely wrong, but it is the coherent outcome of many years of intense effort by right wing thinkers. Its implementation by the Tories represents a determined attempt to come to grips with a problem which governments have evaded for decades.

Let us consider its theory for a moment. The Thatcherites share with the left the view that something is deeply wrong with the British economy and that fundamental changes are needed. However, they have diametrically opposite views about what should be done. Most of the left call for a radical programme of economic and social reforms, including both a new and strongly interventionist role for the state and new forms of democratic control over society and the economy. This, they argue, would strengthen the working class at all levels of society, weaken the power of international capital over the economy, and unleash the creative energies of the British people, so allowing them to tackle Britain's problems in a constructive fashion.

The Thatcherites reject all aspects of this programme. They are opposed to any extension of working class power and to any new limits on the rights of capital, and they reject the usual left demand for import controls and a strongly interventionist industrial strategy. Although it is often expressed in economic terms, their primary motive for opposing such measures is really political, for these are seen as one more step on the road to socialism or, as their mentor Hayek would put it, on the road to 'serfdom'. Having rejected measures of this kind and yet still believing that something radical is required, the Thatcherites are driven to their present position. They really have nowhere else to go. If a major shake-up is needed and if, for political reasons, a major state programme of industrial modernisation is ruled out, the only possible course left is to use competition and market forces to break up the existing structure in the hope that something new and more dynamic will eventually take its place. This course of action involves a number of specific measures.

For a start, an intense economic crisis is required so as to promote competition between both firms and workers. This, it is claimed, will drive some inefficient firms out of business altogether and compel others to change their methods of work. At the same time unemployment and the threat of redundancy is supposed to discipline workers, forcing them to accept lower wages and co-operate more fully with their employers. To make these economic pressures more effective, firms in trouble because of the crisis must be denied financial support, and allowed to go under if they cannot adapt and survive on their own. It is claimed propping them up will only prolong the agony and delay the profound changes which are required. On the workers' side, competition must be made more effective by legal measures to reduce the ability of trade unions to defend their members, and by cutting back the social welfare services so individual workers are forced to make private provision for themselves and their dependents. The aim of such measures is to atomise the working class and to strip workers of their collective protection, thereby making them more vulnerable to economic pressure and less able to resist their employers.

This is clearly an ambitious programme. Its aim is to transform the character of both capital and labour and to lay the basis for a particular form of capitalist recovery in Britain. With a docile labour force and low wages, Britain would supposedly become an attractive location for multinational firms, and those national firms still in existence after the holocaust would be better able to withstand foreign competition.

So much for the theory behind Thatcherism. How far have its hopes been fulfilled in practice? This is not an easy question to answer because most of the long term effects of the Thatcherite strategy are as yet difficult to observe and will only become visible if and when there is an economic recovery at some time in the future. However, the omens are not good for the strategy's supporters and the promised results seem very slow to materialise. There have been certain spectacular gains in productivity in, for example, steel and cars, and there is some anecdotal evidence to suggest that work practices are being modified throughout the economy as employers take the present opportunity to reassert managerial prerogatives and to shed labour. But the long term potential for such changes is limited and the increases in productivity which are now occurring may simply be a once and for all gain as existing production is rationalised. There is, so far, no sign that industry has been infused with the dynamism which the Thatcherite strategy is supposed to generate. Moreover, although militancy is at a low ebb at the moment, the Tories have still not crushed the unions decisively and workers are by no means defeated. Thus, there is little sign that the Tory strategy has yet achieved its long term aim of dynamising British capitalism and atomising the working class.

If the long term consequences of Thatcherism are uncertain, its immediate impact is only too obvious. There has been a slump unprecedented in the whole of British history. In just one year, between December 1979 and December 1980 manufacturing output fell by 15%. This compares with a fall of 5.5% in the worst year of the Great Depression between 1878 and 1879 and a fall of 6.9% in the interwar depression between 1930 and 1931. No other advanced capitalist country has experienced a fall in recent years remotely comparable to that in Britain (see Table 1). The nearest is France, where the Prime Minister, Raymond Barre, pursued a somewhat milder version of Thatcherism until he was thrown out after the elections. And even in France the fall in output was only half that in Britain.

The slump has led to a spectacular fall in employment. Almost as many manufacturing jobs have been lost in the past two years as in the entire 13 years of de-industrialisation between 1966 and 1979 put together. Moreover, in the past, losses in manufacturing have been offset by the new jobs created in the service sector, especially in the public services. Indeed, under Labour, the total number of people employed in Britain actually rose between 1974 and 1979, despite a loss of 700,000 manufacturing jobs. Under the Tories, however, the service sector has been shedding labour under the impact of the slump and the cuts in public expenditure. As a result, total employment has fallen dramatically. This is reflected in the unemployment statistics which, even when doctored by the government, indicate that over three million people are without jobs. In just two years unemployment in Britain doubled to reach nearly 12% of the labour force. No other advanced capitalist country has experienced anything like this, and although unemployment has increased almost everywhere, Thatcherism has made things much worse in Britain (see Figure 1).

A slump of the magnitude we are now witnessing is bound to hurt all but the most fortunate of capitalist firms and it is therefore no surprise to see that profits have fallen dramatically.

Figure 1   Unemployment in Western Europe

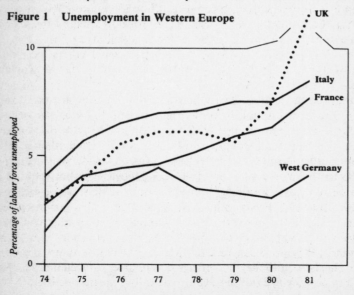

Excluding North Sea oil operations, the real after-tax profit rate of industrial and commercial companies has fallen from around 6% under the last Labour government to around 2% in 1982. Since this is an average figure, it means that even many large firms are now in trouble and must rationalise if they are to survive. This is, of course, exactly the logic of Thatcherism, which seeks to force change upon industrial firms by threatening them with bankruptcy.

SDP-Liberal Alliance

With its harsh free market doctrines, Thatcherism explicitly rejects the consensus approach followed by all preceding postwar governments, both Tory and Labour alike. This consensus approach expressed in political form an 'historic compromise' between capital and the organised working class. Under the terms of this compromise, capital accepted the basic reforms embodied in the welfare state and agreed to provide both rising living standards and full employment, whilst the organised working class confined its demands within narrow economic and political limits, neither seeking too great a share of the national income nor challenging the basic rights of capital.

However, by its very nature, such a compromise assumes that capital is willing and able to keep its side of the bargain, and when this is no longer the case the result is bound to be social conflict and the eventual breakdown of consensus politics. And this is just what occurred in Britain during the 1960s and 70s. For reasons described above, capital prevented the kind of planning and state intervention required to modernise the British economy in a rational and humane way. Government policy towards industry was therefore weak and vacillating, economic difficulties multiplied, and it became increasingly difficult to provide the rising living standards and full employment upon which the compromise between capital and the working class was based. As a result, this compromise broke down and ever since there has been endemic industrial conflict over the past fifteen years as workers have sought to increase, or even maintain, their standard of living in the face of hostile employers. And, at a political level, the forms and practices expressing the compromise between capital and the working class have now almost disintegrated.

The process of disintegration is rather complex and cannot be described in detail, but its main outlines are as follows. Within the two main political parties – Tory and Labour – there have emerged powerful radical currents which reject the consensus approach as a failure and seek a fundamental shift in the balance of power in society. Amongst the Tories this can be seen in the virulent right wing backlash which ousted Edward Heath from leadership of the Tory Party in 1974. And in the Labour Party, it can be seen in the growth of a strong left wing around Tony Benn, whose increasing influence was instrumental in causing certain elements of the party to break away and form a new centre grouping the SDP.

However, this radicalisation within the Tory and Labour Parties has not been matched by a corresponding degree of radicalisation in society at large. Some sections of the population have certainly moved to the right and, to a lesser extent, the left, but many others have simply become confused and have no idea where to place their allegiance, and as a result their voting behaviour has become increasingly volatile. In 1974 there was a big swing from the Tories to the Liberals which, because of the peculiarities of the voting system, put Labour into office. In 1979 there was a big swing away from both the Liberals and Labour towards the Tories. And now, after just two years of the present Thatcher government, there is a big swing away from both Labour and the Tories towards the new SDP-Liberal Alliance.

Thus, as economic problems have multiplied and the compromise between capital and the organised working class has broken down, there has been a radicalisation within the Tory and Labour Parties. But this has not been matched by a corresponding radicalisation in the society at large, and there has emerged a vast and unstable mass of confused voters who are not really committed to any party. It is to these people that the new SDP-Liberal Party appeals. The aim of this alliance is to re-establish consensus politics, not in the old alternating form of moderate Tory and Labour governments – which is no longer possible – but in the form of a national government based on the SDP-Liberal Alliance and supported by sympathetic MPs from all parties. Such a government, it is claimed, would unite all people of goodwill, eliminate the extremism which is supposedly the cause of all our present ills, and allow the British people to work together in a spirit of cooperation. This message is undoubtedly very popular, and it is not impossible that a national government will be formed after the next election.

What would be the fate of such a national government? Would it re-establish a stable consensus in Britain, as its supporters claim, or would it fail, just as previous Tory and Labour governments have done, and collapse amidst the usual recriminations? There are obviously many opposing views and sources of potential conflict within the Alliance, on such matters as nuclear disarmament for example, but the fate of a future national government would hinge mainly on its economic performance. If such a government could achieve anything like full employment, and provide security and prosperity for the British people, it would have a secure future and could survive indefinitely. But if it failed to achieve these objectives, a national government would probably collapse and the SDP-Liberal Alliance would go down with it.

To assess the likely economic performance of such a government requires information: both about its economic programme and about the conditions under which this programme would be implemented. On neither point can we be very sure. The programme of the Alliance is still not very clear, and so far it seems to comprise little more than a limited package of measures, consisting of a mild reflation, a certain amount of public investment, some minor social and economic reforms, together with an incomes policy and a small devaluation of the pound. This modest programme is merely a half-speed version of the Barber 'dash for growth' of 1972-73, and its chances of success are slim under the conditions likely to face a future national government.

If such a government comes to power, the economy will almost certainly be in a very weak condition for, although Thatcher's policies have been successful in some areas, they have merely wrecked others and they are most unlikely to revitalise British industry within the next couple of years. And on the international front, conditions would be equally gloomy, for the world economy is now facing a prolonged period of stagnation, and export markets will remain depressed for some years to come. Given the combination of a weak economy at home and depressed export markets abroad, the reflationary package proposed by the Alliance would have only a marginal impact on the economy. Indeed, even its academic advocates admit that it would create only $\frac{1}{2}$ million jobs which, given the rate at which jobs are disappearing under the Tories, would mean that unemployment would remain above its present level of 3 million.

Thus, unless there is an unforeseen recovery in the world economy, any government based on the policies of the SDP-Liberal Alliance would soon find itself in difficulties and would inevitably be drawn into conflict with the trade unions, just as preceding governments have been. Such a combination of economic failure and social conflict would destroy the credibility and electoral support for a national government, and the SDP-Liberal Alliance would almost certainly disintegrate under the strain. The result of such a collapse would, of course, be a highly unstable political situation. There would be millions of people deeply disillusioned not just with individual political parties, but also with the whole system of parliamentary democracy. This would pose a real challenge for the left. For unless these people could be drawn into a new and effective reforming alliance to replace the old and discredited SDP-Liberal Alliance, many of them could shift radically to the right and provide the mass base for an authoritarian government.

This is, of course, all very speculative. No one can know for certain whether the SDP-Liberal Alliance will be able to form a national government or, if it does so, whether such a government will fail. But even so, there does seem to be a good chance that such a government will be formed, and that it will fail because it is unwilling to take the radical steps needed to solve Britain's economic problems. And if it does fail, the left will face a very difficult situation in which there are new opportunities, but also great dangers.

David Currie

World Capitalism in Recession

From the Second World War through to the late 1960s and early 1970s, the international capitalist economy enjoyed a period of unprecedented expansion. Despite occasional interruptions to this long boom, it appears in retrospect as a period remarkably free from crisis. Since the early 1970s, this has changed abruptly. Because of forces originating, as we shall see, in the long boom, the international economy has been crisis-ridden. A measure of this may be observed in all the major economic indicators: economic growth has remained at relatively low levels; unemployment has remained around the 5 per cent level which it reached in 1975 in the major industrial countries, and shows no sign of falling; inflation is running, on average, at double digit levels, while profitability continues to be under pressure. In certain economies, notably the UK, the crisis has assumed much greater proportions, for reasons we touch on later, but this should not obscure the generality of the problems facing the international capitalist economy.

The continuation of these adverse trends has led to much discussion as to whether this is merely temporary, or whether a new contractionary phase of capitalist development has emerged. As the passage of time brings no sign of a return to the conditions of the long boom, the former position has proved hard to sustain, and the latter view has become more prevalent. Yet very little analysis has been provided of why, in concrete terms, such a shift from the rhythm of expansion to that of relative contraction has taken place. The purpose of this article is to examine the roots of this change in the nature and pattern of accumulation in the long boom. To do this, we seek to provide an account of the forces underlying the long boom and its collapse. This permits us to assess prospective developments in the international capitalist economy, and to consider some implications for socialist strategy.

The marked deterioration in the economic performance of the major capitalist countries over the past decade has had profound political effects. The radical right has flourished in the new climate, arguing the need to abandon consensus policies under the umbrella of the welfare state and to revert to free market economics to resolve the crisis. This renewed political confidence in old solutions has added substantial impetus to the rightward shift of the British Conservative Party under Thatcher, and to Reagan's rise to power in the USA; while the second half of the 1970s saw a strengthening of rightwing influence in Western Europe. But the political change cannot be understood simply in terms of a move to the right, but rather as a shattering of the earlier broad consensus and a polarisation of politics. The electoral victory of Mitterrand in France in 1981, and the significant move to the left of the British Labour Party, as illustrated by the influence of Benn, shows the potential for left advances in the current climate. What remains to be seen is whether the policies of the left can both carry the day and be seen to be viable in practice. The current slump offers challenges and opportunities to the left, if it can propose hard-headed and realistic policies as an alternative to the destructive course espoused by the radical right.

It is against this background that our analysis of economic developments assumes importance, providing a framework within which to assess alternative policies. Limitations of space make our treatment rather schematic and, in places, over-simple. In particular, it needs to be borne in mind that our main concern is with the general trends: while we touch on the particular experiences of certain countries, especially the UK, these are inevitably only by way of illustration.

The Long Boom

The forces underlying the strength of the long boom may be thought of in two categories: first, a set of preconditions without which a phase of rapid accumulation would have been difficult or impossible; and second, a capacity to organise the system in such a way as to take advantage of those favourable preconditions. The two are not independent, as we see in the following.

Much of Europe was a low wage/high profit economy in the decade after the Second World War. To a degree, this was the result of the ravages of the slump of the 1930s and wartime destruction, which created a large pool of unemployed. (This was added to, in the case of West Germany, by the flow of refugees from East Germany). In addition, the continuing dominance of peasant holdings in agriculture meant a large pool of disguised unemployment. Thus by minor rationalisation and consolidation of land holdings, workers could be transferred to the industrial sector from agriculture (or, more realistically, not replaced) without impairing agricultural productivity. Moreover, US dominance in West Germany and Japan in the period of postwar occupation, together with the earlier effects of fascism, ensured the weakening and dismantling of working class organisation. Together with the pressure of unemployed (or disguised) labour reserves, this meant that the terms on which workers were forced to seek employment were favourable to capital. Not only were wages low but capitalists had enormous freedom to adopt new techniques of production and alter work practices to increase profits.

The period of innovation prior to, and during the Second World War, particularly in the electrical and associated sectors, as well as in the aircraft, vehicles and chemicals sectors, provided a considerable backlog of technical knowledge. This was important in two respects: first, new methods of production, based on this advance in knowledge, could be brought into use with considerable gains in productivity; and, secondly, new important markets, particularly those for consumer goods, were waiting to be exploited.

The 1930s had seen a growing volume of investment in third world countries by multinational corporations, overwhelmingly concentrated in the extractive industries. This trend continued after the war, creating a relatively abundant supply of raw materials. Although the 1950s and 1960s saw a rising assertion of independence in the third world, this was first effective in securing political, rather than economic, independence from former colonial ties. Continuing economic dependence left control of raw material supplies with multinational corporations, mainly US-owned. In consequence, the relative price of raw materials to manufactured goods fell throughout the postwar period up to 1970. Thus, for example, crude oil was supplied at very cheap prices throughout the 1950s and 1960s. This acted to boost profitability in the industrial countries, thereby creating conditions favourable to accumulation.

Of equal importance was the expansion and modernisation of state structures. The way in which this took place varied greatly from country to country, depending on political circumstances. In West Germany, the historical legacy of a strong centralised state, together with the effects of fascism, made the task of modernisation straightforward; while in Japan the task was aided by US influence. Elsewhere, the role of the labour movement was often critical. In France, the left played a major part in the process of recovery, while similar gains were made in Britain (though to some extent dissipated by successive Tory governments in the 1950s). In Italy, by contrast, the failure of successive right-wing governments to modernise the state apparatus may be seen as a significant factor in the subsequent fragility of Italian development.

Certain, though not all, of these preconditions were present prior to the Second World War. The period of rapid accumulation in the postwar period depended critically on the capacity of the USA to structure and organise the capitalist system.[1]

The basis for this role was the dominant international position of the US economy, accounting for over 60% of total OECD output in the early 1950s. This strength placed the other advanced capitalist countries in a position of significant dependence on the USA (though this was realised only slowly by the strongest such country, Britain). The USA was able to use this power (together with the political influence deriving from its wartime role), to secure a general commitment to the principle of openness and freedom in trading relations among advanced capitalist countries. This commitment was enshrined in various international agencies, such as the OEEC (later OECD), IMF and GATT; and acted to maintain the cohesiveness of the Western bloc not only in its internal relations but also in its external dealings with the socialist bloc and the third world.

The advantages to the USA were not simply strategic. The openness of Western Europe to trade and capital flows gave US companies freedom to penetrate these markets (from which protection had excluded them in the 1930s), and to buy up significant parts of European industry. In this, they were helped by the central role that the dollar played as a reserve currency in the international monetary system (embodied in the IMF). Despite the contradictions (which we note below) in this arrangement, US capital gained substantially from it in the postwar period. On the other side, the strength of the long boom itself maintained the cohesiveness of the system long after the other industrial countries had emerged from their position of dependence on the USA. The strength of the alliance of advanced capitalist countries, with its commitment to freedom of trade and capital movements, was cemented by the success of the strategy itself. And when that success came into question, the cracks in this commitment started increasingly to appear.

Uneven Development

The favourable factors discussed above which lay behind the long boom did not operate uniformly across countries. Because of this, the historically very rapid rate of expansion of the advanced capitalist countries was associated with marked differences in rates of growth across countries. Thus, of the major economies, West Germany and Japan experienced exceptionally rapid growth; France and Italy grew fast; while the USA and UK experienced relatively slow growth (though still high in comparison with earlier historical periods).

The factors underlying the success of the fast growing economies are complex, but certain points follow from our previous discussion. Abundant labour reserves held down wages, thereby raising profitability. Effective state regulation (particularly in Japan and West Germany, indirectly through the banking system, and in France through newly evolved planning mechanisms) worked to foster accumulation; while the relatively low level of development (particularly in the case of Japan) permitted growth by the adoption of techniques of production evolved elsewhere. Japan (and to a lesser extent continental Europe) also benefited from substantial US assistance, aimed at securing Western Europe and Japan as integral parts of the Western alliance. These factors provided the basis for rapid accumulation domestically, and expansion internationally took place through exports, rather than overseas investment, thereby adding to the strength of domestically based capital.

By contrast, postwar conditions in the USA were rather less

favourable to domestic accumulation. Reserves of unemployed (including disguised unemployment) were, relatively, not large, so that high wages prevailed. Moreover, as the world leader in industrial technology, the USA did not have the possibility, open to other countries, of enjoying fast gains in productivity simply by adopting advanced techniques of production in use elsewhere.[2] Both factors led to rather slow domestic expansion. With rising competition from the more dynamic economies, it is not surprising that the more dynamic sections of US capital seized the opportunity, provided by the removal of international barriers to trade and investment, to locate an increasing proportion of their production activities in Western Europe, where the most rapidly expanding markets lay. At the same time, the US developed major international commitments, including the reserve role of the dollar and a high level of military spending, which further constrained domestic growth.

The position of the UK in the immediate postwar period, intermediate in terms of industrial development between the USA and the economies of continental Europe, gave the UK potential for growth by adopting US technology, but much less than that open to other European countries. In other respects, the factors favourable to growth were marked mainly by their absence. With a virtual absence of labour reserves, and with the labour movement emerging strengthened, rather than weakened, from the Second World War, wages were relatively high and the freedom of capital to restructure production on terms dictated by itself was circumscribed.

It would, however, be wrong to infer from these factors an absence of any potential for rapid expansion: such possibilities were there, particularly in the critical decade after the Second World War. The failure to seize those opportunities must be traced to two further factors. Historically, British capital, particularly its more dynamic sections, was oriented internationally. In the postwar period, this orientation continued, initially towards the countries of the former Empire, and later towards the dynamic economies of Western Europe. Thus, in contrast to the national capital of other European countries, a very high proportion of the production activities of British capital was located overseas.[3] In consequence, the interest of key sections of British capital in the restructuring and dynamism of the domestic economy was weakened. This was reflected in, but also conditioned by, the international role of the British state: the imperial legacy and the attempt to maintain a major international strategic role involved heavy costs in terms of military and other expenditures, and diverted attention from developing problems of the domestic economy. The result was a failure to adapt quickly enough to the new circumstances of the postwar international economy.

Once established, these differences in economic growth proved deep-seated, leading to marked uneven development between national economies. Fast growing economies were able to exploit economies of scale and modern technology, thereby increasing international competitiveness, raising their share of world markets, and thus recreating the conditions for further expansion. By contrast, slow growing economies found themselves in a vicious circle of slow growth, low and inefficient investment, and a shrinking share of world markets.[4]

In the postwar expansion the overall conditions favourable to rapid expansion were gradually eroded, in a way that we discuss in the following section. This caused the long boom to falter and finally collapse in the early 1970s, bringing rapid growth to an end even in the fast growing economies of Japan and Germany. When this happened the effects were felt most acutely in the weaker slow growing economies. In particular, the limping British boom of the 1950s and 1960s, largely carried along by rapid international expansion, disintegrated into major economic crisis in the middle of the 1970s, providing fertile ground for Thatcherism to take root. In the following, our main concern is with the development of problems of the international economy and its effects on individual economies, but the specific features of the UK crisis need to be kept firmly in mind.

Strains in the Long Boom

By the late 1960s, increasing signs of strain were apparent in the international economy. An important indication of this was the generally rising rate of inflation. These points of strain are most easily understood as resulting from the gradual erosion of the favourable factors (discussed above) underlying the long boom; from growing imbalances in the international capitalist economy (one form of which was discussed above); and the reduced ability of the USA to manage the system, this in turn being attributable to the relative decline of its domestic economy and the shift in the international balance of forces. We consider each in turn.

The long boom saw rapid growth in industrial output, matched largely by corresponding gains in labour productivity. Broadly speaking, therefore, the industrial labour force remained relatively constant.[5] But output in the service sector rose more quickly than industrial output, while productivity growth was slower than in industry. In consequence, the service sector increased employment, so that the industrial and service sectors together absorbed labour. Since this increased employment exceeded the growth in the labour force, the result was a reduction in labour reserves, whether from the pool of actual unemployed or the pool of disguised unemployment in agriculture. By the mid to late 1960s, such reserves were largely depleted, despite attempts to maintain labour supply by importing guest-workers from the 'peripheral' countries of Western Europe.[6] This was only one of several forces raising the militancy of working class organisations in Western Europe in this period as it shifted the balance of strength between workers and capitalists; but it was probably a major reason why this rising tide of militancy resulted in an increasing pace of wage settlements.

The resulting rise in wage costs was largely passed forward in the form of higher prices. This may partly be attributable to the power of large monopolistic firms to set prices with relative impunity. But the opening up of domestic markets to foreign competition probably meant that such power was declining in the 1960s and early 1970s, despite the generally growing degree of concentration of production in national economies. A more important factor was the general commitment by nation states to sustain by a variety of means the expansionary impetus of the national economy. These expansionary reflexes meant that in general price increases mitigated the decline in profitability that would otherwise have occurred, but at the cost of an upward twist in the rate of inflation.

At the same time, growing imbalances were emerging. We have already noted the disparities in growth rates between countries. These additional imbalances were of a particular significance. First, the lagging productivity in services noted above had important implications for the balance between the public and the private sector. Since public sector employment is largely concentrated in the service sector, this differential in productivity growth tended to produce a rise in the share of government expenditure in total output. This was financed by increased taxation, or by credit expansion accompanied by government budget deficits. In either case, the result was to add to inflationary pressures: a rising tax burden cut into take-home pay, tending to raise nominal wage claims as workers tried to maintain living standards and adding to the upward pressure on costs and prices; while credit expansion generated high levels of demand, creating upward demand pressures on prices. Through either route, this growing imbalance complemented the inflationary pressures arising anyway from the tightening labour market.

Second, growing imbalances in trading relations between countries were generating persistent current account balance of payments surpluses and deficits. In part, these reflected the differences in growth performance of different economies: thus the fast growing economies, Japan and West Germany, moved into persistent surplus in the middle to late 1960s; while the UK and the USA balance of payments moved into deficit. This resulted in part from the tendency of fast growing economies to expand internationally through exports, with favourable effects on the balance of payments, while US and UK capital grew through an expansion of overseas production. A further factor was the different policy responses amongst states. Thus in West Germany and Japan, the governments did not typically respond to a fall in demand by stimulating domestic demand (by expansionary monetary or fiscal policy); instead they fostered a growth of exports to make up the demand shortfall.[7] By contrast, the response in slower growing economies, such as the USA and the UK, was to stimulate domestic demand, thus tending to suck in imports and generate persistent balance of payments problems. The size of such trade imbalances tended to rise in the late 1960s and early 1970s, causing increasing instability in the international financial sphere. The persistent US balance of payments deficit was of particular significance, because of the key role played by the dollar as an international reserve currency. The ability of the USA to finance this deficit by creating more dollars led to a sharp rise in international liquidity in the late 1960s and early 1970s, adding to inflationary pressures.

Third, from 1970 onwards, there were growing indications of imbalance between raw material production and other sectors, reflected in the sharply rising price of commodities. In the 1950s and 1960s, the trade cycles in the major industrial countries were largely out of phase, so that a high demand for raw materials by one country was offset by a low demand elsewhere. But growing integration in trade tended to bring the cycles together, and this (together with contingent factors related to international financial disturbances) created a sharp, concerted boom in all the major countries from 1971 onwards. The sudden surge in demand (coupled with some supply failures) for raw materials drove their price up sharply. In the case of oil, additional factors were at work. The grip of the major oil companies on world oil production had been loosened by competition from independent companies, and the oil producing countries had been able to assert increasing control over the price and production of oil. Rising nationalism in these countries seized the favourable opportunity of very bouyant demand to create the OPEC cartel, leading to a quadrupling of the price of oil in 1973. The downward trend of primary product prices relative to manufactured prices, which had prevailed up to 1970, was decisively reversed in the period 1971-1973.

Each of these trends acted as a growing barrier to accumulation. All in concert threatened the long boom itself. These barriers were increasingly reflected in profitability, which exhibited a downward trend in each of the major advanced capitalist countries from the late 1960s onwards.[8] To avoid recession would have required much more effective organisation and coordination of the international system. But the declining position of the US internationally made it increasingly hard for the US to maintain, let alone extend, its coordinating role. The military failure in Vietnam generated an isolationist tendency in the USA and impotence in the face of rising third world (particularly Middle East) nationalist forces. The pressures on the dollar forced the USA into a protectionist trade embargo in 1971. Although temporary, it signalled a retreat from the commitment to free trade, and demonstrated openly the divergencies of interest between the major capitalist countries that had emerged. US hegemony was challenged and weakened, but no alternative could replace it. The resulting vacuum meant that the growing barriers to accumulation resulted in 1974 in the worst slump of the postwar period, triggered by the oil crisis and marking the end of the long boom.

The End of the Long Boom

1971-73 had seen a general sharp boom in each of the major advanced capitalist countries, and a generally rising rate of inflation. Some downturn was likely to occur in 1974 or 1975, simply as part of the usual rhythm of the business cycle. However, in the event, the generality and depth of the recession was unprecedented in the postwar period, and in retrospect it may be seen as marking the end of the long expansionary phase of postwar accumulation.

The onset of recession was marked by the very big rise in the price of oil. This sharply raised costs and prices in the industrial countries, increasing the rate of inflation to double digit levels, and also tended to bite into profits. But it created further problems. The price increase transferred revenue to the OPEC countries on a scale which, at least immediately, they could not spend. Although large development plans were initiated, with associated increases in imports, these planned expenditures typically took one or two years to effect. In consequence, the OPEC countries ran massive balance of payments surpluses on current account, and the counterpart of this was that the non-OPEC countries had to run large current account deficits.

With sufficient coordination of the international system, these current account imbalances need not have created major difficulties. For as the counterpart of their collective balance of payments surplus, the OPEC countries had no choice but to redeposit the revenues in the non-OPEC financial markets. Provided that the non-OPEC countries agreed to targets sharing out their collective deficit between individual countries, and provided that suitable swap arrangements to recycle funds to finance these deficits were agreed upon by central banks, the OPEC surplus need not have created problems.[9] Had such coordination occurred, the oil price increase would still have raised the rate of inflation and cut into profitability in the industrial countries; but it seems plausible to argue that the impact of the oil price increase would have been much less than it in fact turned out to be.

In the event, of course, such a degree of coordination was impossible to achieve.[10] It would have been difficult enough to accomplish with a strong hegemonic power, such as the USA was in the 1950s and early 1960s; but with US hegemony weakened and increasing signs of division amongst the major industrial countries, it was impossible to secure agreement. Certain countries (e.g., the UK and USA) attempted to follow the strategy alone by running large current account deficits; but the consequent rise in indebtedness eventually resulted in pressure on their currencies from international financial markets, forcing domestic contraction. Other countries, notably Germany, acted immediately to eliminate their current account deficit by domestic contraction and fostering exports. In consequence, the current account deficits were passed around like hot potatoes, forcing a contractionary response on the holder, and driving the international capitalist economy deeper into recession. The end result was a sharp rise in unemployment, and a fall in output and investment, with the non-OPEC deficit left largely with the third world countries, creating growing problems of indebtedness in developing countries.

Many commentators have suggested that the recession since 1973 is attributable to these factors – the effect of higher oil prices on inflation and profitability; and the lack of international coordination of the policy response of the non-OPEC (especially the major industrial) countries. However, it should be clear from the earlier argument that we do not share this view. Rather than seeing the recession as having a single cause, we see it as the result of a growing number of related structural imbalances and problems that had developed as a result of the nature and pattern of accumulation in the long boom. In summary form, these problems may be stated as:

(a) depletion of labour resources.
(b) sectoral imbalances between the industrial sector and service sector (with implications for the balance between the private sector and the public sector).
(c) uneven development between advanced capitalist countries, both in terms of growth rates and external trade (with the US payments deficit assuming particular importance).
(d) declining US hegemony and consequent leadership vacuum.

(e) growing imbalance between extractive and industrial sectors, together with a transformation in the power of the oil-producing countries.

These problems (which, of course, include the issue of oil supply) were sufficiently acute by the early 1970s to act as an increasing barrier to continued profitable accumulation; they found their expression in a generally declining rate of profit in this period.[11] It is, of course, the case that the oil price increases initiated the 1974 recession and added to its intensity. But the presence of major structural problems made the system particularly vulnerable to such disturbances, and made a major recession highly probable.

Since 1973

The oil price rise of 1973 triggered a fall in output in 1974 and 1975, a marked rise in unemployment and inflation on average in double figures. The rapid rise in manufacturing prices ate into the real price of oil, thereby easing pressures on profitability in individual countries. In addition, this acted to erode the OPEC trade surpluses, already cut into by the implementation of ambitious development plans in OPEC countries. The easing of these problems permitted a tentative revival to start, with output rising though at a rate significantly below the average of the 1950s and 1960s. Unemployment scarcely fell, since a process of rationalisation and restructuring had been initiated by the recession and the intensified international competition that it brought.

By 1979, this halting boom was petering out, and output started to stagnate in the main industrial countries. The doubling of the price of oil in the course of 1979 and early 1980 increased the oil import bill of OECD countries by about 2% of OECD output, and was, therefore, in these terms comparable to the 1973 oil price increase. This increased inflationary pressures in the system, while administering a serious blow to output. During 1980, industrial output fell sharply in the major advanced industrial countries, the decline being particularly acute in the weaker economies such as the UK and Italy. But, since unemployment scarcely fell during the halting expansion up to 1979 (having risen in the UK), unemployment in the current recession has exhibited a further, ratchet-like, upward movement, with all the associated suffering that it brings.

This period since 1974 has been one of marked instability, presenting a somewhat confused picture, with noticeable disparities between countries. The following critical features help us to understand the forces at work.

First, as we have noted in the previous section, attempts at coordination of responses to the recession, inflation and other problems, proved purgatory largely because of rivalries and conflicts among the major capitalist powers. Indeed, policy responses showed marked differences and contradictions. To a large degree, these are explicable in terms of the marked disparities in economic performance conditioning policy responses. Greater international competition in this period of recession intensified the differences in performance, already noticeable in the long boom, which were therefore more pronounced than hitherto (whether measured in terms of output, unemployment or inflation). And the lack of any coordinating force to replace US influence (by now considerably weakened by political and economic events) undoubtedly added to the instability of the international capitalist economy.

Second, one form of this lack of policy coordination was manifest in the gradual spread of protectionism in international trade. This was primarily introduced in an overt form by the advanced capitalist countries against manufacturing imports from the third world (particularly the so-called Newly Industrialising Countries or NICs, e.g., Hong Kong, South Korea, Taiwan), though some rise in trade barriers between third world countries themselves is also discernible.[12] But it seems probable that some rise in covert protection (in the form of non-tariff barriers to trade) has also occurred between the advanced industrial countries. The clearest example of this is growing US and EEC pressure against Japanese exports.

Third, a further instance of the failure of policy coordination was the lack of agreement on any effective, concerted energy-saving programme in response to the 1973 oil price rise. Reliance was placed instead on the price mechanism, though in many countries the rise in energy prices to final users was delayed and muted.[13] The higher price of energy has induced significant reductions in energy consumption only in the early 1980s, after a considerable lag, and the main influence depressing energy consumption in the second half of the 1970s was the depressed level of output. Paradoxically, the contractionary pressures in the system have prevented world energy prices from rising as much as they would otherwise have done; but this, in turn, has impeded the process of energy saving and hence the adaptation of the system to new international circumstances.[14]

Fourth, one form of the more marked instability since 1973 has been the much greater fluctuations in international financial markets, and most importantly in exchange rates. While the gyrations of the pound, down to a rate of $1.56 and then up to $2.32 in the space of a few years, have been larger than most, other exchange rates have exhibited short run movements nearly as large. This has caused sharp volatility in relative price competitiveness with consequent disturbances to international trade. Despite this, the longer run movements in exchange rates have generally been such as to eliminate the major trade imbalances. The devaluation of the dollar in the 1971-73 period helped to reverse the steady decline in US based industry's share of world trade; and the subsequent fall in the dollar in 1977-78 increased still further US competitiveness. On the other side, successive revaluations of the yen and Deutsche Mark have eroded the profitability of Japanese and West German exports. In consequence, by 1979, the current accounts of these major countries were in broad balance.[15] An important result of these changes was the considerable volume of direct investment overseas by Japan and Germany, a significant proportion going to the USA.

Fifth, the balance of accumulation has exhibited an important shift since 1973. The emergence of the newly industrialising countries has demonstrated the strength of accumulation in the third world.[16] These countries have, on average, succeeded in avoiding the worst effects of the post 1973 recession by increasing their share of export markets. Together with the rapid development of certain oil-producing countries, this represents a shift in the dynamic of accumulation towards the third world. Much play has been made of the harmful effects of the NICs on expansion prospects in the advanced capitalist countries, but these are greatly exaggerated. While the NICs may represent an important *future* force in the international economy, for the present their total size is too small for their penetration of the markets to represent a major problem. Thus in total, they account, for example, for only 1% of OECD consumption of manufactures. (Indeed, since they are major importers of capital goods, they represent important new markets for the advanced industrial countries, and it is noticeable that Japan and West Germany had been quick to exploit these possibilities.) But since their exports are concentrated in specific products and within narrow sectors, and since their export strategy is one of concentrated promotion of products, leading to a sudden upsurge of imports of certain items, acute problems have been created for particular firms or sectors in the advanced capitalist countries. In these circumstances, a combination of forces, including chauvinistic tendencies, has led to growing protection (noted above) by the advanced industrial countries against these imports (as for example against textile imports through the GATT multifibre-agreement).

The sixth feature has important, and potentially pessimistic, implications for the balance of forces between capital and labour in the future. The generally low rate of growth since 1973 has meant a depressed level of investment. This has had the effect of reducing the growth in industrial capacity well below its earlier trend. Moreover, this effect has been magnified because much investment has gone into rationalisation and replacement of existing capacity, rather than extensions to capacity.[17] This slow growth in output since 1973 has been matched by a similar slow growth in industrial capacity so that capacity utilisation has remained fairly high. Because of this capacity utilisation in 1979 in the main OECD countries is estimated to have been at around its average level for 1964-73, a period of rapid expansion in which capacity utilisation was generally high. It is therefore wrong to infer from slow growth in output and the high level of unemployment that there are ample possibilities for expansion in the world economy since capacity (rather than labour) constraints may well curtail such expansion rather quickly.

The evidence for the UK on this point is very sparse, since no reliable measure of capacity utilisation exists. But business responses suggest such a shift, and circumstantial evidence is provided by the relatively buoyant level of investment in the 1974-79 period despite low growth and low profits, pointing to a high level of utilisation of effective capacity. Moreover, the Thatcher Government's policies, which are acting to accelerate closures and bankruptcies, are causing capacity to shrink still more rapidly.

The implications of this shift are profound. If spare capacity remains low (or worse, continues to decline) relative to unemployment, unemployment will remain at high, or rising, levels. Sustained unemployment at these levels will greatly increase the power of capital to dictate its terms to the working class, and push through rationalisation of work practices. In effect, the last few years have seen trends recreating the labour reserves depleted in the long boom. It remains to be seen whether effective mobilisation by the labour movement can prevent this from shifting the balance of forces back in favour of capital.

The final major change has resulted from shifts at the political level. The governments of Western Europe and the USA have pursued more conservative policies since 1974, under the influence of both deteriorating economic circumstances and of the increased influence of the radical right. (It remains to be seen how successfully the new Mitterrand administration can reverse this tendency.) Most governments have been, and continue to be, committed to a deflationary, monetarist policy at the macroeconomic level, involving tight monetary control and cutbacks in the public sector. This is not surprising, for in a highly integrated international economy, expansionary measures by individual countries will quickly run into the barriers of a weakening trading position and rising inflation; to avoid this requires either a degree of international coordination of policy that has been lacking, or radical measures that strike at the freedom of the international market to dictate domestic developments. (This represents a major, but not insuperable, obstacle to the implementation of the Mitterrand programme.) In any event, the consequence, as we have noted, has been a gradual but persistent drift into slump that invites parallels with the slide towards the international depression of the 1930s.

Despite this common shift towards a more contractionary stance of policy, the scope and effects of government involvement have differed markedly between countries. In part, this reflects the differing conditions of different national capitals: those such as Japan and West Germany with relatively high profitability and a strong dynamic industrial base have been able

successfully to weather the more adverse conditions induced by
monetarist policies; whereas weak capitals, notably the UK
bloc, have experienced an almost complete erosion of
profitability that may well prove fatal to important sections.
Thus the impact of contractionary policy has operated unevenly
between countries. Moreover, in the more dynamic economies,
governments have encouraged, whether by direct intervention or
indirectly, an active process of restructuring in response to the
changed circumstances of the world economy. The consequence
has been to foster investment and research and development in
new branches of industry, such as micro-electronics, and to
support declining industries by attempting to plan their phased
run-down. Elsewhere, particularly in the UK, government has
expressed a conscious aim of withdrawing from involvement in
industry, leaving it to market processes and the supposed
incentives of lower taxation to restructure the economy. The
practice has been rather different from this objective. In the
event, the precipitate collapse of British industry has forced
government to provide substantial funds to major sectors such
as British Leyland and steel to ensure their continued survival;
but such help has been piecemeal and has not formed part of a
conscious overall strategy. Moreover, the collapse of the
economy has disrupted government finances, forcing an increase
in the overall tax burden. It is still too early to observe whether
the rather similar strategy (going under the label of 'supply side
economics') of the Reagan administration in the US will also run
into the sand, or whether the UK failures reflect the deep
structural weaknesses of the domestic economy.

Prospects for world Capitalism

The international economy experienced almost stagnant output
in 1980/82 as OECD trade fell significantly. This resulted from
a slackening of the tentative boom of 1976-78, and from the
doubling of the price of oil in 1978/80. We are in the midst of a
replay of the recession of 1974/75, but at a much higher level of
unemployment.

There are, however, certain differences between the
prospective recession and the previous one. The synchronisation
in 1972-73 of the booms of the major capitalist countries was
not observable in the 1976-78 boom (thereby contributing, in
part, to its weakness). Thus whereas output in the USA seems to

have been faltering, that in Japan and West Germany retained its buoyancy, at least until the recent sharp rise in oil prices. But this factor may be outweighed by two further factors, both of which suggest a rather more prolonged recession than in 1974-75.

After the 1973 oil price increase, inflation in the advanced industrial countries led to a sharp fall in the real oil price, thereby eroding the contradictory effects of the OPEC oil price rises. But with generally contractionary policies by states, such an inflationary response is likely to be rather more muted. Moreover, the OPEC countries have become increasingly aware of this possibility, and have proved much more ready to make good any decline in the real price by a suitable adjustment of the dollar price of oil.

Furthermore, in 1974-75 a number of OPEC countries launched ambitious development programmes, which ran into problems of finance subsequently. But the upsurge in expenditure helped to eliminate rather more quickly the problem of OPEC surpluses. This time round a much more cautious response has resulted (particularly given the political changes in Iran), so that the OPEC surpluses are likely to be a larger, and longer-lasting, problem for the advanced capitalist countries.

On balance, therefore, the prospects are for a continued recession, of a fairly prolonged character. While some revival of output is to be expected, such expansion as there is will be weak and hesitant. Against this background, the prospects for unemployment are grim, rising in the early 1980s in a ratchet-like progression. Within the total view, the prospects for weaker countries, like the UK, are correspondingly worse. What we are experiencing is a protracted slump that bears serious comparison with the 1930s depression.

Such crystal-ball gazing is, of course, speculative. Moreover, from the perspective of capital, all is not gloomy. We have already noted the limited recreation of labour reserves, threatening to shift the balance of economic forces away from labour in favour of capital. The microprocessor revolution, as it becomes applied, may take this process further, particularly in the service sector, thereby acting to rectify the imbalance (discussed previously) between productivity performance in services and industry. The evidence of significant restructuring in all branches of industry indicate that the conditions for a renewed phase of accumulation are gradually being recreated.

However, such a restructuring process is likely to be a long and prolonged one. Moreover, as we noted in discussing the origins of the long boom, the re-establishment of such preconditions is not sufficient to permit profitable accumulation to restart. The hegemonic, coordinating role needs also to be assumed. Thus the 1930s saw a major process of innovation and restructuring in the midst of depression, but it was only after a lengthy period of time, including a world war, that the political conditions, in the form of the dominance of the USA, for hegemonic direction of the system were created. History, we must hope, does not repeat itself, but it is now hard to see the emergence of any effective coordinating force (whether a single country or an effective coalition) even as a result of major international political upheaval.

The prospect, therefore, is for a long, depressed phase of capitalist development. This phase offers the left both opportunities and problems, to which we now turn in conclusion.

Issues for Socialist Strategy

In this concluding section, we turn to consider briefly some implications of the above analysis for the left and for economic strategies advanced by the left. These strategies and the specific context within which they have been worked out vary from country to country, though it is also true to say that, for example, the Alternative Economic Strategy (AES) of the British left has major elements in common with the Mitterrand programme. Here we focus on common issues and problems, most notably those posed by the high degree of integration of Western European economies in the international economy.

At the outset, it is important to stress the obvious point that the current slump reveals with brutal clarity the need for the democratic socialist alternative to capitalist regulation. Unacceptable unemployment, depressed living standards, cuts in social services and high inflation all point to the failures of contemporary capitalism, and would create conditions propitious to the propagation of an effective alternative. This is not to argue that conditions of slump are necessarily simply periods of advance for the left, since historical experience suggests that such periods generate contradictory cross-currents within society, and specifically within the working class. (Thus the 1930s, with the rise both of the Popular Front and of fascism, indicate the manner in which periods of crisis force a major questioning and reassessment, but simultaneously a polarisation and radicalisation of society.) But if the left cannot establish a mass base of support for such a programme in the coming period, when the system is in crisis and capitalist responses are divided and hesitant, then the possibility of acceptance at other times must be slim indeed.

In Britain, despite the major setback of the Thatcher government, signs of the growing awareness of the need for *elements* of the AES are apparent. The intellectual barrenness of the right wing of the Labour Party; the growing indications of divisions within the Conservative Party, with signs of revolt against the stringent cuts in government spending, against the willingness of the present government to abandon large sections of industry to international competition, and against the freeing of control over international finance with the abolition of exchange controls; the growing sections of British industry pressing for protection (in a significant number of cases in response to corresponding protection overseas); and the general signs of a broad movement against monetarism – all these indicate the signs of rejection of current strategy in favour of particular components of the AES. But as yet these represent mainly reactions to adverse trends without any commitment to any viable, well-thought out alternative strategy. Thus the lack of any effective opposition by the right of the Labour Party springs from its lack of any real alternative, as the 1976-79 monetarist policies of the Callaghan/Healey axis made all too clear. The left alternative strategy is the only coherent alternative to monetarist policies, and it is the growing support for this programme in the Labour Party and the broader labour movement that is the most significant and hopeful development for the left. What is vital is for this movement to be broadened still further, to forge alliances between diverse groupings, to make a reality of the broad democratic alliance on the left. In this, the example and experiences of the Mitterrand programme may prove critical in winning wider support for the AES in Britain. But the winning of the political and intellectual argument for the AES requires the left to face squarely the new trends and issues thrown up by the current slump.

It is clear that the economic strategies advanced by the left in each country must provide a coherent and effective framework for economic recovery in the particular country. In this respect, it must be nationally oriented and address the specific problems and weaknesses of the national economy. But, in this, it should not lose sight of the fact that each country is heavily integrated into the international economy, and that this imposes both problems and obligations. In seeking national solutions, the left should not lose sight of its internationalist traditions. But all too often the AES is presented in its national dimension, without adequate consideration of the associated international issues.

The areas of interdependence of policy between countries are legion. Major industries, such as steel, chemicals, cars, and electronics, face similar problems in a number of Western European countries, and need coordination of policies to tackle them. We have already noted the interdependence of demand management policies, whereby domestic expansion is more easily sustainable in the context of a wider, general economic expansion. The volatile exchange rates of the 1970s and early 1980s represent problems that can only be fully tackled in a coordinated fashion, as can issues of balance of payments correction. And the critical issues raised by the North/South dialogue and policies towards restructuring the international economic order can only be thought about in a framework of international cooperation.

These issues represent an agenda for policy, and it is not the role of this chapter to discuss these issues or to develop proposals. Rather the point is that the left needs to take the offensive in the intellectual debates surrounding these issues, offering positive ideas for cooperation and development. Use needs to be made of existing institutional structures in this debate, the result of which may be reform and adaptation of existing institutions to new circumstances. In this, the institutions comprising the EEC form an important focus: it may, after all, not be impossible for the EEC, under pressure from an assertive left, to permit greater democratic planning of economic developments. It might even countenance differential protection: the EEC accepted effective tariffs on agricultural trade in the form of the 'green' currencies; and it is conceivable that it might evolve a system of 'black' currencies applying to industrial products. Only if the left abdicates its responsibilities and withdraws from these debates is the outcome clear: that progressive, democratic changes will be removed from the agenda.

Having said this, it is also clear that national developments cannot await international cooperation, because such cooperation will depend on the strengths of national movements. (Thus Mitterrand's success in implementing his national plan for economic expansion in France will be critical in determining his ability to influence Western European policy-making.) These national movements must formulate their own national strategy for economic revival, while bearing international considerations carefully in mind. In the UK, the AES represents this strategy, envisaging economic expansion based on planning of imports, coupled with an extension of democratic planning and control to major areas of the economy.[18] Our discussion of trends in the international economy suggests three issues that require careful consideration in the AES in the context of the UK.

First, there is the issue of the retaliation against import controls. The demand for general import controls is not, of course, a demand to *reduce* imports; rather, it is a demand to expand the economy while preventing the level of imports from *rising* as a consequence. It is therefore a demand not for *protection*, but rather for the *management* of trade. Since such controls will not reduce imports, the economic justification for retaliation is, on average, absent (though it must be admitted that some countries would gain and others lose).

However, the argument does not dispose of the risk of retaliation. We have already noted that the degree of covert protection has risen significantly in the recession since 1973, and several advanced capitalist countries have shown their willingness to resort to protectionist measures. The advent of a left government, introducing general controls, may provide the convenient excuse for such action, particularly given the intensified competition of the present slump. Moreover, there will be numerous pressures, notably from international capital (whose underlying interests is in unfettered trade), to introduce retaliatory measures with the effect of destabilising the economy and bringing down the left government. And given the dependence of the British economy on exports, it could not withstand a major retaliatory protectionist war.

This is not to argue against import controls, which must be regarded as a major and essential plank of the AES. Rather it is to argue that the left must give serious attention to the strategic and tactical issues involved, and specifically to the considerable bargaining power that the UK would have in such a position and to how it can best be deployed to *minimise* the risk of large scale retaliatory action by other advanced capitalist powers. One objective of the left must be to aim for a reform of international agreements and institutions that make such action more difficult. Thus it might press for a ban on discriminatory responses to non-discriminatory protection (aimed at economic expansion), backed-up by the threat of discriminatory action against offenders.

The second issue is raised by the continuing rapid decline of the UK relative to other advanced capitalist countries and relates to longer run supply considerations in the UK economy. A major longer run objective of any left strategy must be to reverse the decline, and maintain or improve the relative economic strength of the UK. But to do this is must be recognised that the UK record of industrial innovation has also deteriorated markedly, and that this is a significant factor in UK decline. A major part of the strategy for economic revival must be to raise the innovatory performance of British industry. But this in itself will not suffice. Given the small relative size of the UK, it must be expected that the vast bulk of innovations will take place in other countries. The UK will clearly have to import this technology, as indeed it is increasingly doing already (as reflected in the rising share of imported capital goods), by a variety of means, whether by foreign ownership or the direct impact of capital equipment. Such arrangements pose important issues for the left of a kind familiar to third world countries: how to import essential technology on which future growth depends on terms which retain democratic control over the developments in the economy. Once again, such problems can be resolved, but only by serious analysis by the left of the issues involved.

Finally we consider one further question: the problem raised previously concerning short run capacity constraints in the British economy. Central to the AES is the demand that unemployment is reduced decisively by expansionary policies. But there must now be serious questions concerning the degree of spare capacity in British industry, because much old plant has been rendered obsolete by the upheavals since 1973 and because of the low level of net investment since that date. In these conditions, an expansion of demand may not be able to stimulate home production to the extent required to cut unemployment sufficiently. This problem is being made steadily worse by the current policies of the Thatcher government, which are acting to accelerate closures and bankruptcies. Any estimate of the magnitude of the problem would be a mere guess, since information on such matters is so poor, but unemployment might only drop to one and a half million before all effective existing plant is working near to capacity. Any further stimulus (with suitable control of imports) would merely generate acute inflationary pressures, which would sabotage any left strategy for economic revival.

The AES envisages a solution to this problem. By reversing current cuts in the public sector, and indeed aiming for further expansion, the AES involves a significant expansion of public sector employment, so that unemployment can be cut to acceptable levels despite the capacity constraint on employment in the public sector. But this is not without its attendant dangers (relating back to the issue of the balance between the provision of public services and private goods). For it implies that the main thrust of short run expansion will be in the public sector, not in a greatly increased supply of industrial goods. And this means that any short term rise in take-home pay will have to be restricted, with the fruits of expansion being enjoyed in the form of a rise in the social provision of services (i.e., the social wage). This need not be unappealing, particularly since the left should be able to devise imaginative new forms of social provision (particularly at the community level) to replace the atomistic structure of many aspects of our lives under contemporary capitalism. But this requirement needs to be considered carefully and absorbed into our political campaigning if false expectations are not to be aroused. In particular, the presentation in certain quarters of the AES as 'more of everything' must be carefully avoided.

This problem of short term capacity pushes to the very forefront of the AES the demand for a planned investment drive in British industry on terms determined by democratic control. Without a major lift in the level of investment, with the object of re-equipping and modernising British industry, the other objectives of the AES will fail. The concrete means by which this will be accomplished in each sector (i.e., the precise balance between planning agreements and nationalisation) needs much more serious consideration by the movement. The substantial future revenues from North Sea oil provides the means by which this investment boom could be financed without the need for any real short term sacrifice in terms of living standards, and the left demand that North Sea oil should be earmarked for this purpose is clearly correct. But if the disastrous policies of the Thatcher government continue, the resulting damage to British industry could be so severe that North Sea oil revenues are squandered on a flood of imported consumer goods. The essential unity between opposition to the Thatcher government and the struggle for the AES is revealed sharply on this issue.

Notes

[1] For a brief but lucid statement of this role, see Ron Smith, 'The Decline of the US Economy', *Marxism Today*, December 1979.

[2] This is over-simple, in that West European technology was more advanced in certain sectors. But such cases were the exception, and overall the argument is valid.

[3] In 1971, UK overseas production as a % of GDP is estimated at 55%; figures for other countries are: USA 22%, France 16%, Italy 9%, West Germany 8% and Japan 4% (UN, *Multinational Corporations in World Development*).

[4] The shares of world manufacturing exports were:

	1950	1977
UK	25.5	9.3
US	27.3	15.9
West Germany	7.3	20.8
Japan	3.4	15.4

[5] There were, of course, different national trends. Thus the UK and US shed labour in the industrial sector, while Japan, West Germany and France expanded employment.

[6] The extent to which guest-workers could relieve labour shortages was limited by constraints (political and social) on the amount of such workers and also by their general lack of the required industrial skills. The UK position was rather different: imports of Commonwealth workers took place on a large scale in the 1950s and early 1960s; by the time labour constraints started to bite in other European countries, the failure of the UK to compete internationally was leading to a falling demand for labour and a movement towards increasing restrictions on immigration.

[7] The resulting structural current account surplus led to considerable market pressure to revalue the exchange rate. The powerful pressures from export-oriented industries blocked this for some considerable time, because of the harmful effects it would have had on export sales. An additional factor in the case of Japan may have been worries about *future* deficits: high growth required a rapid increase in imports of raw materials, and the danger was that other industrial countries would not permit the rate of increase of exports required to finance this.

[8] See T.P. Hill, Profits and Rates of Return, OECD, 1979.

[9] Some further complications would have arisen from any wish by OPEC countries to buy real assets, such as property or gold, but at least in this period such problems were minor.

[10] Had it been so, other possibilities, such as coordinated action by the oil consuming countries against the OPEC cartel, might have been attempted. Although the idea was floated, rivalries amongst the oil consumers precluded action.

[11] See T.P. Hill, *op. cit.*

[12] See S.A.B. Page, 'The Management of International Trade' in R. Major, *Britain's Trade and Exchange Rate Policy*, Heinemann/NIESR, 1979.

[13] For the UK, see: J. Morel, 'Real Prices of Energy', *National Institute Economic Review*, August, 1980. See also OECD Economic Outlook, July 1981.

[14] For a careful exposition of this argument, see *World Trade and Finance: Prospects for the 1980s, Cambridge Economic Policy Review*, Vol. 6, No. 3, December 1980.

[15] Since then, the oil price rise has pushed the major industrial countries into deficit. The exception is, of course, the UK, which now has overall self-sufficiency in oil. It should be noted that in the UK the combination of severely contractionary domestic policies in conjunction with North Sea oil has meant that external balance has been achieved by a sharply rising exchange rate during 1979/80, with consequent damage to UK domestically based industry.

[16] For a useful discussion, see OECD, *The Impact of the Newly Industralising Countries*, 1979. In this report, the NICs are taken to be Hong Kong, South Korea, Taiwan, Brazil, Greece, Mexico, Portugal, Singapore and Yugoslavia; the first three have exhibited the most spectacular growth.

[17] Thus a 20% growth in non-residential investment in Japan up to mid-1979 is estimated to have raised capacity by only 1%. See OECD *Economic Outlook*, December 1979.

[18] For a lucid exposition of the AES, and the currents of debate surrounding it, see S. Aaronovitch, *The Road from Thatcherism*, London 1981.

II Thatcherism

Andrew Gamble

Thatcherism and Conservative Politics

Introduction

In April 1979 the willingness of the minor parties to sustain the Labour administration finally fell away, bringing to a close another period of dispiriting and ineffectual Labour government. Labour had returned to office in 1974 in the midst of an industrial and political crisis and at the beginning of a major downturn in the world economy. It was ejected once more following the collapse of its pay policy and its devolution policy. A Labour administration had presided over a further episode in Britain's economic decline. It had attempted to mitigate the worst effects of the recession, but increasingly without any clear policy or strategy other than day-to-day survival. The control of inflation had become its chief priority, and unemployment had risen to 1.5 million. At the general election in May 1979 the Conservatives won a decisive parliamentary majority. It would have been surprising had they not done so. Since 1959 no government after serving a full term had been re-elected, chiefly because no government had succeeded in interrupting the record of deepening economic failure. The Callaghan administration was certainly no exception.

In terms of votes the Conservative victory in 1979 was less impressive. The parliamentary majority of the new government was 43, but it enjoyed the support of less than half of those actually voting (44.9%) and only a third of those entitled to vote. But this was a significant advance over October 1974 when only one in three voters and only one in four electors had supported the Conservatives – the lowest level of support the party had recorded at any general election this century. The revival of electoral support for the Conservatives was most marked in England, particularly in the South and in the Midlands.[1] But the movement was not uniform. The swing of support to the Tories in Scotland and the North of England was significantly lower, and this increased still further the already marked regional bias of Conservative support. In 1955 the Conservatives had won 111 seats in Scotland and the North of England, but they only managed 78 in 1979; in the South, by contrast, the Conservatives captured 261 seats (as against 223 in 1955).

The revival of Conservative electoral fortunes therefore did not mark any great popular landslide towards them, nor did it assure them an impregnable electoral position, but it did allow the Conservative leaders to claim a mandate, and in marked contrast to the behaviour of Labour administrations, to set about the implementation of a highly partisan programme with great vigour, enthusiasm, and confidence. As a result the significance of May 1979 for many of the architects and advocates of the Government's new strategy, and for many of its opponents on the left, went beyond electoral arithmetic. It signalled the crossing of a major political watershed, the decisive break with the social democratic consensus, the marking out of a new terrain for British politics. The Thatcher Government was soon being described as the most radical government in Britain since the war, and as the most reactionary government in Europe.

This reputation rested on the programme which became known as Thatcherism. Thatcherism does constitute a major new perspective and strategy for the Conservatives, although it also re-activates and continues certain traditions of the party. Its rise within the party is a response to the party's gradual long-term decline. But the Conservatives are not alone in their plight – in the last twenty years the strength of the support for both major parties had been noticeably undermined and along with it the legitimacy and stability of parliamentary government.

Thatcherism and the Politics of Support

The reasons for the deepening crisis of the British party system lie in the wider political and economic decline of the British state. The inability of either party to come to terms with this decline, or to reverse it, has caused a long-drawn out crisis of identity and purpose for both of them. For the Conservatives the loss of British world power and the continuing relative failure of

British industry to become internationally competitive has threatened the ability of the party to identify itself and win support either as the party of nation and of national institutes, or as the party of competent government and prosperity.

The dilemma for the Conservatives is acute. Ever since the rise of mass democracy it has had to rely on working-class votes, and since the 1920s it has had to maintain its working-class support against the competition of a party claiming to be the exclusive representative of the interests of that class. Since 1918 occupational class identity has been the most important factor in determining the way in which the majority of people cast their votes in Britain, yet the party which has won most general elections and which has been most frequently in government has been the Conservatives. This means that the party has always had to draw at least half its support from across that occupational class divide. Conservative leaders have generally been acutely aware of the precariousness of their position, and of the need constantly to win over working-class opinion by articulating national interests and concerns, maintaining a popular bloc, and presenting themselves as governing for the people rather than for any one section of it. But Conservatives have never been primarily a party of the nation but a party of the state. Their objective in organising and maintaining a broad national coalition has not been to force demands on government but to ensure popular support for whatever policies the Conservative leadership judge are necessary.

The party's electoral fortunes after 1880 were built upon projecting itself as the party of the Union, the Empire, and the Constitution, and identifying the party with the established institutions and the symbols of national legitimacy. National issues and national causes were used to great effect to rally a substantial section of working-class and trade unionist support behind Conservatism, and the Falklands War shows that they still can. The Empire, however, has gone, the Constitution is in disarray, and even the Union has recently proved unsteady. The identity of the Conservatives as the national party is no longer so automatic or so easy, especially after Macmillan and Heath had identified the party so strongly with the Common Market, and Labour had developed its own national rather than class appeal. The Falklands War tells us more about Britain's past than its future.

The end of British expansion and world power was always
certain to damage the Conservatives more than their electoral
rivals. As the themes of patriotism and national greatness
dimmed, so the Conservatives came to rely more on their appeal
and standing as the party of prosperity, the party which knew
how to manage the national economy – 'Life's better under the
Conservatives: don't let Labour ruin it', as the famous 1959
election poster proclaimed. This approach appeared to pay
handsomely in the 1950s, when the Conservatives presided over
an economy comfortably afloat in the backwash created by the
boom in the world economy. In the last twenty years, however,
the problem of the relative decline of the British economy and
the steady worsening of Britain's economic problems,
particularly since the deepening world recession after 1974, have
made all British governments appear powerless. Support as
measured by opinion polls, by-elections and general elections
has fluctuated violently, in marked contrast with the period from
1945 to 1959 (when no government lost a by-election until
1957).

The Conservatives particularly suffered from their spell in
office from 1970-74, which saw four states of emergency, an
unprecedented post-war level of industrial conflict, high
unemployment, high inflation, and the spectacular shipwreck of
the Government's attempt to expand the economy on the rocks
of the oil crisis, the miners' strike, and the three-day week. After
that experience and the earlier one between 1960 and 1964, the
Conservatives could no longer very plausibly claim to be the
party of prosperity and successful economic management. They
were further handicapped by having moved from being the party
of Empire and protection to becoming the party of free trade
and Europe. The Conservatives were finding it increasingly
difficult to project themselves as the defenders of the national
economy, since so much of domestic capital had made their
operations international and powerfully reinforced the
traditional pressure from the City for free movement of goods
and capital.

It is against this background that the rise of Thatcherism
must be seen. The last twenty years have produced major
debates and rifts within the party and at times the Conservatives
have seemed on the way to becoming a party of ideology and
doctrine, the very things they derided in their political

opponents. Conservatives have normally prided themselves on their unity and the absence of factions and splits, which used to make the party very different from many mass parties of the right elsewhere, such as the Italian Christian Democrats. The new preoccupation of the party with ideological debate has originated from a ferment amongst party supporters which precedes the current recession but has been enormously amplified by it.

When the Conservatives were in Opposition between 1964 and 1970, a New Right took shape in the party which was distinct from the traditional right (although membership often overlapped) in so far as it drew its strength from a rejection of the consensus around social-democratic values and objectives that had been established ever since the war-time coalition. The New Right is the seedbed from which Thatcherism has grown, and is composed of two rather different strands. There is the revival of liberal political economy, which seeks the abandonment of Keynesianism and any kinds of government intervention; and there is a new populism – the focusing on issues like immigration, crime and punishment, strikes, social security abuse, taxation and bureaucracy.

Central to the gospel of the new economic liberalism is the doctrine of the social market economy and the concept of a market order.[3] These notions can be traced back a long way in liberal thought, and they have been restated with great clarity by Friedrich von Hayek, the most important theorist of the new liberal political economy. He makes three crucial theoretical distinctions – between liberty and democracy, between law and bureaucracy, and between the market and planning. The ideal society is a market order in which all actions and choices and exchanges between individuals are regulated by general rules which are known in advance and apply to all indiscriminately. The existence of such general rules permits a sphere of economic liberty to arise, but only if a strong public power is organised to enforce them. Such a power must exist if all individuals are to enjoy liberty, but what safeguards can be created to prevent the public power itself from taking away the liberty of individuals? If liberty is to be preserved then this public power must refrain from trying to influence the choices and outcomes of the market, and limit itself to guaranteeing the framework (in particular property and contract, free competition, and sound money) and removing all obstacles to the unimpeded development of free choice.

The doctrine reconsecrates the divide between the public and the private. All collective measures to regulate industry or to provide welfare benefits or services are infringements of individual liberty and substitute the arbitrariness of bureaucracy for the impersonality and even-handedness of the rule of law. The results are both morally wrong and economically inefficient. The doctrine does not suggest that there should be no state welfare services and no collective provision. A *social* market economy is intended to guarantee certain minimum standards. But beyond those the freest possible scope is to be given to private initiative, individual responsibility, and free choice. Such an economy is expected to generate high and rising levels of welfare spending, but only because an increasing proportion is provided through the market itself. Market outcomes are preferred to planning outcomes and have to be accepted, whatever they are. There is no justification for any collective redistribution of resources, except for the provision of certain minimum standards, and this is because there is no sense in which market outcomes can be regarded in ethical terms at all. Social justice resides not in what individuals get, but in the rules governing how they get it. In return for economic liberty, individuals must reconcile themselves to great and often arbitrary inequalities.

The doctrine supplies a most powerful set of ideological weapons against social democracy. For social democracy involves constant interference with market outcomes in the name of popular sovereignty and the claims of the community over the individual. The new liberal political economy attacks this at its root. The economic demands of the New Right are not primarily tactical or opportunistic but are grounded in ideological principles which are fundamentally hostile to the principles of social democracy. This can be seen by looking at the main economic doctrines proclaimed by Thatcherism. There are three key propositions:

(1) The public sector is an unproductive burden on the wealth-creating sector in general and on taxpayers in particular. From this follows the need to drastically reduce public expenditure and to return as many services in the public sector as possible to the market and to the family. The aim is firstly to

prevent the real cost of public services rising at a time when output and productivity are stagnant or falling. But it is also to permit the kind of tax cuts that are intended both to secure electoral support and to encourage the revival of private enterprise, the regeneration of the capitalist class, and to restore family and individual responsibility.

(2) The chief aim of government economic policy should be maintaining price stability by firm control of the money supply. This is because control of the money supply is believed (though many economists doubt it and events in 1980 belied it) to be the one thing that governments actually can control in a capitalist economy. The money supply can be controlled if governments steadily reduce their borrowing, so removing any temptation to resort to the printing press to increase revenue, and if government sets monetary targets and controls the volume of private credit in line with them.

To believe that governments can and should control the money supply means believing that governments are directly responsible for whatever rate of inflation exists. Wage demands by trade unions, according to monetarist doctrine, do not by themselves raise or lower the rate of inflation, so income policies and the involvement of unions in discussions about general economic policy are entirely unnecessary. But trade unions are directly responsible for the level of unemployment if they insist on a level of real wages which firms cannot pay. Trade unions are also responsible for stagnation and a slow rate of growth to the extent that they are capable of resisting rationalisation and reorganisation of the labour process aimed at raising productivity. The effects of high unemployment and stagnant or falling living standards can create political pressures for an expansion of money supply which governments find hard to resist. If they give in to them, higher rates of inflation will result, which will indirectly be the consequence of trade-union action. But it is a key doctrine of monetarism that government efforts to realise a higher level of employment or a faster rate of growth by expanding demand (the mainstream Keynesian prescription) are doomed to failure because of the existence of a 'natural' rate of unemployment and a 'natural' rate of growth. These are determined not by the level of demand but by the institutional organisation of markets. Expanding demand can only raise the rate of inflation.

(3) The role of government in the economy should accordingly be confined to maintaining the conditions for markets to function properly. Stable money is one such condition, security of property and enforceability of contracts are others. In addition governments have the duty to intervene to remove any obstacles which prevent markets functioning properly. Taken together these tasks do not imply a small role for government or a non-interventionist role. On the contrary it signifies not a withdrawal but a redirection of state energies and goals, and constant vigilance to maintain and extend the market order. The free economy requires a strong state.

Thatcher and Heath

How far do these doctrines and the strategy which is based upon them represent a break with the strategies employed by Conservative Governments in the past, and in particular by the Heath Government? There are certain undeniable resemblances between the two. Both the Heath and Thatcher administrations presented programmes which ostensibly broke with central priorities of the social democratic consensus. Both followed periods of ineffectual Labour government and intense internal ideological ferment directed against social democracy. Both began with aggression and confidence. The Heath Government proclaimed a withdrawal from intervention, it ended assistance to lame ducks, it conducted a selective massacre of the Quangos, it committed itself to reducing public expenditure and proposed a series of new charges on public services, and it put forward a wide-ranging programme of trade-union reform.

But these similarities should not blind us to the essential differences. Although Heath's policy appeared at the time to mark a break with social democracy, in retrospect it can be seen as a last attempt to operate within its confines. The Heath Government sought to put British capitalism on a new course, to arrest national economic decline, and make British companies competitive within the EEC. Heath's competition policy was an attempt to overcome the specific competitive weaknesses of British capital. The means tried at first were certainly influenced by the new current of social market thinking, but once these failed to produce faster growth because of the scale of unemployment and working-class resistance they created, the Government made significant changes in its policies (the so-called U-turns), and opted instead for statutory wage controls, increased public expenditure and much greater intervention in industry. The basic aim remained the same – achieving a higher rate of growth in the British economy. Faster growth was seen as indispensable to enable British capital to succeed in the EEC, to ease the problems of funding the public sector, and to restore the Conservatives' reputation for successful economic management to which their electoral fortunes since the war had become so closely linked.

The Thatcher Government began operating in very different circumstances. The world recession had changed the framework of political calculation. Since growth in the world economy can no longer be assumed, the whole basis of social-democratic politics – increasing public provision and a measure of redistribution finances out of steadily expanding output – has been undermined. The recession has at the same time made the relative decline of the British economy potentially catastrophic. British capitalism is now the weakest national capitalism amongst the developed capitalist states. In the last world recession in the 1930s it was one of the strongest, and did not suffer the worst effects. The loss of empire is only partly offset by the good fortune of North Sea oil.

One consequence of Britain's deteriorating economic position has been that a significant section of the Conservative leadership has now broken with social-democratic politics. It does not believe social democracy can be resuscitated nor does it wish it to be, although it disagrees on how fast and how far the party should proceed in dismantling it. This is the reason for a remarkable paradox. The Heath Government, committed to making social democracy work, was prepared to take greater political risks and pursue more radical policies than the Thatcher government.

The Thatcher Government in its first two years proceeded cautiously, particularly as regards trade union reform. But although it is more cautious there is also much less chance that it will indulge in the kind of U-turns the Heath Government performed. This is because those kinds of U-turns could only be performed by a government still committed to the social-democratic goals of full employment and growth. The Heath leadership flirted with the doctrines of the social market economy as techniques for improving efficiency and raising growth. Since they were only seen as techniques they could always be changed. For Thatcher and her supporters they were not techniques but principles. The resolve of the Thatcher Government was much more solid because clear alternatives were so much less evident.

A majority of Thatcher's Cabinet believed from the outset that the economic strategy would fail. But they were also convinced that the strategy would have to be seen to fail comprehensively before a major change was possible. The confidence of Tory leaders in their traditional governing style of pragmatism, compromise and flexibility has temporarily left them, as a result of the seriousness of the plight of the national economy and the precariousness of their own party's electoral fortunes. If Thatcherism were to succeed in restabilising the economy, shifting the political balance permanently and creating a new and broader working-class constituency for the Conservatives, the bulk of the present leadership, reared amidst the constraints and procedures of social democratic politics, would speedily adapt to ruling in the new set of circumstances. On this basis Thatcherism was seen as worth exploring and supporting for a while. But some of Thatcher's Conservative critics still fear that a resort by the Conservatives to doctrinal and partisan politics and an explicit reopening of long-settled class questions risks a similar response from the left, and a dangerous polarisation between the two main parties. This could endanger a political system which, though outwardly characterised by the elaborate rituals of adversary politics, inwardly relies upon a fundamental consensus derived from the institutional continuity of the state and the acceptance of both party leaderships when in government of the need to govern within the constraints which the permanent agencies of the state do not hesitate to point out to them.

Thatcherism and Conservatism

In one sense at least Thatcherism is very alien to Conservative traditions — because of its acceptance of certain of the doctrines of liberal political economy as a guide and criterion for its policies. This supreme old bourgeois party once took pride in distancing itself from the most characteristic expression of bourgeois ideology. The Conservatives presented themselves as the party of the national economy and the state, the party of the community rather than the market, the party of protection, imperialism, paternalism, and intervention, not the party of free trade, cosmopolitanism, self-help, and laissez-faire. Before 1914 Tory hostility to liberal political economy was pronounced, particularly because it promoted individualism and questioned the authority of established institutions, and encouraged selfishness and competition between individuals and classes. The Conservatives believed that there were some things worth dying in the last ditch for – the Union of the United Kingdom and the rights of property being two – but the preservation of an egalitarian and competitive market order was not among them. The Conservatives were always renowned for their hostility to doctrine and their lack of principle. Churchill once described the Conservatives as 'a party of great vested interests, banded together in a formidable confederation ... corruption at home, aggression to cover it up abroad; the trickery of tariff juggles, the tyranny of a party machine; sentiment by the bucketful; patriotism by the imperial pint; the open hand at the public exchequer, the open door at the public house; dear food for the million, cheap labour for the millionaire.'

The hostility of Conservatism to liberalism and individualism was modified in the 1920s with the break-up of the old Liberal party and the entry of large numbers of former Liberals, including Churchill himself, into the Conservative Party to the despair of the imperialist and protectionist wing of the party.

However, although these new elements created a new ideological bloc – Liberal Conservatism – and helped tip the balance of party opinion towards orthodoxy in economic policy, it did not mean the implanting of a doctrinal liberal political economy in the party. The Conservatives became the dominant governing party and increasingly the umbrella party for the defence of all the interests of property against the threat posed by the rise of Labour at home and world revolution abroad. This meant that the party accepted the main lines of the foreign economic policy of the British state – the commitment to free trade and the international role of sterling, the recreation of a world liberal economic order, rather than a protectionist and self-sufficient imperial federation. This was accompanied by domestic policies emphasising financial retrenchment. Neither policy involved, however, a crusading commitment to restore and develop the principles of a market order, rather an acceptance of policies that had become orthodoxies and which expressed the enduring facts of Britain's external position and the influence the doctrines of liberal political economy had exercised over economic policy-making for seventy years.[4]

The revival of liberal political economy which began in the 1960s and which has become steadily more influential in the Conservative Party is different from the liberal Conservatism of the 1920s in that it does not reflect an established policy consensus, but on the contrary seeks to break with established policies and challenges the essential assumptions and priorities of economic management which social democracy and Keynesian economics established. One of the most striking features of present British politics is the absence of protectionism in the Conservative party. This favourite refuge of right-wing parties in the face of world depression and external economic challenge holds only the National Front at present in Britain. Some of the most nationalistic British politicians are also those most committed to the social market doctrine and therefore to the standpoint of the world economy and of international capital which it dictates. This reflects in part the far-reaching accommodation and subordination of British strategic and economic interests to those of the United States since 1941, and also the degree to which British capital has been internationalised. A viable protectionist strategy would necessarily attack the interests of the dominant multinational and financial sectors of the British economy. Like many other states Britain no longer has a unified national bourgeosie and its governments must balance the needs and pressures of the national economy and national electorate on one side with the needs and pressures of international capital on the other.

A liberal foreign economic policy has been maintained by all governments in Britain since the war. The new social market doctrine is aimed not at the external policy but the internal policy of economic management. It criticises, firstly, the techniques of demand management whose purpose is to achieve full employment by smoothing out cycles and raising the rate of growth; secondly, the considerable increase in the volume and range of public expenditure and public involvement at all levels in the economy.

Liberal political economy is not a single doctrine, and Thatcherism represents a specific combination of its key elements – the family, economy and state. The emphasis of Thatcherism upon a free economy, an unfettered market order is what has attracted most comment and which appears most at variance with traditional Conservative ideology. But the other terms of the trinity are interpreted in ways which are much more closely linked to traditional Conservative ideological concerns. All versions of liberal political economy prescribe a strong state, able to establish the highly artificial conditions of a market order, but whereas a strong state can also be a minimal state, Thatcherism seeks a greater not a smaller role for the agencies charged with internal security and external defence. The state is to be rolled back in some areas and rolled forward in others. Similarly Thatcherism does not seek to reduce but to enlarge the scope of the family. Its emphasis upon family responsibility is accompanied by an emphasis upon family morality and the need for greater discipline and higher moral standards. The real innovation of Thatcherism is the way it has linked traditional Conservative concern with the basis of authority in social institutions and the importance of internal order and external security, with a new emphasis upon re-establishing free markets and extending market criteria into new fields.

Through its revival of several of the key doctrines of liberal political economy and the restating of them in terms of populist causes, Thatcherism created a much closer identity than has been usual in the Conservative party between the ideologies that mobilise support and the principles that guide the formulation of government policy. Thatcherism reactivated what has been for the last fifty years one of the central features of the Conservative party's appeal to the electorate – its hostility to the state sector and to the trade unions. The party has long won the support of significant numbers of workers in the private sector and in non-unionised occupations. In its policies in government, however, between 1951 and 1964, the Conservatives proved far from hostile either to the trade unions or to the state sector, and showed themselves quite content to negotiate with the former and to administer the latter. In electoral terms Thatcherism repaired the ravages wrought by the highly interventionist policies of the Heath administration, and re-established the identity of the party as the 'anti-state' party on economic policy. This was the same strategy the Conservatives pursued in opposition in 1964-70 or indeed between 1945 and 1951. What proved different after 1979 was that once the Conservatives were back in government this electoral ideology, far from being discarded having served its purpose, formed the basis for the economic programme the Government attempted to implement.

What nobody foresaw was the opportunity created by the Falklands War for Thatcher to combine the populist anti-state programme with the traditional One Nation theme of strong leadership and national greatness. By this means the criteria for judging the Conservatives' economic policy were changed. Fitness for national leadership, resoluteness and determination came to count for more in 1982 than the actual consequences of the policies themselves. Strong leadership appeared for a time to be compensation enough.

Thatcherism and the Politics of Power

Thatcherism has so far been examined as a bid to establish a new electoral coalition and as an ideological break with post-war consensus politics and with post-war Conservatism. But when we pass from the glitter and media dazzle of electoral politics to the prosaic realities of government, a different question arises. What is the relationship of Thatcherism as an ideological doctrine to Thatcherism as a programme for government? In the realm of government, questions of strategy become not ideological but technical questions. Policies are expected to work and to produce results. Is Thatcherism simply a response to popular discontent with social democracy and discontent within the party to post-war Conservatism? Is it mainly a means by which the legitimacy of the state is refurbished, or does it also represent a shift in the kind of policies that can be implemented? Is it in fact a response to certain objective interests of the British ruling class?

The general interests of the ruling class are the preservation of capital and the conditions for its reproduction and accumulation. But the practical political task of defining these general interests and identifying these specific conditions gives rise at any one time to several different strategies for securing them. Such strategies have to embody not merely economic realism but political realism; they must take account of the complex field of pressures within which governments move. The sources of such pressures include the state bureaucracy, organised interests, and foreign governments. Governments must also keep the confidence of the agents in the main markets which sustain the conditions for the economic and political reproduction of capital; these include the financial, commercial, labour, and political markets. The task of knitting together policies that are practicable at the level of government with a programme and an electoral image that can win popular endorsement for the government, falls on the political parties.

British capitalism as a whole is weaker than at any time this century, but there is a clear division between those sectors of business, including much of the financial sector and the multinational sector of big business which operate internationally and remain internationally competitive, and those sectors which are confined entirely to the national economy and have found it increasingly difficult to compete. The international and financial sectors of British capital have long reinforced the policy of maintaining the openness of the British economy. But the consequernce of that policy, particularly in the post-war era, has been to accelerate the decline of the national economy. At the root of this relative decline have been the persistent lower levels of productivity and the associated higher rates of inflation and falling share of world trade. After the failure of the different attempts in the 1960s and early 1970s to pursue a modernisation strategy and following the onset of the world recession after 1974, the comfortable economic decline of the years of the long boom has threatened to become something much more serious. Political positions and technical prescriptions have polarised, and three broad stategic options have emerged.

1. *De-industrialisation.* In many ways this is not an option, simply the line of least resistance. It is the necessary consequence of pursuing the kind of disinflationary policies which have been in force since 1976. They entail high and rising unemployment, and stagnant or falling output, and the progressive run-down of all those industries unable to compete

internationally. A slow demoralisation sets in as factories close
and public expenditure is subjected to round after round of cuts.
The political effects of high unemployment are contained
because it is confined to certain areas, and because some of its
effects can be offset by using North Sea oil revenues to maintain
unemployment benefit at a sufficient level, and by strong
security forces. At the same time the service sector and the high-
technology sector of the economy expand, and these together
with the multinational and financial sectors earn enough export
and rentier incomes to keep a sizeable part of the economy
afloat. The industrial decline is inexorable and no determined
attempt made to reverse it. Trade union membership begins to
fall and the unions are outflanked rather than confronted, their
rank-and-file demoralised and divided by the disinflationary
policy. The problem of the strength of the British working class
is dealt with by shifting the economy away from those sectors
where union strength is greatest. This is at the expense of Britain
remaining a major industrial power, but the policy carries least
political risk and least challenge to established interests. In
particular the openness of the British economy to world trade
and world capital is not questioned. What is incalculable is the
effect of the world recession and the possibility that de-
industrialisation is turned from a slow retreat into a headlong
rout.

2. *Industrial Regeneration I.* The second option is much
bolder. It is to use the political opportunity of the present
recession to restructure the industrial base of the economy and
to confront and materially weaken the power of organised
labour. Trade union power is not outflanked but confronted and
destroyed. The internal barriers to accumulation are removed;
particularly the ability and willingness of workers to resist
changes in work practices and the introduction of new
machinery; and the tax burden of the state, involving major
cutbacks in the collective provision of welfare, health and
education. Such policies would mean an open and bitter
onslaught on trade unions as independent organisations on a
much bigger scale than was attempted by the Heath
government. The major risk involved is the likely scale of
resistance to direct attacks upon the unions as organisations.
The Conservatives have unhappy memories of the last such

attempt. A second drawback is that removing the internal obstacles to internal accumulation is no guarantee of success so long as the external obstacles remain.

3. *Industrial Regeneration II.* The third option is the one least canvassed amongst economic policy makers because it involves some sacrifices from capital. Here industrial regeneration would be carried out by a large increase in state involvement in the economy — state investment, planning agreements, and wage controls. They would have to be accompanied by import and foreign exchange controls, as well as a continuation and extension of egalitarian welfare measures, particularly to assist in redeployment of the labour force. This kind of strategy has never been resorted to in Britain except during war, in 1916 and 1940. It involves the suspension of the market in many areas and an attempt to manage the economy through direct collaboration between the classes. Such strategies, although, when implemented, often seen in retrospect as being in the long-term interests of capital, are rarely in the short-term interests of individual capitals, and so are employed only in conditions of extreme crisis. This is partly because such strategies, although options for the ruling class, are also options for the working class, and their outcome depends on the respective strengths of capital and labour. They provide openings to the left as well as the right and can precipitate more radical challenges to the social order.

There is scarcely any need to remark on how distant Thatcherism is from this last option. For many reasons such a programme is anathema to almost all sections of British business and would only be accepted in dire circumstances. Big and small capital alike are willing and often anxious for specific and limited state interventions to reduce their costs, but a wholesale programme of national reconstruction is very different. Ideological suspicion of the state is still very strong. In these circumstances only the second option — the social market strategy — is a plausible alternative to accepting further de-industrialisation. A roll-back of the state, a reduction of taxes, a restoration of incentives, an end to bureaucratic meddling in industry's affairs — all these are measures strongly supported by all sectors of business. The priority given to the control of inflation is also welcomed.

But whilst all sectors of British business declaim the language of economic realism, endorsing the social market strategy in practice has not been so easy. The ambition of the social market strategy is breath-taking. It seeks decisively to reverse all the gains and encroachments which the labour movement has made both politically and industrially in the last fifty years. It was always inevitable that if it were to be seriously implemented it would hurt not only organised labour but would squeeze large sections of British capital and eliminate some of them. This is the strength of the strategy — that it recognises that if state intervention and class collaboration is ruled out, the only way for a thoroughgoing revival of British capitalism is for a decisive defeat of shop-floor power at the point of production, to raise the rate of exploitation and so ensure a major leap in productivity.

Yet political support for it from business remains relatively limited. The low risk first option is preferred, particularly by those firms which already operate internationally and do not welcome any policy that might threaten their British operations. The Conservatives found the de-industrialisation option already well established when they entered office in May 1979. The Labour Government had pioneered monetarism in Britain, and was the first administration to set monetary targets, introduce cash limits, and attempt the containment of public expenditure, at the same time that it emasculated its own industrial strategy and resisted pressure for import controls. This disinflationary policy, which necessarily meant the abandonment of the goal of full employment was carried through on the basis of formal cooperation between the trade unions and the government, an agreement not threatened until the Callaghan Government's last winter.

The first two years of the Thatcher Government were a remarkable period in British poltics. The Cabinet was uneasily balanced from the start between a small group of committed monetarists, whom Thatcher appointed, to the main economic ministries and the bulk of the leadership, many of whom had held office under Heath and whose instincts inclined them to traditional Conservative policy.

This attitude may be summed up as governing according to circumstances rather than principles, making careful assessment of the political balance between classes and interests, being prepared to make concessions where necessary, and only pursuing those lines of action for which support can be won and which do not threaten the security of the state. Since 1940 this had meant governing within the limits imposed by social democracy, using government powers to promote full employment and prosperity, accepting a considerable public sector alongside the private, financing high government spending on welfare out of high taxation, and conciliating trade-union power.

The bulk of the leadership in 1979 would have been quite content to continue the main line of the Labour Government's policy. But Thatcher herself and her closest supporters were determined that the social market strategy should have a trial. From the start, however, they were confronted by an extremely difficult tactical problem. They had to choose between fighting a war of manoeuvre, aimed at storming all the important positions of social democracy simultaneously, or settling for a much more drawn-out war of position, gradually transforming the context within which government operated. Hayek himself urged the first tactic, the *Blitzkrieg*, on the grounds that the government would run out of time if it did not act quickly and decisively. He suggested a referendum on the issue of abolishing all trade union legal immunities granted since 1906. He also favoured policies to precipitate a short but very severe slump by the sudden withdrawal of all subsidies to industry, by drastic reductions in public expenditure, and by an immediate return to 'sound finance'. The rewards would be considerable; trade-union power would be broken, the market order would be repaired, and major cuts in personal and business taxation would be possible.

Some of the advocates of the social market strategy were undoubtedly tempted by the idea of a *Blitzkrieg* on social democracy. But the divisions in the Conservative Party and the Cabinet, and the scale of the political risk involved in openly confronting the labour movement, persuaded Thatcher to settle for the less dramatic war of position, a series of engagements on many separate fronts. The government aimed to press forward whenever conditions were favourable. But because the struggle as a result became so diffuse it became difficult to maintain any overall strategic control, and numerous reverses began to accumulate. This was made worse because, although the government had in practice chosen to conduct a war of position, much of its rhetoric suggested that it was actually engaged on a war of manoeuvre. For example, it kept taking credit for the recession by describing it as a necessary medicine which the British economy had to take if it was to recover, whilst constantly intervening to stop the recession developing into a slump.

The attempt to implement the social market strategy was also gravely weakened because of the Government's adherence to inconsistent objectives. The manifesto commitments to lower direct taxation, higher defence spending, and higher pay for the armed forces and the police were implemented immediately, although they were obviously inconsistent with the overriding priority to bring inflation down by establishing firm control over public spending and the money supply. So, too, was the surprising decision to honour the Clegg pay settlements. The consequence was that the Government lost control of public spending and was forced onto the defensive right at the beginning of its term of office. In order to maintain its financial objectives it found itself obliged to allow first interest rates and then taxation to rise.

By the time of the third Conservative budget in 1981 Britain was suffering a more severe recession than any other major capitalist economy. Unemployment was close to $2\frac{1}{2}$ million whilst manufacturing output had fallen by $15\frac{1}{2}\%$ during 1980. The recession had outflanked and significantly weakened the organised labour movement and strengthened the hand of management. A major shakeout of labour was in progress throughout British industry, and the number of industrial disputes had fallen sharply. Inflation was moving towards single figures and interest rates were beginning to come down. But on most other fronts the Government's strategy was in disarray. It had proposed only relatively minor new curbs on trade-union powers, and had publicly backed away from a confrontation with the miners in February 1981. So trade union power had not been broken, only contained. The Government had also failed to control either public spending or the money supply. The borrowing requirement in 1980-81 was £4 billion more than planned, and the money supply (sterling M3) was twice as high as the target announced in the 1980 budget. This failure to control public spending reflected the earlier decision over Clegg awards and tax cuts, but also the extra cost of dole for the unemployed and the successful resistance to public spending cuts mounted by Cabinet ministers in the Autumn of 1980, and by the series of decisions to continue supporting major industries such as British Leyland and the British Steel Corporation.

A pragmatic Tory Government at this stage might well have abandoned its monetarist doctrines and launched a new industrial strategy. But this was not the path Thatcher chose. She decided instead to stick to the financial targets announced in the first two budgets and to seek to realise them by making whatever short-term increases in taxation were necessary. This decision created a storm of protest from business, the unions and the media, and widespread unease in the Conservative Party. It meant that the burden of taxation two years after the Conservatives took office was significantly higher than it had been under Labour. Even the proportion of direct taxation was higher. After a period which had seen such steep falls in industrial output and such large rises in unemployment the Government introduced a budget which, combined with falling pay settlements, was sure to severely reduce living standards over the next two years.

The 1981 Budget was a notable expression of the internal contradictions of Thatcherism. As one of the Treasury Ministers admitted, the retreat which had been forced on the Government meant that if the Conservatives were to realise their 1979 manifesto pledge to cut income tax, they would need to achieve new additional cuts in public expenditure of £6,000 million. Most commentators concluded that the budget was the last chance for maintaining even the financial part of the strategy. The defeats on so many fronts and the numerous predictions that unemployment was set to climb above three million, and that the living standards of those in work which hitherto had been protected were about to fall sharply, faced the party with the possibility of an electoral collapse. Only a major economic recovery could rescue the Government, but the Government had hardly begun to do the things which in terms of its own strategy it had to do in order to bring such a recovery about.

If the Thatcher experiment does indeed prove transitional, its failure in the eyes of its supporters will be clearly linked to the inability or unwillingness of the leadership to take decisive radical, and internally consistent measures at the outset. By the spring of 1981 the fate of the Thatcher Government was closely tied to the question of when the slump would bottom out, and how broad based the recovery would prove to be. The electoral and political bases for Thatcherism were visibly declining and other electoral alternatives, particularly the possibility of an alliance between the Liberals and the Social Democrats, looked formidable.[5] Yet even if Thatcherism does collapse, the problem of Britain's economic decline will still be there. It will not mean that the social market strategy is dead or that it may not be revived at some time in the future. The kind of decline that Britain is now experiencing cannot go on indefinitely. At some point it will precipitate a crisis which will decisively alter the balance of forces in British politics.

The arrival of the Thatcher Government marked the moment that the break with social-democratic politics was explicitly acknowledged. The disinflationary strategy which had led to a shrinking industrial base was no longer justified as an expedient and temporary tactic, but as the only possible course of action for restoring prosperity. But like so many of its predecessors, the new Government failed to take the more radical measures which seem certain to be needed if the British economy is to be restored as a major site for the accumulation of capital. This failure casts a long shadow over the Thatcher experiment, and makes its eventual failure more probable. If it should fail, it may well be followed by a government which continues the same policies and for which Thatcherism has prepared the ground.

In the short term the Falklands War in 1982 transformed the prospects for the government, and the Thatcher experiment. The economic record on which to fight an election remained extremely weak. Inflation had come down but at the expense of the deepest slump since the war from which there were still no sure signs of recovery. Nevertheless there was some evidence that the Government was not widely blamed for the recession, while at the same time it was receiving enormous credit for its handling of the Falklands War. Despite the bleak economic prospect the Conservatives had become favourites to win the election due by 1984. This would give the Thatcher experiment the second term its adherents had always thought would be necessary to carry through the full programme. A second term would consolidate the new directions for British politics which had emerged in the 1970s and marked the ending of the post-war consensus on the right balance between the public and private sectors, on the priority to be given to full employment, on universal welfare provision, on free state education, and on trade union rights. But while the Thatcher Government had proclaimed in its rhetoric the end of this consensus, it had failed in its actions to halt the decline of the British economy. The consequences of this failure are still to come.

Notes

Versions of this chapter first appeared in *Marxism Today* in November 1979 and November 1980. My thanks are due to Martin Jacques for encouraging me to write the original articles.

[1] See Michael Steed and John Curtice, 'An Analysis of the Voting' in D.E. Butler and D. Kavanagh, *The British General Election of 1979*, (Macmillan, 1980). The South East, South West, East and West Midlands all registered swings of over 6%. It is calculated that skilled workers swung $11\frac{1}{2}$% to the Conservatives, unskilled workers 9%, and that as a result the Labour Party attracted only 50% of the trade-union vote and only 45% of the working-class vote.

[2] In Scotland the swing to the Tories was 0.7%. In Greater Clydeside and Glasgow there was a small swing to Labour. Elsewhere in the north the swing to the Conservatives averaged 4%. The Conservatives were also weakened because their long-standing alliance with Ulster Unionism, sundered in 1972 when direct rule was declared, had still not been restored by 1979. Steed and Curtice summarise the result of the election as follows; the swing 'gave the Conservatives as large a plurality of votes (7%) over the next largest party as any party had enjoyed since Labour's 1945 landslide ... Yet Mrs Thatcher took office with a smaller share of the national vote than any Prime Minister enjoying a secure parliamentary majority since Bonar Law in 1922' (p. 393).

[3] I have explored this doctrine at greater length in 'The Free Economy and the Strong State', *Socialist Register 1979*, pp. 1-25.

[4] Once the gold standard collapsed in 1931 the National Government, having purged itself of the few doctrinaire economic liberals like Philip Snowden in its ranks, imposed a measure of protection and encouraged the formation of cartels and a range of means for reducing competition in the home market because of the depressed state of world demand.

[5] An alliance between the SDP and the Liberals was subsequently arranged and the impact of this and of the 1981 Cabinet reshuffle were discussed in a later article in *Marxism Today*, November 1981.

Michael Bleaney

Conservative Economic Strategy

The policy of the Conservative Government under Mrs Thatcher has had spectacular and potentially highly destructive effects on the British economy. The manufacturing sector in particular has suffered very badly: industrial production in 1981 was 12 per cent below the 1979 level (minus 14 per cent when mineral oil and gas are excluded), which itself represented only a very limited recovery from the 1975 slump. Many plants have been closed down for good. The service sector too has contracted, for the first time since the war, and the collapse of employment in combination with an expanding labour force has taken the figures for registered unemployment to almost four million. Any recovery in output looks likely to be so weak that it will be difficult to stop that total from rising further, let alone bring it down.

What exactly are the Conservatives up to? Can this possibly be in the interests of British capital? Is it just the relentless pursuit of misguided ideas? Or is it such a far-sighted move on the chessboard that we are unable to understand its relevance to the present situation?

These are questions which every person in Britain must have asked himself or herself many times since May 1979. Practically every news bulletin prompts them. Those who remain unconvinced by the Government's defence of its economic strategy have found offered to them two sorts of answers. The first, which I shall describe as the SDP line since it fits well into the ideology of that party, regards Thatcherism as a fundamentally irrational phenomenon. It is ideology run riot so that it no longer responds to reality but pursues its blinkered course regardless of where it culminates. The Tories, in other words, are so convinced of the correctness of their own world that they do not adjust to the obvious destruction of the economy, to the criticisms of the majority of economists, to the human misery involved or even to sheer common sense, but take all the adverse evidence merely as proof of how much harder they have to push their preconceived policies. If they are not stopped, the results could cripple the British economy for decades. Markets are being lost, industrial capacity is being destroyed, profits are rock-bottom, and much-needed new investment is being discouraged by high interest rates and bleak prospects for the future. The essence of this critique is that although nominally designed to revitalise private enterprise, Thatcherism runs contrary to the interests of British capital and indeed to those of every other class in society.

The second type of analysis of Thatcherism is in many ways the antithesis of the first, and is widespread on the Marxist left and in the trade union movement. This strand of thought sees Conservative strategy as an unusually energetic and forthright expression of the class interests of British capital. Through a sustained onslaught on the trade union movement and the public sector, the Tories aim to inflict a historic defeat on the working class and in particular to reverse most of the gains which that class has made since 1945. This is intended to lay the basis for an economic revival in which Britain can use its relatively low real wages and experienced labour force to attract investment which would otherwise have gone elsewhere in the EEC. British capital has been forced into this strategy, which is risky because it cannot be certain of winning the resulting confrontation, by the desperate situation brought about by its own prolonged decline. Deflation is an integral part of this strategy since mass unemployment is needed to undermine the self-confidence of the working class and throw it on the defensive. This analysis, in other words, sees the programme of the Thatcher Government as a considered and highly dangerous and unusual mobilisation of the total resources of the ruling class in order to effect a permanent shift in the balance of class forces in Britain. In purely intellectual terms, this view regards Thatcherism with much greater respect than the SDP line.

These are clearly two very different ways of looking at Conservative strategy. Yet most of us on the left, when speaking, thinking or writing about Thatcherism, combine elements of both views, as if we had never really sorted out which horse we really wanted to back. What I shall attempt to do in this essay, by looking in a certain amount of detail at Conservative economic policy, is to show that both views contain important elements of truth, but both are at the same time partial and inadequate. I shall argue that the first view involves a much more subtle appreciation of what might be termed the pure mechanics of economic policy problems and the consequences of the particular aims of economic policy which the Government chose, but has very little to say beyond these relatively superficial technicalities. By contrast the second view embodies a much more accurate interpretation of the historical and political background to Thatcherism and of its deeper motivation, but has difficulty in explaining some of the particular consequences and failures of Conservative economic policy. Nevertheless, it is possible, and indeed necessary, to marry these two approaches in such a way as to reach a deeper understanding of Thatcherism.

The Conservative Election Programme

When the Conservatives won the election in May 1979 they defeated a Labour government which was not only, by then, a minority government, but also one which had exhausted its already depleted fund of initiatives and ideas. It was fifteen years since the centre right of the Labour Party had been able to formulate anything new and exciting in its politics: since then it had traded largely on its claim to superiority in economic management and a more subtle approach to dealing with the trade unions. What new ideas did emerge from the period of opposition from 1970 to 1974 were pushed into the Labour programme by the left, and were for the most part forgotten or hopelessly watered down once election victory had propelled Labour into government. Once in government, Labour's strategy for dealing with the economic crisis was a sustained campaign to dampen down popular aspirations in the face of an adverse economic environment. Public services were cut back to make room for tax cuts, but private incomes were controlled (or at least meant to be) by an endless succession of incomes policies. Labour, once become 'the natural party of government' in Harold Wilson's famous phrase, had almost inadvertently become the main bulwark of an unsatisfactory status quo.

Meanwhile the Conservatives, under the leadership of Mrs

Thatcher since 1975, had developed a coherent and strident political challenge, and one which implicitly rejected much of what not only Labour but also previous Conservative Governments had done. They argued that the whole drift of British society since around 1960 (or even before) had been for the worse, and that economic revival required radical changes which would reverse that drift. In particular, drastic reductions in the economic role of the state and the burden of taxation were necessary in order to liberate private enterprise. The whole programme bore a distinct family resemblance to 'Selsdon man', the programme on which the Tories had fought and won the 1970 election. Up until its famous U-turn, the Heath Government had tried to strengthen British capital by opening it up to market forces and by tough anti-union legislation, but had abandoned this approach when it seemed not to be producing results. Similar ideas animated the 1979 election programme, though it was now bolstered by a judicious admixture of monetarism and promises of tax cuts, and by the failures of five more years of Labour government. I propose to examine separately what seem to me to be the three main dimensions of the Conservative programme: monetarism, the rolling back of the state, and the trade union question.

When the Conservatives first came into office the catchword most often used to describe their economic policy was 'monetarism' (more recently the failure of money supply control and the apparently reduced emphasis on it by the Government have caused a decline in this form of description). By referring to the topical and long-running disputes in academic economics, this label seemed at once to capture both the distinctive intellectual antecedents of Conservative thought and the determination to change some of the major principles of policy-making. Emphasis on the control of the money supply and the virtues of free enterprise and the free market have after all been the most prominent features of academic monetarism, as expressed through the writings and speeches of its founder and leader, Milton Friedman. Under the Conservatives a new emphasis has been placed on money supply control, despite the fact that money supply targets have been in operation since 1976. This new emphasis has not grown out of a critique of the way in which monetary policy was operated under Labour (indeed in retrospect Labour's monetary policy now seems exceptionally competent). It is the consequence of the fact that *the money supply is now expected to take on the role that was formerly played by incomes policies.*

Money supply control is regarded by the Conservative right as superior to any formal incomes policy, primarily because it is thought to contain a built-in sanction against wage militancy. If wages and prices rise faster than desired by the government, it is expected that this will lead to a contraction of real output and a loss of jobs. In other words, the Conservatives believed that strict money supply control offered a relatively painless solution to the twin problems of trade union militancy and inflation, because workers in the aggregate could only defy the implied wage norms at the expense of their own employment; sooner or later, whatever their trade union leaderships might say, they would recognise this and go along with the Government's desires. Why things have not turned out quite like this I shall discuss later; the point I wish to stress at the moment is that 'monetarism' was intended primarily as a big stick to keep the trade union movement in order.

The second significant aspect of the Conservative economic programme was the wide-ranging attack on the state. Nationalised industries were condemned as inefficient, and widespread sales of state assets were promised, along with the admission of private capital into certain profitable nationalised industries. State intervention was castigated as inimical to the development of private initiative and enterprise, and reductions in public expenditure (other than defence and law and order) were planned in order to liberate the private sector from its 'excessive' tax burden. Public borrowing was to be reduced. The centre of gravity of taxation was to be shifted away from income tax and towards taxes on expenditure, and taxes on higher incomes and on capital sharply reduced. In fact, on the whole the firm commitments that were made were rather moderate compared with the rhetoric. For example the Government did not commit itself to a long-term reduction in public expenditure in real terms but only to a reduction in its share of national income; during the election campaign it was promised that all the economies would come from eliminating waste. It was also promised that public sector borrowing would be reduced steadily as a proportion of national income.

All this was presented as part of a plan to revive the British economy by giving freedom of scope to private enterprise: the catchword was 'incentives'. At one level this 'incentives' argument is highly unconvincing. To raise the rate of VAT to 15 per cent in order to reduce income tax, as happened in Sir Geoffrey Howe's first Budget, is only an incentive to someone with a very peculiar pattern of consumption, or to someone who intends to save all their extra income or spend a large part of the year abroad. Moreover, a reduced tax burden is just as likely to induce someone to work shorter hours (because they can earn the same take-home pay in less time) as to work longer, and there is little hard evidence of any significant effect in either direction. Furthermore it would be difficult to argue that the benefits to society from the sharp reductions in taxes on capital and on higher incomes (top rate of income tax down from 83 to 60 per cent) in the June 1979 Budget were significant compared to the benefit to the individuals concerned.

But these arguments really miss the point. Mrs Thatcher and her colleagues did not arrive at their position through detailed economic analysis of this kind. They are deeply convinced, like most right-wing radicals, of the virtues of free market capitalism. By casual observation they have formed an assessment of the recent economic history of Britain in which pride of place as a cause of decline is given to the erosion of the elementary principles of a healthy capitalism through the growth of the welfare state, egalitarianism and a self-confident and militant working class. These are seen as the end-product of decades of domination of social-democratic ideology under Labour and Conservative governments alike, and they are supposed to have sapped the spirit of enterprise from the British people. Britain has lost its economic dynamism, the Conservatives believe, because those who have a real contribution to make can no longer get their proper rewards: they are obstructed by trade unions and labour legislation, the state creams off most of the cake as taxes, and society does not appreciate them. The argument is, in short, that entrepreneurship has been crushed by a state whose modern ideology has been built around the social-democratic principles of protection of the weak, even if they contribute little to society, instead of promotion of the strong and productive.

Thus the Conservatives see themselves as leading a counter-revolution against the whole drift of British society in recent times. When they talk of incentives they do not have in mind the worker considering whether to do overtime; they are thinking of entrepreneurs who are looking for new ideas to exploit, new ways of making money (hence the concern with the prospects of small business). Their model individual is one who is searching out ways to rise above his or her peers. The argument is that such frankly self-interested spirits have been discouraged by an unfavourable social atmosphere and high taxation. At the same time the principle of individual self-reliance has been undermined by the massive growth of social provision. Not only has this been expensive, but it has cushioned people from harsh economic realities and encouraged them to seek protection against adversity in state subsidy rather than individual effort. When the Conservatives deride 'socialism', they refer to a collectivist mentality which has grown up with the social changes and government policies of the post-war period, and which it is a basic objective of their strategy to root out.

An outlook such as this is far-reaching in its consequences. It implies a programme of major structural change, not just in taxation or the balance of public and private ownership, but also in social ideology. Such a programme may well require the lifetime of several governments to complete. Indeed it is one of the weaknesses of the Conservatives that they have become so used to looking at their economic programme in this way that they have been blind to the immediate damage (which may well have long-term consequences) which their economic policies are causing.

The third major aspect of the Conservative programme has been a new, hard line towards the trade union movement. For the last two decades or so governments have tended to take the attitude that the trade unions are one of the keys to Britain's economic problems, and of course the last Conservative Government tried to bring in new punitive legislation in the form of the Industrial Relations Act. But under Labour's 'Social Contract' trade union leaders were consulted by government more frequently and on a broader range of issues than ever before. Mrs Thatcher brought all these forms of consultation to a sudden end. The fundamental attitude of the Conservative Government is that trade unions in their present form represent one of the least desirable aspects of social democracy, and cannot be regarded as the legitimate expression of working-class interests. They should therefore be weakened and isolated as much as possible.

The lessons of Mr Heath's experience have however been well learned. Indeed this dramatic demonstration that a determined Government could provoke a major confrontation with the trade unions, and lose it, has been a major formative influence on the whole Thatcherist programme. It has been the main impetus behind the notion that the problems of British society are at bottom ideological, and have first to be attacked on that level. For it is only when some significant shift has occurred in the ideological balance that the support for trade unionism will be weakened and the unions can be confronted more directly. In line with this theory, the Government has adopted a strategy towards the trade union movement akin to that of a guerrilla war: to mount continuous attacks without getting involved in a major confrontation with the big battalions which might serve as a focus to mobilise opposition. Accordingly, the Government's original proposals for industrial relations legislation were fairly mild and concerned with relatively minor matters such as secondary picketing. It has gone out of its way to avoid confrontations with the most powerful groups of public sector workers (e.g. the backing down over coal imports in the face of the NUM in June 1981). And one of the perceived advantages of the money supply as a form of wages policy was that it offered no targets to attack.

The long-term strategy has been that the ideological changes which the Government is trying to effect would gradually weaken the hold on the working class of the collectivist mentality symbolised by the trade unions. People would increasingly search for individual advancement rather than collective security. The public ostracism to which the trade unions are now subject is part of this strategy. The TUC must not be allowed to establish its own legitimacy in the eyes of the public as a representative of working-class opinion, and this has been a factor in the rejection of incomes policy: every government which has had an incomes policy has sooner or later been seduced into some form of negotiation with the TUC because of the critical importance of TUC attitudes to the success of the policy. This is precisely what Mrs Thatcher wishes to avoid, and it is a safe bet that although she has never ruled out the possibility of a pay freeze, what she has in mind is something unilaterally imposed by the Government and not subject to negotiation.

The Government's trade union policy therefore conveys the impression of a studied and well-thought-out response to the debacle of the early 1970s. The situation has however been changed somewhat by the recession. The very swift and very large rise in unemployment has caused considerable demoralisation and disarray throughout the trade union movement, and the Government has seen its opportunity to bring in much more bold and sweeping legislative changes – but I shall return to this topic later.

The Conduct of Macroeconomic Policy

The major issue of the Conservatives' economic policy management must be the recession. At its worst one million people were added to the unemployment register in just twelve months. Why has the UK experienced such a deep recession since the Conservatives came to power, declining much more swiftly than other advanced capitalist countries even though the recession is world-wide? Is it deliberate?

It has sometimes been argued that the Tories are pursuing the classic Marxist prescription of engineering a major crisis in order to inflict resounding defeats on the working class, thus laying the foundations for a new boom. If this is intended to mean that the Government is simply increasing the rate of unemployment to whatever level is necessary to break the spirit and organisation of workers, it seems to me to be a misreading of the situation. Whilst the Conservatives are striving to extract every possible advantage out of mass unemployment, the fact that it has occurred can be explained as a by-product of their stated economic strategy rather than as an *intended* result.

The evidence suggests that, if anything, the Conservatives believed that their structural reforms could be carried through without much of an increase in unemployment, the mere threat of it being sufficient to keep trade unions under control during the transition period, and that after that unemployment would be dramatically reduced. Whilst the Government's policy has indeed involved a massive deflation, they themselves have refused to see it that way. Thus when Sir Geoffrey Howe's first Budget was condemned as deflationary, the reply was that the forecasts generated by the Treasury or any other economic model were far too pessimistic because they took no account of the stimulating effect of the extra incentives to private enterprise. There is an underlying belief that unemployment is an index of the broad state of health of the economy and when the Government's medicine starts to take effect, it will automatically come down. The Government appears not to accept what everyone else has believed since the Keynesian Revolution, namely that whether jobs are lost and firms go bust can depend on the state of demand. Since the Government does not believe this, it does not accept that its policies have been deflationary: it views reflation simply as an abandonment of its strategy and something which would therefore create only 'phoney' jobs.

This attitude may allow Mrs Thatcher to brush off any responsibility for the recession but it does not explain why the Government's policies have taken the particular course they have. To explain this we must turn to the Medium Term Financial Strategy (MTFS) published along with the Budget of March 1980. This laid down target ranges for the growth of the money supply for several years ahead, declining steadily from 7-11 per cent in 1980-81 to 4-8 per cent in 1983-84. It therefore implied a steady deceleration on the monetary front, the intention being that there would be an accompanying decline in the rate of inflation. But the MTFS also laid down a similar reduction in the Public Sector Borrowing Requirement (or PSBR – a measure of the budget deficit, after allowing for various government lending activities) from $5\frac{1}{2}$ per cent of gross domestic product in 1978-79 to $1\frac{1}{2}$ per cent in 1983-84. This implied a steady fall in government expenditure relative to tax receipts. If the economy had been on an expansionary path, this need not have caused any great difficulty, because the growth in real income would have automatically increased tax receipts, and all that the government would have had to do was to keep its own expenditure growing at a somewhat smaller rate. Since, however, the economy was already moving into recession when the Conservative Government came into office, this strategy has come close to pushing the economy into an inescapable deflationary whirlpool. For each addition to the unemployment register adds several thousand pounds to the PSBR as a result of the extra benefit payments and lost tax revenue. The recession itself was therefore raising the PSBR just as the Government was trying to reduce it, and the only way it could reduce it was to bring forward in each Budget a new package of expenditure cuts and/or tax increases, which would inevitably exacerbate the recession.

The stated reason for this planned reduction in the PSBR was to keep down interest rates, and there is a logic in this, for with a given money supply target a larger PSBR is likely to imply higher interest rates. Nevertheless it is hard to escape the impression that the Government's hostility to budget deficits also reflects a deep-seated and not entirely rational belief in the virtues of sound finance.

The effects of the immediate policy actions of the Government have therefore been to exacerbate the recession. A further very important factor, however, has been the massive rise in the exchange rate which took place in 1979 and 1980. This caused a decline in international competitiveness of over 30 per cent (a truly massive amount) and explains why the manufacturing sector has suffered so badly. The Government has always blamed this on oil prices, describing sterling as a 'petro-currency'. Oil prices have certainly been an element in the situation, but secondary to the impact of the Government's own policy. The fiscal deflation has depressed imports and high interest rates have attracted inflows of short-term capital, whilst the promises of further fiscal and monetary stringency in the MTFS have transformed the pound into a hard currency. The rise in the exchange rate was partially reversed in 1981, but much of this reflected a soaring dollar as monetarism came to power in the United States. The decline against EEC currencies has been only a few per cent. Moreover since the autumn of 1981 the Bank of England has been intervening to prevent any further falls, in the hope of keeping the inflation rate moving downwards.

It is well known that the Government's monetary policy has in practice been something of a debacle. In each year the money supply has grown considerably more than laid down in the targets. The main reason for this is that the Government has been very sensitive about interest rates. Each time the money supply has started to rise too fast, the Government has been scared to push interest rates, which were already high, to the level necessary to rein the money supply back, so that it has just had to accept the over-run. In the 1981 Budget a determined attempt to save the face of the MTFS by a massive deflation almost caused a Cabinet revolt. And even then the money supply growth targets for 1981-2 were being maintained as stated the year before, without any attempt to claw back the excess from the previous year. In the 1982 Budget, after another year of excessive monetary growth, the monetary dimension of the MTFS was effectively killed off by a relaxation of the target to 8-12 per cent instead of the prescribed 5-9 per cent.

This political anxiety about interest rates is in fact the key to the Government's behaviour. It explains why it has effectively abandoned the monetary part of the MTFS, while substantially maintaining the fiscal part (the reductions in the PSBR). For in the Budget at the beginning of each financial year, the aim has been to get the PSBR forecast low enough to persuade the financial markets that the monetary targets are consistent with reasonably low interest rates. But when, in the course of the financial year, the money supply has been found to be growing too fast, the measures requires to rein it back have been regarded as politically unacceptable.

As mentioned earlier, Conservative rhetoric has suggested a major onslaught on public expenditure. In practice the Government has found precious few easy targets (partly because large cuts in capital expenditure had already been made under Labour). The task has been made more difficult by the commitment to increase defence spending and the growth in the social security budget as a result of the recession. But the basic problem is that even quite small cuts have aroused some considerable opposition (e.g. the proposal to charge for school transport, or not to compensate pensioners for the difference between actual and expected inflation in 1981). The outcome has been that in real terms public expenditure has not fallen at all, and its share of national income has risen (not fallen as promised) because of the recession. The fall of four per cent in real terms by 1983-4 promised in the MTFS looks unlikely to be fulfilled, and was in any case dependent on greatly reduced borrowing by nationalised industries; this can only mean higher prices, which is more akin to a tax increase than an expenditure cut (one result has been that in 1981 nationalised industry prices rose considerably faster than the Retail Price Index).

As a consequence, the PSBR gap has been closed by raising the burden of taxation. In the June 1979 Budget the standard

rate of income tax was reduced from 33 to 30 per cent, and
VAT raised to 15 per cent, where it has stayed. But in 1980
income tax allowances were only partially indexed for inflation,
and in 1981 not at all. In 1982 allowances were increased by
two per cent more than the rate of inflation, but in both 1981
and 1982 employees' national insurance contributions took an
extra one per cent of gross pay. As a result the tax burden on an
average household has increased considerably, and it is only the
relatively small percentage of households on high incomes for
whom the relaxation of taxes on capital and higher rate bands of
income tax have outweighed the increase in VAT and national
insurance contributions.

On the inflation front, the Conservatives have had
considerable difficulty in getting back even to where they were
when they came into office. The measures in the June 1979
Budget themselves added over three per cent to the Retail Price
Index, which in combination with the ending of incomes policy
led to an acceleration of wage increases, to which firms
responded by increasing prices. At its peak in May 1980 the
Retail Price Index was over 20 per cent above what it had been
a year before. At this time the Government was taking a
surprisingly soft line on wages, and it paid the public sector
increases recommended by the Clegg Commission. Almost
certainly it was over-optimistic about the ability of its monetary
targets to influence wage settlements. By the summer of 1980
fear for jobs stimulated by the accelerating stream of
redundancies had brought private sector wage increases down
sharply, and the Government began to take a tough line in the
public sector (though they were notably more lenient with the
stronger groups). By 1982 it was imposing a four per cent limit
for the public sector, whilst high and rising unemployment
continued to keep private sector settlements in or close to single
figures. The inflation rate came down, but stuck at around 12
per cent in 1981, only moving below that in 1982.

A New Pragmatism?

Until the summer of 1981 the main plank of the Government's
policy was monetarism: money supply targets combined with
successive attempts to prune public spending. Despite the oft-
leaked complaints of the Wets that some modification was

required in the face of a massive rise in unemployment, the Government seemed to be sticking to the path laid down by its doctrine. But around this time there were a number of significant changes. First of all, a likely election date was now only two years away, so that the minds of Conservative backbenchers and the Government were focusing more and more on how its economic policy could be made more presentable to the electorate. Secondly, the money supply was running a long way outside its target for the second year in a row, and the targets were being tacitly abandoned. This disillusionment with monetarism was confirmed by the 1982 Budget, when the MTFS was effectively thrown out of the window.

However, this has not led to the sort of wide-ranging reassessment of the Government's strategy which the Wets would have liked. Mrs Thatcher has not retreated into the manipulative economic management of her predecessors: her perspective is still very much that of a structural rejuvenation of British capitalism. Indeed in the Cabinet reshuffle of September 1981 the Wets lost their power base and are now, at least temporarily, and possibly permanently, a spent force. The disillusionment with monetarism did, however, lead to a search for new initiatives in other directions. The two which stand out are the sale of state assets and industrial relations legislation.

Over the first couple of years of Conservative rule it seemed as if most of the denationalisation plans had been temporarily shelved in the face of technical difficulties. But from late 1981 all state assets came under close scrutiny for possible sale, from the obviously profitable, such as BNOC, to the obviously uprofitable, such as British Airways. Such sales do have certain short-term advantages in reducing the PSBR, but the main motivation is clearly a belief in the merits of privatisation.

The replacement of James Prior by Norman Tebbit at the Department of Employment was the prelude to much tougher anti-union legislation. It is more or less certain that Prior would not have been willing to introduce such legislation. More to the point, however, was the Government's appreciation of the demoralising effect of the recession on the trade union movement. It recognised that the TUC would no longer be able to mount opposition on anything like the scale of the struggle against the Industrial Relations Act, and it seized its opportunity.

The object of these new moves is to keep up the momentum of structural reform which is the animating spirit of Thatcherism. But are there any tangible signs that this programme could be successful? In spring 1982 the only statistic to which the Government could point with some satisfaction was the rise in industrial productivity which occurred in 1981 (but slowed down in 1982). The Government would like to believe that this increase in productivity, which goes against the pattern of most previous recessions, is a reflection of new attitudes to work and a new flexibility of labour in British industry, as unions are weakened and management reasserts its authority. There is some evidence for this explanation: there have been considerable rises in labour productivity in British Steel and British Leyland, where the tangible threat of closure has enabled management to force through major changes. But the statistics may simply be reflecting a combination of (1) the closure of the least profitable and least efficient plants which were pulling down the average before; and (2) a greater readiness to lay off workers because of financial pressures and pessimism about future orders.

However, the Government is really clutching at straws here: there is a very long way to go before it could claim that it had managed to raise the economy's long-term rate of productivity growth, and meanwhile almost every other indicator is flashing gloom and despondency. Output has fallen and unemployment has risen dramatically and looks unlikely to decrease significantly over the next few years. Profits and investment are extremely depressed. Inflation has come down, but only slowly until 1982, and the remarkable drop in the second half of 1982 may well prove unsustainable. If this sort of pressure does not force British capital to do vigorous battle with its workers and wring some major concessions from them, then the prolonged stagnation will leave it still more gravely weakened than when the Thatcher experiment started.

The political problem which the economic situation poses for the Government is how to bring about some improvement by the time of the next general election without performing an obvious U-turn. Otherwise the experiment runs the risk of being condemned by the electorate as a catastrophic failure. Here the 1982 Budget gave a clear indication of the Government's tactics. Since a fiscal reflation through large public expenditure increases or tax cuts would undoubtedly be perceived as an abandonment of its previous strategy, the Government eschewed this course, maintaining a fairly neutral Budget, though it has been attempting to massage the unemployment figures downwards by an expansion of various special employment and training schemes for young people (and by manipulation of the qualifications for inclusion in the count). Instead it has opted for monetary relaxation, in the hope of keeping interest rates moving downwards through 1982 and 1983. Meanwhile it is holding the exchange rate up, in order to try to keep the inflation rate moving downwards also. This latter part of the strategy may yet be defeated by speculative pressures, but the reckoning is that, for the electorate as a whole, inflation and interest rates are much more important than a few hundred thousand less on the unemployment register. From the Conservatives' point of view, this looks like very astute tactics, and given the unwillingness of the electorate to turn to Labour and the uncertainties surrounding the SDP – Liberal Alliance, it could yet give them victory at the next general election.

Ian Gough

Thatcherism and the Welfare State

'Minister, how exactly will shutting down old peoples' homes revitalise the British economy?' *(Robin Day in a radio interview with a Conservative government minister)*

The British welfare state is under attack today, that much is clear. But why? What is the nature of the attack? How does the 'new conservatism' of the Thatcher Government differ from the 'traditional Toryism' of Macmillan and Heath? What is the link between the government's monetarist economic policies and its anti-welfarism? And will either work? These are some of the questions I want to tackle here.

The current crisis in the welfare state has a quantitative and a qualitative dimension. Let us look at each in turn. Since the mid-1970s first a Labour then a Tory government have successfully attempted to restrain the previously rapid growth of expenditure on the major social services (see table, p. 149). Between 1975/6 and 1977/8 the Labour Government cut back housing and education spending, held spending on personal social services constant and thereby stabilised total social expenditure. The newly instituted cash limit system clearly did its work, especially in cutting back these local authority provided services.

A slight easing of controls on social spending occurred in the last year of the Labour Government, but planned spending for the next year (1979/80) allowed for virtually no growth, and included the centrally provided social security and health services in the cutbacks. Though the Tories' June 1979 Budget made further immediate cuts in the housing and education programme, raised prescription charges and cut back on employment services for that year, the basic plans for this next squeeze on social spending had already been decided on by the outgoing Labour Government. The outcome was zero change in real terms in social spending for 1978/79 – 1979/80.

SOCIAL EXPENDITURE IN THE U.K.
% changes at constant prices (see below)

	1975/6 –77/8 (2 yrs)	1977/8 –79/80 (2 yrs)	1979/80 –80/1	1980/1 –81/2	1981/2 –82/3	1982/3 –83/4	1979/80 –83/4 (4 yrs)
Social security	8.6	1.1[3]	2.2	9.8	6.0	0.9	19.9
NHS	2.1	4.7	8.5 (3.9)	1.72 (–0.8)	0.6	0.8	12.1
Personal social services	0.5	7.2	5.0 (0.6)	–0.6 (–3.2)	4.8	–3.1	5.9
Education	–4.3	–1.8	3.0 (–1.3)	–2.0 (–4.5)	–0.7	–5.3	–5.0
Housing	–15.7	2.1	–16.5 (–20.0)	–36.4 (–38.0)	–23.5	3.1	–58.1
Employment services	10.7	–0.2	32.6 (27.1)	4.6 (1.9)	4.5	14.2	65.4
TOTAL SOCIAL SERVICES	–0.4[2]	1.3[3]	2.4 (0.0)	1.4 (0.0)	1.9	0.1	6.0 (2.0)
TOTAL PUBLIC EXPENDITURE[1]	–7.4	6.2	2.3	2.3	0.3	0.9	6.0

Sources:
1975/76–77/8: Public Expenditure White Paper, Cmnd 8175, March 1981
1977/78–83/4: Public Expenditure White Paper, Cmnd 8789, vols I & II, February 1983, mainly table I.14.

Calculation of constant price figures:
1975/6–77/8: volume terms.
1977/8–83/4: cost terms, i.e. cash spending deflated by increase in total home costs. The government assumes an increase in costs of 7½% in 1982/3 over the previous year, and of 5% in 1983/4. The first may now be an overestimate. The figures in brackets deflate cash spending by the rise in 'general government final consumption' costs taken from CSO, *National Income and Expenditure 1982*, table 2.6. This reveals the following increases in GDP costs and general government costs for the following *calendar* years:

	1979-80	1980-81
GDP	18.4%	10.7%
General government	23.6%	13.6%

These differentials were then applied to the constant cost figures to obtain the percentage changes in brackets.

Notes:
1. 'Planning total' + net debt interest.
2. The total is adjusted to include the phasing out of food subsidies over these two years.
3. The social security figure (and consequently that for total social spending) is adjusted to eliminate the effect of the switch from family allowances plus child tax allowances to child benefit in these two years. Without this adjustment social security rose by 7.8% and total social services by 4.3%.

In November 1979 and March 1980 the Thatcher Government took two more swings of the axe against the welfare state and planned for a real fall in spending in 1980/81. Much has recently been made of its failure to control public spending, but if any sector was out of control it certainly was not social spending, which barely changed for the second year running. True it was planned to fall by around 1%, but the main increases reflected the catastrophic climb in unemployment during the year: spending on all employment services (redundancy payments, special employment measures, Youth Opportunities Programmes etc.) shot up by 41%, and the cost of all unemployment benefits by 31%. The overshoot in these two programmes was counterbalanced by serious cutbacks in the local authority services – education, personal social services and especially housing – which all fell roughly according to plan. Nevertheless total public expenditure rose by 2.3% due to some belated U-turns in industrial support and not least to rising interest charges, plus planned expansion in the military and law and order services.

So in November 1980 and March 1981 the Government entered round three. Level funding was planned for the social services in 1981/2, but once again a large increase in social security (unemployment costs up by a further 29%) plus some growth in total NHS and employment services, was to be financed by swingeing cuts in housing and education.

Round four was inaugurated by the combined Budget and Public Expenditure White Paper in March 1982. The Medium Term Financial Strategy was reaffirmed, some taxes were cut, and for the first time public expenditure was planned solely in cash terms which allowed for no cost increase outside those budgeted for. More was to be spent on defence, law and order, special employment services and health, but education was still squeezed and total housing expenditure was to be reduced by a further quarter.

By the time of the Chancellor's November 1982 Budget statement and the February 1983 White Paper he was able to record real satisfaction that public expenditure plans could be revised downwards for the first time for many years: the public sector was under control. Defence costs were up due to the Falklands War, and social security benefits were to be uprated by a figure lower than the inflation rate in 1983 to counteract the 'windfall' benefits claimants received in 1982 due to the lower than forecast inflation rate. Apart from that the pattern of social spending followed the previous years except for a belated planned increase in capital spending on housing.

What is the upshot of all this for the funding of social services in real terms? In recent years it is peculiarly difficult to tell due to the government's switch to full cash planning in 1982. The table is derived from the government's own figures, in the 1983 White Paper on Public Expenditure, of spending in cost terms. These were obtained by deflating cash spending by the rise in total home costs (the GDP deflator) in each year since 1977/8. *But* it is well known that the costs of public social services tend to rise faster due to their labour intensive nature, so these figures *over*estimate the amount of actual services that can be bought with the money. This excessive cost inflation was particularly important in the two years from 1979 to 1981, partly due to above average public sector wage increases then. So the table also attempts to correct for this factor (the figures in brackets) for these two years. Despite their rough and ready nature (the method is described at the foot of the table) they probably give a better indication of the real funding of the welfare state over this period.

The overall picture is as follows. After a rapid growth in total social spending in the first half of the 1970s (up to 28%), it has virtually stagnated since 1975. For the remainder of the Labour administration and the first year of the Conservative one (when spending was pretty much determined in advance), a slight fall was followed by a slight rise resulting in an overall increase of less than 1% over the four years. The next four years of Thatcher Government will by 1983/4 have increased real spending on the welfare state by just 2% according to my calculations (though the lower than expected inflation now may provide a slight bonus for 1982/3). When interpreting these figures two things should be remembered. First, the period has witnessed an unprecedented growth in unemployment and the Exchequer costs associated with it. Second, the growing needs of the population often means that social service spending must run to stand still. For example, the growing number of elderly people means that personal social services such as home helps need to rise by 2% each year just to keep pace. In relation to real social needs the welfare services have undoubtedly been cut back.

When we turn to individual services the picture is still more stark. Once social security and the employment services are excluded, due to their dependence on the deepening recession, the remaining services in kind, with the exception of the NHS, have suffered almost continuous cutbacks. Housing expenditure was reduced by about 13% under Labour and has been further cut by at least three-fifths under the Tories (helped by the strength of council house sales and rapidly rising council rents). Education has been cut 6% by Labour and by a further 12% under the Tories. Spending on the personal social services grew 8% under Labour but has stagnated since. Only the NHS has been spared real cuts in funding, but when account is taken of real cost increases the extra funding under the Tories will amount to about 4.5% over four years, less than that necessary to maintain services in relation to needs. There can be no doubt that in quantitative terms the welfare state is under attack, and that the attack began with the Wilson/Callaghan administrations in 1975.

It is when we turn to the qualitative shifts in social policy that we see more clearly the distinct ideological reversal championed by the Thatcher government. Its policy changes have included the following. Sitting council house tenants have the right to buy their houses at very large discounts, council rents are going up sharply (which will further 'encourage' the sale of council houses), new housing programmes are pared to the bone and new controls are to be introduced over councils' direct works departments. In education the trend to comprehensives is being halted, overseas students fees are being raised to their full economic cost, plans to introduce student loans are mooted, and the new assisted places scheme will provide more public money for private schools. And in social security the 1980 Budget marked the most significant attack on social rights since the war: benefits to strikers' families were cut by £12 a week, 'short-term' benefits for the sick, unemployed and disabled were cut by 5% in real terms in 1980/81, earnings-related short-term benefits were abolished in January 1982 (but not earnings-related contributions), and responsibility for payment of basic sick pay during the first eight weeks of sickness devolved on employers in 1983.

Indications of government thinking about the future of the welfare state were revealed in the 'Think Tank' proposals leaked in the *Economist* of 18 September 1982. The Central Policy Review Staff outlined the following options for radical cuts in public spending up to the end of the decade:

- ending state funding of higher education and (less certainly) a system of educational vouchers for schooling.
- raising social security by less than the rate of inflation.

     — replacing the National Health Service with private health insurance, and in the meantime charging for visits to the doctor and more for drugs.

(Incidentally the Think Tank was 'short of bright ideas' on how to curb the other big spending department — the armed forces.) When the Cabinet 'wets' protested the paper was shelved for the time being, much to Mrs Thatcher's fury, but we may not have heard the last of these proposals.

Drawing together the threads of these policies, we see a major attempt to reprivatise parts of the welfare state (housing, education), higher charges on consumers (health, housing), and in social security explicit decisions to weaken the organised working class, to widen the gap between 'deserving' and 'undeserving' claimants and to encourage work incentives (at the same time that some employment schemes are eliminated and unemployment will escalate). This is not to mention the encouragement of police and law and order services, or the overt attack on progressive education. It is difficult to avoid the conclusion that the welfare state is attacked by the new conservatism at least as much for ideological as for economic reasons. Some of their policies (the assisted places scheme, possibly council house sales) will *raise* net costs to the Exchequer.

Restructuring the Welfare State Under Thatcher

In *The Political Economy of the Welfare State*[1] I argued:

> There are four ways amongst others in which the state, acting in the long-term interests of capital, may seek to restructure the welfare state at a time of economic crisis like the present: by adapting policies to secure more efficient reproduction of the labour force, by shifting emphasis to the social control of destabilising groups in society, by raising productivity within the social services and possibly by reprivatising parts of the welfare state.

However I also argued that this process of restructuring needs to be situated within an overall strategy for counteracting the crisis, and that there were, in Britain today, two alternative capitalist strategies available: the radical right strategy and the 'corporatist' strategy. The Labour administrations of 1974-79 practised a degenerate form of corporatism increasingly watered down with various monetarist elements. In the 1979 election a clear choice was expressed (at least in the southern half of England) for an undiluted form of the right wing strategy. But what are the crucial elements of the 'new conservatism' and how have they affected the restructuring of the welfare state?

In answering this question I am drawing on some previous articles in *Marxism Today*. Peter Leonard[2] has explored different ways in which this restructuring takes place under social democracy and under the 'radical right'. Together with earlier articles by Stuart Hall[3] and Andrew Gamble,[4] he emphasises the specific role of political and ideological elements in this particular response to the contemporary crisis of British capitalism. I wish to consider the links between these and the Tories' economic strategy analysed by Michael Bleaney.[5]

According to Hall and Gamble, Thatcherism is a political formation that combines the principles of the 'social market economy' with a new 'authoritarian populism'. The social market economy represents a return to some of the precepts of nineteenth century liberalism; a limited role for government, an emphasis on the responsibilities of the individual and so forth. In Britain and the Anglo-Saxon world generally this has taken the form of a resurgence of monetarism as advocated by Milton Friedman. Populism represents an appeal to national interests which are supposedly above class interests, drawing on the ideology of a neutral market place working in the interests of all. In its attack on immigrants, welfare recipients and unions, for example, it stresses the need for a strong state to represent national over sectional interests, though Thatcherism clearly differs from a truly authoritarian movement. Crudely speaking the Thatcherism = monetarism + authoritarian populism though the two threads of this ideology clearly complement each other.

What is striking for our purposes is the position of the welfare state at the heart of these two strands. The welfare state is the central target for the radical right on both counts. First, because it allegedly generates even higher tax levels, budget deficits, disincentives to work and save, and a bloated class of unproductive workers. Second, because it encourages 'soft' attitudes towards crime, immigrants, the idle, the feckless, strikers, the sexually aberrant and so forth. Economic prescriptions and populist incantations are harnessed together, and their prime target is the expanded sphere of state responsibility, state regulation and state-provided benefits which constitute the modern welfare state. As Hall stresses, this new right ideology did not appear out of thin air; it needed to be constructed, though it utilised existing elements. And, as Gamble shows, it had to be welded into a party political programme which could be electorally successful.

The process of restructuring the welfare state can now be situated within the political formation of the radical right. First, the *quantitative* role of cuts follows from the precepts of monetarism: strict control of the money supply, a substantial reduction in the level of government expenditure and taxation and a shift towards indirect taxation. A reduction in the public sector borrowing requirement is a key object of policy because of its impact on the money supply (or on interest rates if government securities are to be sold to the non-banking sector). Given the commitment to lower tax levels in order to encourage incentives to work and invest, this must involve even faster cuts in public spending. Given the commitment to higher defence spending, this must involve still greater cuts in social and economic expenditures. This has as another aim the weakening of the power of organised labour via higher rates of unemployment (and the threat of still higher levels if wage claims are 'excessive'). The goal is to use market forces (together with new legal restrictions) to reduce real wages and augment profits. A cut in the 'social wage', for example reducing housing subsidies or personal social services, augments this pressure to reduce labour's share in the national income. It thus provides an indirect route to encourage profitability and re-investment in British industry, even if a sound monetarist government like the present one disclaims any responsibility for the national rate of economic growth.

Second, the *qualitative* shifts in social policy are designed to reassert individualism, self-reliance and family responsibility, and to reverse the collective social provision of the post-war era. Present attempts to impose a national curriculum and 'raise standards' in public education provide a striking example of the social programme of the new conservatism. In many ways, though not all, these qualitative shifts complement the absolute cuts in expenditure: cutting social benefits to working age adults saves money and panders to the anti-scrounger mentality of the new populism. Together these two sets of forces have generated the most sustained attack on the welfare state since the war. The restructing of the welfare state has begun in earnest.

Welfare Under Capitalism

To understand why the welfare state is under attack today, we must first understand why it developed so markedly this century and in particular since the Second World War. This section summarises the analysis developed at greater length in my book. The welfare state in modern capitalist countries comprises public cash benefits (such as pensions), public benefits in kind (such as education), public regulation of the activities of individuals and corporations (such as consumer or labour legislation) and the taxation system. This complex of measures serves two major goals: the reproduction of labour-power, and the maintenance and control of the non-working population. Both involve quantitative and qualitative aspects; the state ensures directly or indirectly a minimum level of consumption for different groups in the population, and at the same time it modifies the pattern of socialisation, behaviour and abilities within the population. Since it is a capitalist welfare state it imposes sanctions and controls at the same time that it provides benefits (take council housing, for example, or education or supplementary benefit).

These goals can be grouped together and constitute *the state organisation of social reproduction.* As Engels pointed out, reproduction is just as essential an activity in all societies as production. The process of social reproduction refers to the processes of biological reproduction, of economic consumption and of socialisation: in short to the way individuals as social beings are 'produced' rather than goods and services in the process of production. Of course the family has played, and continues to play, a crucial function here, but when we refer to the state organisation of social reproduction we are referring to the way the welfare state has modified and partially supplemented the family in the twentieth century. From supplementary benefit to child care officers the welfare state today is intimately involved in this process. But our definition also reminds us how contentious this process is: after all the radical right are questioning precisely the respective roles of state, family and market in the sphere of social reproduction.

Reproduction is only one of the activities of the modern capitalist state. Modifying James O'Connor's analysis in *The Fiscal Crisis of the State*[6] we can identify three broad functions that it performs:

1. accumulation
2. reproduction
3. legitimation/repression

The first refers to all the means by which the state tries to maintain favourable conditions for the accumulation of capital. The third refers to the means by which it attempts to maintain social order and social control whilst at the same time trying to preserve social harmony and avoid harmful conflict (harmful, that is, to the state and private capital). Social policies clearly have implications for these other goals of the modern state: for example some policies (like the redundancy payments scheme or parts of higher education) are designed to achieve economic benefits for the private sector; while others (such as some aspects of education) perform a social control job, and many help to legitimise the system and reduce dissension in society. So the welfare state is involved in all three areas of activity, though I would argue its prime concern is with maintaining and adapting social reproduction.

But this does no more than provide a framework for understanding particular social policies such as those of the Thatcher Government. In fact it scarcely does this, for there is a danger in the above account of *explaining* the modern welfare state in terms of the *functions* that it performs in capitalist society – the danger, in short, of a crudely functionalist account. But class conflict, in particular pressure from the organised working class, has played a major role in the origins and spread of welfare services. Indeed for many the British welfare state is the child of the labour movement and the post-war Labour government. How can this be reconciled with the role that, we have argued, it plays in securing capital accumulation, social reproduction and political legitimation?

The brief answer is that the welfare state is the vector of two sets of political forces: 'pressure from below' and 'reform from above'. The first refers to the myriad ways in which class movements together with social and community movements demand social reforms to protect or extend their interests. This may result from pressure group politics within the state at one extreme to direct action and street conflict at the other. 'Reform from above' refers to the various ways in which the state seeks to implement social reform which will serve the longer-term economic, social and political interests of capital, or particular sections of capital. The state does not automatically perform this job: it requires at the least the executive and administrative wherewithal and a form of political mobilisation. I believe these are more readily available the more centralised is the apparatus of the state. The stronger is the role of the executive and senior civil service *vis-a-vis* parliament, for example, the more can they override short-term pressures from representatives of particular capitalist interests and impose a longer-term, more class-oriented strategy.

I would argue that these two sets of forces have *both* strengthened, and partially reinforced one another, over the last 40 years particularly in Britain. Their interaction led to two especially notable periods of social reform in the 1940s and the 1960s. During the Second World War the foundations of the Keynesian-welfare state were established. Though many of the reforms were enacted by the post-war Attlee Government, it is notable that most were the product of the war-time Coalition Government – the Beveridge report, the Butler Education Act. They represented the outcome of pressures from below – war-time radicalisation and a spirit of 'no going back to the thirties' – plus reforming drives from above – a recognition of the political and economic necessity of greater state responsibility for economic performance, notably through Keynesian demand management techniques. Thus in Britain Keynes and Beveridge represented a linked response to the pre-war crisis focusing respectively on demand management (part, but only part, of the economic sphere) and the sphere of social reproduction. Together they formed the core of the 'post-war settlement' between capital and labour which was to prove so successful a basis for post-war prosperity.

The 1960s and early 1970s saw a second wave of reforms as social and economic policy was slowly restructured in the face of a faltering rate of accumulation in Britain. The development of incomes policies, industrial strategies, the modification of Beveridge's social security principles, the expansion of higher education: all these represented a further extension of state intervention and a closer gearing of economic and social policy. Again there were pressures from below, from a labour movement of greater defensive economic strength, and from newer social and community movements; and pressures from above as reformers and spokesmen for capital understood the limited role of Keynesian policies and advocated more systematic economic and social intervention in order to restructure British capital in the face of overseas competition, domestic class pressures and a falling rate of profit. Again, though the Labour election victory in 1964 signalled the shift in direction, many of the individual reforms had been initiated in the last years of the previous Conservative administration.

So the British welfare state represents the outcome of growing working class pressure for economic and social reforms, modified by the desire of a more centralised state apparatus to restructure economic and social policies for its own reasons. In part the post-war Keynesian-welfare state generated its own momentum for further state intervention, to secure economic growth and capital accumulation within a new balance of class forces that it had itself helped to shape. It follows from this that the development of Keynesian economic policy and modern social policy were interlinked and formed the two central planks of the post-war political consensus between the parties. It therefore comes as no surprise to find that both planks are simultaneously under attack from the new radical right.

The Welfare State and the Economic Crisis

But what, if any, is the link between an expanded welfare state and a declining economy? Is the British economic crisis the result of an overgrown public sector, as the present Government would have it, or are the two unconnected? My own view is that there is a link, but that it is not so straightforward or unambiguous as the new conservatism suggests. After all, a recent EEC report showed that government spending as a share of GDP is lower in the UK than any other country in the EEC. On the other hand socialist reformers and others who deny any link and who reiterate Keynesian nostrums about the need for more public spending in order to pull us out of recession do a disservice to the socialist movement. The Keynesian welfare state *has* generated new contradictions working as it is within the framework of a private capitalist economy. It is not possible for state spending to rise inexorably as a share of GNP without adverse consequences for its domestic capital. What then are these limits?

I believe there are two main limits. First, a growing level of state expenditure exacerbates the post-war conflict between capital and labour over the *distribution* of national output. Given the centralisation of capital within an expanding international economy, and given a stronger, more organised labour movement, then inflation becomes inbuilt within advanced capitalist countries, as capital and labour can in turn offset higher wage costs or higher prices. When the state then lays claim to a higher share of resources this two-way conflict becomes a three-way conflict adding to the inflationary pressure. For however the state seeks to finance this expenditure – via higher taxes on the working class, or on corporations (very unusual), or via higher indirect taxes, or via higher state borrowing – the result is to exacerbate the spiral of wage costs and prices. At a time of economic slowdown and increasing international competition, this has also contributed to the squeeze on profit rates.

Second, the growing level of state expenditure and intervention interferes with the *production* of surplus value and profit.[7] The growth of the 'social wage' and 'collective consumption' means that the operation of the labour market and the reserve army of labour is impaired, and the bargaining strength of the working class increased. Unemployment benefits, family benefits, public assistance, state health and social services, housing subsidies, etc., all remove part of the real living standards of the working class from the wage system, and allocate this part according to some criteria of social need and citizenship. Citizenship rights are counterposed to property rights, and the ability of capital to transform labour power into labour performed is impaired.

The precise impact of welfare policies on capital accumulation will depend in practice on the criteria according to which social benefits are distributed, and will vary between countries. Are they predominantly distributed on some criterion of need, or do they take into account the labour market position of men and women, the impact on work incentives, and so forth? In other words the extent to which particular social policies *subvert* or *complement* the market mechanism can only be answered after detailed research on the way in which they operate. Generally speaking, one may assume that the impact of welfare policies on capital accumulation will be more favourable the more they follow market criteria in distributing and awarding benefits, and the more closely are social and economic policies integrated. But of course the further social policies are shifted in this direction, the more they may interfere with social reproduction and political legitimation.

In the light of this what has been the impact of the welfare state on British capitalism? Two peculiar facts about Britain must be borne in mind in answering this question. First, the position of Britain within the world economy is a declining one, and the deep-seated weaknesses of our economic structure are now super-imposed on a world-wide recession which has marked the end of the post-war boom. Second, the defensive economic strength of the British trade union movement has prevented the strategy of industrial restructuring attempted by Labour and Conservative administrations since the early 1960s from being successfully implemented (Purdy, Jacques).[8] This defensively strong, decentralised labour movement with extensive shop-floor organisation has also hindered the restructuring of the welfare state. Unlike the USA, Britain has a developed set of social services available in the main for the whole population rather than certain privileged strata within it. But unlike Sweden and West Germany, for example, these are not closely integrated with economic policy to achieve greater mobility of labour or to encourage labour force participation. Council housing policy, for example, may well restrict the mobility of labour demanded by capital and interfere with the operation of labour markets. Furthermore, British unions managed to maintain their members' post-tax incomes in the face of slow growth, rising tax levels and periodic incomes policies at least until the mid-1970s. But unlike Sweden this was not achieved by means of a corporatist-style social contract which would yield some tangible benefits to capital. In an environment of relative economic decline, it is likely that the British welfare system has contributed to the British economic crisis by exacerbating inflation and undermining market mechanisms. But these very features stem from the particular ways social policy has developed in post-war Britain, outlined above.

It is perhaps not surprising, then, that monetarist and populist attacks on the welfare state have established themselves here. Given the failure of Keynesianism, and the progressive degeneration of the Labour Governments' corporatist experiments after the 1974 Social Contract, a vacuum opened up which first Powell, then Thatcher, Joseph *et al* were quick to exploit. The defeat of the left in the EEC referendum of 1975 under a Labour government helped prepare the ground for this move to the right. The indigenous populist ideology, analysed by Hall and Gamble; the reluctance of British capital to opt for Continental-style interventionism; and the failure of the Labour leadership to develop an alternative strategy to replace the wilting nostrums of Keynesianism, all left the way open for a tax-welfare backlash culminating in the victory of the new conservatism in the last election. The left is also implicated in its failure to unify around some coherent transitional strategy as an alternative to both Labour reformism and the new conservatism. The alternative economic strategy adopted at the Labour Party conference in 1973 represented an important stage in this process of re-thinking. But as Hodgson[9] has argued it was conceived by the left of the Labour Party, in particular the Tribune group, as a Parliamentary policy without the need for mobilisation at the local level, which emasculated its socialist content and meant that it differed from corporatist-style interventionism.

The result is that Britain is experiencing the most far-reaching experiment in 'new right' politics in the Western world. The Thatcher government alone has received Milton Friedman's blessing. Its underlying aim is to attack the labour movement on the economic and ideological fronts. The policy shifts outlined earlier on can all be seen to contribute to this aim: legal sanctions against unions, mass unemployment by means of tight monetary controls, the cutting of social benefits for the families of strikers, a reduction in the social wage on several fronts, and a shift to more authoritarian practices in the welfare field. It represents one coherent strategy for managing the British crisis, a strategy aimed at the heart of the post-war Keynesian-welfare state settlement.

The Future Prospects For Thatcherism

Will it work? In trying to answer this question, I will address in
turn each of the three functions of the state mentioned earlier on.

1. *Accumulation*. All economic forecasters now agree that the
prospects for the British economy are grim. Unemployment has
risen to well over 3 million. In the single month of December
1980, the equivalent of Bradford's entire workforce was added
to Britain's dole queues. Manufacturing output fell at a rate
unprecedented this century — 15% between late 1979 and early
1981. In the eighteen months since the dramatic fall it has
remained unchanged. After a 2% fall in gross domestic product
in 1980, it rose only 1% in the following eighteen months. The
tight fiscal squeeze maintained by the Thatcher government has
resulted in Britain having the lowest budget deficit of the major
OECD countries. When it is adjusted for the increased 'costs' of
unemployment, Britain has, since 1981, run a budget surplus
during the most severe slump since the 1930s. Thus the
deflationary monetary and fiscal policies of the present
government hardly provide the basis for a recovery in
profitability and capital accumulation in the short-to-medium
term: instead they are making matters much worse.

The cuts in social expenditure will have an impact not only on
the recipients of the services, but on sections of private capital as
well. So far it is capital spending that has borne the brunt of the
cuts, so that government demand for the output of the
construction industry for example has fallen dramatically. The
new cuts announced recently will only exacerbate this problem.
One half of NHS expenditure for example consists of purchases
from the private and nationalised sectors (drugs, supplies, oil,
electricity), so that government cuts here directly harm private
industry. Even if the Government manages to impose its future
cuts on transfer payments, public sector employment and wage
and salary levels, this will still have a multiplier effect on private
sector output. The Chancellor's intention to reduce public sector
borrowing sharply to £8½ billion in 1980, only 3¾% of GDP, will
exacerbate the already deep recession.

How can it happen that a policy intentionally designed to

revitalise British capitalism should have this opposite effect? It stems from a contradiction within the accumulation process long ago noted by Marx. For capital accumulation to proceed two conditions must be fulfilled: first, profits must be produced by successfully exploiting labour within the production process; second, these profits must then be realised by the exchange of commodities in the circulation process. These two movements of the process are now in contradiction. Keynesian policies by sustaining aggregate demand overcame the inter-war crisis of underconsumption but over the long-term have contributed to a falling rate of profit and undermined the production of surplus value. In reaction to this the present Government is attempting to alter the class balance of forces to raise the rate of exploitation, but in so doing it will worsen in the short-term the domestic conditions for realising this surplus value. That is, a deflationary policy results in excess capacity and falling profit margins (unless exports can rise to make up the loss, a scenario that looks increasingly unlikely). In short, higher government spending facilitates the realisation of profits in the short term, but interferes with their production of profits in the longer term, whereas cuts in spending may aid the production of profits in the longer term, but at their short-term expense. The conclusion is that an approach relying on market forces to expand accumulation in the longer-term worsens its prospects on the short to medium term.

2. *Reproduction.* The new conservatism believes that the welfare state, the state organisation of social reproduction, has proceeded too far, that individual and family responsibility are undermined by this process and need to be restored. But to what extent can this twentieth century process be put into reverse? In my view the problems generated by a substantial dismantling of welfare services would be great, a fact reflected in the hesitancy even of this Government in implementing spending cuts in, for example, the health service. First, it would throw a greater burden back on individual families and in particular the women within them. (Moroney[10] documents the enormous burden borne by, for example, middle-aged women in caring for their elderly relatives.) But rising numbers of conventional nuclear families are breaking up in divorce and a growing proportion of them are not being reconstituted. The numbers of children living with

single parents is increasing, adding to the demand for, for instance, supplementary benefit. Furthermore the women's movement is now a force capable of resisting some of the more overt attempts at a 'back to the family' approach, as its success in deflecting attempts to retract the abortion laws testifies. Second, social needs are not something objectively identifiable; they are interpreted and new needs engendered in the process of class and social conflict. Community-based movements such as Women's Aid or law centres have helped recognise and define previously personal problems as new social needs. So too have state social services, as when the introduction of the NHS in 1948 revealed a large unmet need for medical services. These discoveries are not easily unlearnt and the gains in social provision not easily reversed.

Thatcherism, in attacking the Keynesian-welfare state couplet, thus risks regenerating many of the problems these policies were initially designed to overcome; mass unemployment, renewed poverty (particularly amongst children), uneven regional development and urban decay amongst others. But it will be attempting to reverse a process that has generated an entirely different environment to that of the thirties. Two factors have changed: expectations for social provision now exist amongst a majority of the population; and new movements exist, premissed on the welfare state, to extend and defend existing social and community provision.

3. *Legitimation/repression.* The present Government seeks legitimacy for its policies in the ideologies of economic realism and authoritarian populism, but these may prove to be a fragile basis, for several reasons. First the purely electoral consequences are hazardous because, as we noted above, the immediate impact of the policies is to worsen recession and unemployment and to lower real incomes. Some monetarists appreciate that the long time-span of their policies conflicts with the election cycle of liberal democracies, and either bemoan the constraints this imposes on 'sound' government policies (something missing after all in the Chilean monetarist experiment) or conduct a vigorous ideological offensive to convince the electorate that theirs is the only sure way forward. But pressure is building up on the Thatcher Government from within the Conservative Party to moderate its monetarist zeal, if

not yet to undertake a U-turn. Second, one fifth of the labour force is employed by central and local government and has a direct interest in maintaining the level of pulic expenditure and employment. Furthermore a majority of the population are consumers in one way or another of social services and many will resent falling standards in their particular sector, even if supporting the Government's broad objectives. Third, fears are growing (witness the post-mortems held on the riots) about the threats to law and order and the growth of widening social divisions and conflict which present social policies will exacerbate. Growing numbers of unemployed school leavers, or the ghettoisation of the council house estates remaining after the sale of the better local authority housing, are two examples of the political dangers in dismantling socially-provided services too far. It is true that the Government is developing a more repressing strategy in some areas of the welfare services and in its law and order policies generally, but the harm to its legitimacy should not be underestimated particularly if major opposition to its policies develops amongst those most affected by them. Lastly, the attempt by the Thatcher Government deliberately to depoliticise areas of social life by disclaiming government responsibility and returning them to the anonymity of the market may itself be politically unacceptable. After several decades in which the state has accepted responsibility for the rate of unemployment, it is hazardous for it now to claim that it has been powerless all along.

Towards a Left Alternative

I have tried to suggest some of the problems which Thatcherism is likely to encounter in the near future. In the process I am conscious that I have underplayed many of the strengths of Thatcherism as a political movement emphasised by Hall and Leonard: the contradictions inherent in the traditional social democracy of the Labour Party; the popular appeal of anti-collectivist anti-state sentiments given the experience of the state (including its welfare apparatus) as a bureaucratic, oppressive imposition; the ability to tap resentment against what Hall labels the '1968' movement for greater democracy and personal freedom. But to list these resources of the new conservatism is not to demonstrate that they will necessarily succeed as a political movement.

However, the future of both Thatcherism and the welfare state will depend in part on the alternatives on offer. At the time of writing the political viability of a new centre coalition of the Liberals and Social Democrats is unclear. Just as unclear is the strategy they would offer in the field of economic and social policy to tackle Britain's deep-seated crisis. Attempts to decry the usefulness of any strategic approach at a time of great uncertainty, and to uphold the virtues of pragmatism, will soon run foul of the contradictions noted above, though North Sea oil may provide a temporary buffer. Given the bankcruptcy of Keynesian/welfare state reformism, the alternative to Thatcherism offered by a new Centre coalition would most likely be a further step forward in state centralisation and state intervention, obscured by a rhetoric of decentralisation.

It is important to recognise that there is nothing inherently socialist in further state intervention and that either option will threaten some of the political and social rights established since the war. It is also important in opposing both strategies to recognise the contradictory nature of the contemporary welfare state: it signals a collective responsibility for meeting an array of social problems and social needs certainly, but it achieves this through a process of centralisation in which social policies are deformed and adapted to suit the requirements of capital and to minimise democratic control.

The need is to move beyond the traditional politics of the Labour Party by harnessing the labour movement to the social, community, women's and other democratic movements that have partly developed in and against the welfare state. But secondly to combine this with an alternative economic strategy to be implemented by a future left government at the national level. An urgent task in both respects is to develop a parallel alternative *social* strategy, that will propose new priorities for social policy together with new forms of implementing and controlling it. Insofar as this is not achieved, the Thatcherist strategy, despite its problems outlined above, could win by default.

Notes

[1] I. Gough, *The Political Economy of the Welfare State*, London 1979.

[2] P. Leonard, 'Restructuring the Welfare State: from social democracy to the radical right', *Marxism Today*, December 1979.

[3] S. Hall, 'The Great Moving Right Show', *Marxism Today*, January 1979 (see this volume p. 19).

[4] A. Gamble, 'The Decline of the Conservative Party', *Marxism Today*, November 1979 (see this volume p. 109).

[5] M. Bleaney, 'The Tories' Economic Strategy', *Marxism Today*, November 1979 (see this volume, p. 132).

[6] J. O'Connor, *The Fiscal Crisis of the State*, St James Press, 1973.

[7] This second limit imposed by the welfare state on capital accumulation is a serious omission in my book. Its importance is well argued by John Harrison in his review, 'State expenditure and capital', *Cambridge Journal of Economics*, Volume 4, No. 4, 1980.

[8] D. Purdy, 'British capitalism since the war', *Marxism Today*, September 1976; M. Jacques, 'Thatcherism — Breaking Out of the Impasse', *Marxism Today*, November 1979 (see this volume, p. 40).

[9] G. Hodgson, *Socialist Economic Strategy*, ILP Square One Publications, 1979.

[10] R. Moroney, *The Family and the State*, Longman, 1976.

[*] This article is a reprint of one first published in *Marxism Today*, July 1980, with updating only of the facts and figures presented in the first and last sections. Subsequent events have discredited some of the arguments and predictions in the last section. Whilst the pessimistic analysis of the prospects for accumulation have been amply borne out over the last three years and the perceived problems in the sphere of social reproduction have grown, the predictions of a 'legitimation crisis' have not been realised. This may well reflect an inherent ambiguity in the concept of legitimation. In any case it demonstrates that my original approach was still too deterministic. It derived political outcomes too directly from an analysis of the contradictions of Thatcherite policies without giving sufficient weight to the political, ideological and cultural mediations — which now seem likely to reward her government with a second term of office.

Tony Lane

The Tories and the Trade Unions: Rhetoric and Reality

Employers take trade unionism as medicine they have got to take. They keep hoping that they will be fit enough without it. I don't think I know of any employers who would take trade unionism as their daily food.

(George Woodcock)[1]

Maggie doesn't want to take us back to the *1930s*. She wants to take us back to the *1830s*.

(Tim Lynch, senior shop steward in a Liverpool factory)

Introduction

The range of interests that the Tory Party embraces and the inter-class accommodations necessary to sustain them, has always involved the Party in an internal ideological struggle. That struggle has always been at its sharpest over the question of how to manage labour and its organisations. The issue was put bluntly enough by Winston Churchill's father, Lord Randolph Churchill in 1892:

If Labour ... found that it could 'obtain its objectives and secure its own advantage' under the existing constitution – which it was the Tories' business to preserve – then all would be well, but if the Conservatives stubbornly resisted these demands in 'unreasoning and shortsighted support of all the present rights of property', then Labour would be ranged against them. Since the Tories were a minority in the country, it was incumbent on them to enlist in their support 'a majority of the votes of the masses of Labour'.[2]

Nothing much has changed. It is just that economic exigencies have once again sharpened the polarities within the party.

That Tories have never liked trade unionism is an elementary truism. But that generalisation glosses over considerable variations in Tory thought and ideology. On trade unionism as on no other question have matters of doctrine and calculation of political expediency coexisted so uneasily. Still, and for all that, the pragmatism of Churchill the elder prevailed. Rules and conventions, organisations and departments of state, new professions and even a new vocabulary were built on and out of that pragmatic acceptance of the existence of organised labour. New generations of trade unionists have grown up in that environment and have come to look upon the edifices of Tory pragmatism as if they were natural features of the landscape. It is not therefore surprising that most trade unionists find it hard to believe that the dominant faction in Thatcher's government really is determined to obliterate them as an effective force.

The Rhetoric ...

Throughout the post-war period, and markedly since the mid-1950s when workplace trade unionism began to emerge as a potent force, there has been a continuing and ever-noisier tension in the Tory Party on the question of trade union power. The import of these disputes, and the recent conversion of major elements within the party to an explicit economic doctrine in which trade union power centrally figures, requires some exploration.

To simplify somewhat − because lines crossed on some specific issues − there have been the One Nation Tories as exemplified latterly by the Macmillan-Butler-Macleod axis. And there are now the free market ideologues as represented by Joseph-Biffen-Nott. With the key exception of Enoch Powell this second group was, until the late 1960s, comprised of uninfluential backbenchers.

The One Nation Tories have drawn their inspiration and rhetoric from successive re-statements of Disraeli's novel *Sybil, or The Two Nations*. Following in like vein have been Macmillan's *The Middle Way*, published in the 1930s, and Lord Hailsham's *The Conservative Case*, published as a Penguin Special for the 1959 election. In each of these statements, re-echoed less eloquently in the speeches of James Prior, William Whitelaw and Peter Walker, is the theme of a people divided by function but organically unified in The Nation. Some must rule and others be ruled and if the ruled have obligations, then by the same token the rulers have duties. The overriding duty is to preserve the nation and in this pursuit the ruled must be protected from predators and injustice lest they become restless. Hence the recurrent warnings to Tory activists against 'opening up old divisions' and resort to an extensive and evocative vocabulary which speaks of the perils of conflict and disunity.

The socio-economic basis of One Nation Toryism is not now always obvious, though it is of interest that Whitelaw, Prior and Walker all have agribusiness interests. It is, in any case, typically difficult directly to relate the ideological position of *individuals* to economic interests. In general, we need only note that One Nation Toryism draws upon the landed aristocracy's tradition of *noblesse oblige* which is eminently well-suited to late capitalism where large firms place a high premium on political stability.

Tory Party conferences have regularly revealed the schisms between the One Nation leadership and the aspirations of constituency activists. In the urban areas, which the Tories must win in elections, the rank and file is an amalgam of accountants, solicitors, shopkeepers, small businessmen, self-employed, plus a leavening of foremen, supervisors and clerks from industry and commerce. In short, much of the party organisation in the localities is in the hands of the petty bourgeoisie and low level industrial functionaries. It is this stratum which forms the right-populist basis of Thatcherism and which makes the most noise about 'iniquitous' trade unions.

The vocal rank and file populists have a sizeable public constituency. They speak for those first line supervisors in industry whose authority has been increasingly challenged; for those clerks and secretaries whose status has been eroded; for all those shop-keepers, small-businessmen and self-employed who cannot organise collectively and who resent the organised strength of waged labour. Their economic marginality and the struggle for survival which that entails seems, to them, to contrast sharply with factory and public service workers who are alleged to work less hard, to lack the sturdy virtues of independence and self-improvement – and yet have substantial economic and political power.

The Tory rank and file may have a substantial constituency in public sentiment but lacks a power base of its own. Attempts at forming 'unions' of shopkeepers, the self-employed and small businesses have tended to collapse in ignominy or remain small in scale and devoid of influence. Their only hope has been in the Tory Party whose One Nation leadership has sometimes found it difficult to conceal its distaste for petty bourgeois rhetoric and its cruder policy demands.

During his stint, first as shadow spokesman on employment and then as minister of that department, James Prior was swimming against the conference tide on trade union questions but nevertheless had his way. The manner and consequences of his victories deserve a brief diversion for the light they throw on important and adjacent issues.

Tory conferences are exercises in stage management and provide a vivid contrast with the Labour affairs. Labour conferences are egalitarian in tone. Debates are debates even if cookery is involved in agendas and compositing resolutions. The party leadership may sometimes be accorded more respect than is its due, but the general style of proceedings is such that one person is no better than another.

Tory conferences are more like a blend of a revival meeting and joint consultation in an old-style paternalist company. The tone is one of benevolent hierarchy where the peasants may have their say but where the lord of the manor retains his privileges. 'Deference' may be an unsatisfactory concept, but it is nevertheless a remarkable fact that due authority in the Tory Party conference can have its way to an extent unheard of in the Labour Party. This can only be satisfactorily explained by saying that a belief in hierarchy *as a matter of principle* is a central feature of Tory ideology. This being so, it is obvious that the question of *who* has the leadership is not a negligible one.

With the accession of Margaret Thatcher to the leadership, the One Nation Tories lost *control* of the party for the first time in their history. It is true that Bonar Law and Edward Heath both had dalliances with the hard-nosed right of the party but these were short-lived and tradition was restored — as indeed it will be again if the Tories lose the next election. In the meantime the right-populists are totally in control. The One Nation group, having cravenly retreated, has been routed and the credibility of its leading figures all but destroyed.

But having said that right-populism now controls the party, does it follow that the Tory attack on the unions would have been any different under a One Nation leadership? Obviously there can be no precise answer to such a question. The balance of probability, however, is that the provisions of the 1980 Employment Act would have been little different. No doubt the accompanying rhetoric would have been milder, the consultative processes with the TUC more extensive and a few innocuous clauses conceded as a diplomatic gesture: the only difference would have been in the salesmanship and this, we may be confident, would not have gulled the TUC.

To reach this conclusion is to reach another. Namely that so far as trade union activity in furtherance of disputes is concerned, there is now substantial common ground between the two factions. This is a far cry from the balance of intra-party forces in the Macmillan period. Several things need to be said about this, some briefly and others more extensively.

On the brief side first. The half-hearted attempts by the Tories to modernise British industrial capital from the late 1950s through to 1964 failed. Furthermore, we know now after the slightly more determined and imaginative efforts by Labour in 1964-70, by the Tories in 1972-74 and by Labour again in 1974-79, that the forms of intervention and management launched first by Macmillan could not have succeeded even with a longer trial period.

Tory disillusionment with such strategies was patently well-established by the late 1960s, hence the early Heath commitment to an unleashing of market forces. That he subsequently retreated and has never recanted may be attributed to his mauling by the trade unions over the Industrial Relations Act. This particular defeat, not to mention the miners' strikes of 1972 and 1974, undermined the One Nation faction in two ways. Firstly it showed that negotiated, as distinct from legislated, agreements with the TUC could deliver no significant goods. Secondly, and by extension, it discredited the whole notion that government could beneficially intervene in industrial reorganisation and detailed economic management.

These conditions presented the right-populists, now stronger and more intellectually respectable, with their opportunity. Throughout the long period of One Nation control, the party continuously reaffirmed its belief in the virtues of a capitalist market economy. Its practice, however, of regulating markets in the interests of maintaining a 'unified' people kept this doctrinal aspect in the background. The assumption was always that judicious interventionism would of itself protect market mechanisms. As we have seen, events undermined this assumption.

These developments deprived the One Nation faction of its *raison d'être* and left it with its ill-defined defence of the market economy. Meanwhile the right-populists had gathered strength, secured the defection of prominent figures like Sir Keith Joseph from the One Nation faction, and developed a sustained defence of the market in which an attack on the unions figures prominently.

Here then were two broad factions, one suffering from a loss of credibility and confidence, the other equipped with a coherent case and promulgated by authoritative figures with energy and ability. The latter, furthermore, could draw upon the support of the party's rank and file. In these conditions the One Nation group were forced to cede ground and become *junior* partners in an uneasy alliance with the right-populists.

One final point on the formation of this new alliance is worth mentioning. There is no doubt that if in the history of the Industrial Relations Act, Tories like Heath and Prior became totally convinced of the need for great caution in the area of trade union legislation, others drew opposite conclusions which were fuelled by the miners' tactics in the 1974 strike. In that historic dispute, the highly successful use of flying and massed pickets raised the spectre of 'mob rule' in Tory breasts. The portrayal of these disputes in the mass media and in the private reports of Chief Constables as threatening, intimidating and verging on organised physical violence, stoked the fires of petty bourgeois prejudice. More significantly, they also frightened the One Nation faction.

That ideology has always expressed a public current of feeling wherein working people are characterised as splendid sturdy figures so long as they are treated decently. But the counterpart to this is the subterranean sentiment and these same people are untamed savages underneath. Untutored and unlettered, working people are barbarians who might rise up and destroy their civilised world of good taste, decorum and cultural accomplishment. Displays of organised working class power brought these normally dormant sentiments bubbling to the surface – and created a certain limited common ground with the right-populists.

Sentiments and prejudices, bigotry and fear, all combine to a greater or lesser extent in Tory ideology (and in others too, for that matter). But without a kernel of doctrine or 'theory' those elements cannot be sufficient for a political programme. *That* began to be constructed on a new footing in the 1960s when Enoch Powell cut himself adrift from mainstream Toryism.

Powell, now mainly remembered for his attacks on immigration, was in fact much more important in the second half of the 1960s for the revival of thinking on the market economy. Forcefully logical in argument and impressive in his integrity, Powell's *intellectual* influence was quite extraordinary by giving clarity and coherence to what had been a hotch-potch of vague and disconnected ideas. On the specific question of trade unionism however, Powell has never been hostile. Indeed, unlike Hayek whose views have resurfaced in the last decade, Powell has dismissed trade unionism as having any economic significance.

The 'theoretical' attack on the unions draws extensively on F.A. Hayek. An Austrian political economist who enjoyed a vogue in the 1940s, resurrected by the Institute for Economic Affairs since the late 1960s and whose ideas have been paraded with increasing frequency in the 1970s, Hayek has a politics readily guessed at by the titles of three volumes published between 1973 and 1979: *Rules and Order, The Mirage of Social Justice, The Political Order of a Free People.*

There is no space here to embark upon an extended analysis of Hayek's work though somebody, somewhere and soon could usefully undertake the task. A few comments will have to suffice to convey the general flavour – but first a series of quotations by way of illustration:

Most people probably still believe that a 'labour dispute' normally means a disagreement about remuneration and the conditions of employment, while as often as not its role purpose is an attempt on the part of unions to force unwilling workers to join.[3]

... the whole basis of our free society is gravely threatened by the powers arrogated by the unions.[4]

It cannot be stressed enough that the coercion which unions have been permitted to exercise contrary to all principles of freedom under the law is primarily the coercion of fellow workers, Whatever true coercive power unions may be able to wield over employers is a consequence of this primary power of coercing other workers; the coercion of employers would lose most of its objectionable character if unions were deprived of this power to exact unwilling support.[5]

It is true that any union effectively controlling all potential workers of a firm or industry can exercise almost unlimited pressure on the employer and that, particularly where a great amount of capital has been invested in specialised equipment, such a union can practically expropriate the owner and command nearly the whole return of his enterprise.[6]

Far from being a public calamity, it would indeed be a highly desirable state of affairs if the workers should not feel it necessary to form unions.[7]

This assortment of quotations does not exhaust Hayek's views on the role of trade unionism. Enough have been provided to show the similarities with Tory rhetoric and certain principles half-established in the 1980 Employment Act.

The first quote can be flatly contradicted. Whereas Hayek says that 50% of disputes in an unspecified period were on the issue of the closed shop, the Donovan Report showed that in the years 1964-66 out of a total of 2,196 unofficial strikes, 1.3% were in pursuit of the closed shop. Even if it were assumed that *all* the official strikes in that period (approximately 180) were over the same issue, the percentage only rises to 9.5.[8]

The fourth quotation can also be flatly rejected. The most capital intensive of industries, chemicals, is not only virtually strike free: it has also been highly profitable. Between 1971 and 1973, 96% of all chemical plants experienced no strikes,[9] and throughout the 1970s ICI has continuously ranked as the fourth most profitable UK company, showing an average return on capital of 17.5% between 1970 and 1977.[10]

This fourth quotation is especially interesting because it depends upon a confused definition of trade unions. As in Hayek, so in Tory rhetoric, there is a blindness to the distinction between the formal apparatus of trade unions (its lay and full-time officers) and the membership. So accustomed to thinking in terms of hierarchy, our ideologues seem unable to appreciate that trade unions have neither a command structure nor an elaborate bureaucracy. Far from being like the giant octopuses of science fiction and popular imagination, the trade unions are highly *de*centralised and organisationally inefficient to a quite startling degree. But even if they had an efficient bureaucracy with an extensive division of labour, the democratic sentiments of the membership and its sectionalised industrial circumstances would make it impossible for members to be dragooned, coerced, or otherwise directed.

In the trade unions the *real* power lies with the workers, for only they can decide to withdraw their labour. The most that the formal apparatus can do is to inform, exhort and lend its collective resources: it can persuade with varying degrees of success but not command. Such elementary truths may not be apparent to Professor Hayek or to his students amongst right-populists, but not all Tories are so blind. At the 1956 conference the late Iain Macleod responded to a motion demanding secret ballots before strikes were called:

> Macleod replied that there was no objection in principle to a secret ballot. But would it contribute to industrial peace … Underlying the motion was the idea that workers are less militant than their leaders. 'All I can say to you, speaking quite frankly, is that this is not my experience, nor is it the experience of any Minister of Labour.' Macleod had no faith in the theory that the great mass of wage earners was fundamentally sound and sober, but at times led astray by cunning leaders.[11]

Industrial management, we may be certain, continues to understand the Macleod truth. Robert Taylor, writing in *Management Today*, the journal of the British Institute of Management, said:

> The unions have long been the scapegoats for UK economic troubles; but are the unions to blame for Britain's feeble productivity performance? It is often the work groups, not the unions themselves, that control disruptive strikes and restrictive practices …[12]

The third quotation also hints at another theme which is more explicit elsewhere in Hayek's writings: namely that trade unions form monopolies in labour markets. This view now enjoys something of a vogue amongst right-populist economists, and, like much else in their writings, it is asserted rather than argued. Samuel Brittan, a *Financial Times* columnist, is the leader of the pack. In his book, *The Economic Consequences of Democracy*, the term 'trade union monopoly power' is employed on eight separate occasions, but is nowhere explained, justified or even defined.[13] On the other hand, the general drift is pretty obvious. In any given bargaining situation where workers are unionised, all workers within a grade are obliged to sell their labour at the negotiated price. This, it is implicitly argued, must therefore distort the market for labour. Such a view is based on the assumption that if workers *individually* negotiated their own rates of pay, there would follow, first, a wide range of wage rates and, second, no possibility of any coercive power being used against employers. If this is what 'trade union monopoly power' means, then its assumptions are correct.

Trade unions, by definition, are concerned with collective organisation as a means of coercing employers. Existing law (which Hayek attacks) even as recently amended, recognises the right to exercise this coercion by generally exempting employees from being sued for damages by their employers when in dispute. It need hardly be said that in providing this exemption, the law (i.e. the political forces that make it) recognises an imbalance of power as between an individual workers and an employer. While the law has never approved the 'right to strike', it has enabled the collective ability to make a strike effective.

Now Hayek and his attentive students are willing to concede that in a free society workers may form unions. What they object to is the possibility of effective collective action against employers. This view is splendidly satirised in Michael Frayn's, 'A Perfect Strike', which begins: 'Public opinion, so far as I can tell, unquestioningly concedes the right of men in a free society to withdraw their labour. It just draws the line at strikes.'[14]

The right-populist attack on trade unions is exactly as portrayed at the beginning of this article by Tim Lynch, the senior shop steward from a Liverpool factory. This faction really does want to eliminate the possibility of effective coercive power and thereby return the law to where it stood in the early nineteenth century. This is no exaggeration. *No other plausible interpretation can be put upon attacks on union monopoly power*. But this is right-Utopianism. If trade unions did not exist they would assuredly be reinvented. In which case the right-populists, to achieve their ends, would need to re-enact the Combination Laws of 1799 and 1800. In a *parliamentary democracy* such aspirations are the purest moonshine.

Much could be made of Hayek's ignorance, his argument by assertion and his highly selective use of evidence.[15] But in the end, so far as he and his followers are concerned, it is a question of a fundamentalist belief requiring an act of faith. Underpinning it all is a theological belief that a capitalism based on the operation of unhampered markets is the surest guarantee of individual liberty. It therefore follows that organisations, such as trade unions, which attempt to regulate markets are pernicious by definition.[16] Accordingly, and in Hayek's own words, it would be '... a highly desirable state of affairs if the workers should not feel it necessary to form unions'.

... and the Reality

Conspicuously absent from public Tory activity is that industrial, technocratic stratum of senior and plant management. Such people, naturally, and in the main, vote Tory. Some may contribute financially. But activists they are not. Their absence from Tory councils, though having an effect in the internal politicking, is not crucial when it comes to policy. Where policy and legislation on the trade unions is concerned, these are the people who have to carry the costs. Thus, while some may inwardly subscribe to right-populist rhetoric, they nevertheless have to contend with organised workers on a daily basis. Even the calculated thundering at CBI conferences sounds more like an empty stomach by the time the industrial relations managers, industry's professional politicians, have got to work.

George Woodcock of course was right. If management were to design an ideal world then trade unions would not feature in it. *People* are a nuisance and insist on having minds of their own. It would be so much more convenient if they were like visual display units and showed the right signals when a key was punched. Order and predictability are what managers want, and preferably of the sort that can be mathematicised. Hence the managerial paradox. On the one hand they would do without trade unions. On the other hand, factories and offices have to be run; their workers are members of trade unions; and so managers collaborate in procedures so as to maximise order and predictability.

It was not for nothing that many large companies were apprehensive about the attack on the closed shop enshrined in the 1972 Industrial Relations Act. With established procedures probable outcomes can be calculated and contingency plans drawn up. External changes, imposed by law, might disrupt all of those carefully nurtured political balances and diplomatic channels and with unknown consequences for productivity and output. Resistance to far-reaching changes in trade union status will, accordingly, be registered by this Tory constituency. The *sense* of this is captured in the following passage from Samuel Brittan although the context is different:

> ... the minority among the intellectual classes who bother to read the standard defences of capitalism by writers such as Friedman or Hayek soon find that the contemporary business leader ... has seldom heard of [their] key propositions ... On the contrary, his ideal is often that of negotiated deals with government officials on a 'power game basis' ... None of this is any cause for surprise ... The typical businessman is, after all, more often an administrator or manager than an entrepreneur.[17]

That caution is the watchword amongst industrial management is confirmed in the official view of the British Institute of Management. That body, though welcoming the Employment Act, said:

> Managers are not looking for wholesale changes in the law and in no way are they seeking to attack legitimate trade union rights ... While the need for change in the law is obvious, it is significant that in two recent samples of BIM members' opinions, managers asked only for limited changes in legislation ... [Managers] want a climate in which they can work *with* responsible trade unionists to attack and to overcome the problems which are holding us back.[18]

There is no reason to suppose that this statement contained any duplicity. In responding to the 'Draft Codes of Practice on Picketing and the Closed Shop' published by the Department of Employment in August 1980, the BIM objected to the wording of several clauses which it said were 'political and exhortatory' and 'unnecessarily provocative'.[19]

Even technocrats may dream. But down there on the shop and office floor it's hard-headed realism and a keen eye for the possible. In a recent article in *Management Today* a senior consultant for Urwick, Orr & Partners expresses what is assuredly the guiding philosophy of industrial relations management:

> ... where management has to do business with the unions, two fundamental problems of industrial relations are unlikely to change. First, it will continue to be what in essence it has always been – a power game. Conflicts of interest are inevitable ... Each side has the power to force the other to take account of its interests ...
>
> The recession will change none of this. If the balance of power has shifted in management's favour, it is because the economic climate has changed, not because management has suddenly become more competent or the unions have grown tired of being in permanent opposition. Pendulums swing both ways. When the economy picks up, the unions will come fighting back to recover what they see as ground lost at the last pay settlement – and how many managements, long starved of orders, will want to lose previous new business because of a strike?[20]

That the BIM and CBI have exerted both negative and positive pressure on the Tories is but a minor expression of a major political reality: the existence of a reciprocal client relationship between the Tories and industrial-commercial interests.

In one aspect the Tories are the clients of industry in the sense that anything a Tory government does with regard to industry must ultimately secure its acquiescence: otherwise its policies must be ineffective or inoperable. In another aspect industry assumed the client role. What industry wants must be conditioned by the government's own need to satisfy its activists and other constituencies (including the trade unions) which can make life difficult.

Within this matrix of forces, and on the particular question of the trade unions, the cautious route was taken as compared with the Industrial Relations Act of 1972 until the autumn of 1981. The government, it appeared, had given the local activists enough to prevent too much pressure for harsher remedies, enough to industry to enhance its muscle and insufficient to provoke organised opposition from labour.

So far as industry was concerned the resultant balance,

though providing less than hoped for, was a reasonable start. The very last thing industry wanted in a recession was a full-scale frontal assault. Despite the fighting words of some company chairmen, when it comes to the point they are willing to be guided by the *realpolitik* of their industrial relations professionals: dogs are kept for barking.

The professionals, many of them with a trade union background, are more conscious than any other managerial or executive stratum of the delicacies of procedures, protocols and the power potential of certain workforce sections. They are jealous of their assiduously cultivated relationships with full-time officers and convenors and are usually the last people in the world to flirt with right-populism.

Others might think they know what *ought* to be so. Our professionals reckon to know what *can* be so — though their confidence has been eroded since Prior's departure. Growing numbers of company chairmen and managing directors, untutored and unlettered in the identification and interpretation of political trends, have convinced themselves that Thatcher has mass popular support, ignore the advice of their dogs and throw their weight behind Tebbit. Inside the Department of Employment the civil servants may well prefer the style and tone of the BIM and the Institute of Personnel Management and privately regard the Institute of Directors as madmen on parole. Their master, following Mao's precept, has put *politics* in command.

And the Next Round?

That the 1980 Employment Act diminished the potential effectiveness of collective action by labour is unquestionable. On the other hand it is not clear, as the TUC claimed at the time, that it was '... an attack on trade union rights that is certainly equal to that contained in the bitterly-fought Industrial Relations Act.'[21] A distinction has to be drawn between the political import of the attack and the legal measures.

The political import was unmistakeable in tendency, though hedged and fudged as a consequence of the divisions in the Tory ranks both inside and outside the party organisation. The most serious legal measures related to redefinitions of what was to be permissible in furtherance of a dispute. The attack was not upon straightforward withdrawals of labour or other in-plant actions, but upon such secondary actions as boycotts. In such cases employers were empowered to take legal action against individuals but not against trade unions.

The situation as Prior saw it on leaving office at the Department of Employment was that for the time being the 1980 Act was sufficient and that nothing further should be done until the law had been thoroughly tested. With some hesitancy, that also seemed to be the view of the CBI at its autumn conference in 1981. At that time, and indeed until early 1983, there were insufficient cases to test the law.

But then came the famous cabinet re-shuffle: forecasted to result in a One Nation revolt, it produced not a whimper. No doubt the arrival of the politically preposterous yet politically plausible SDP greatly dampened the ardour of the much-billed dissidents. Prior in particular, presumably acting on the maxim that 'he who fights and runs away, lives to fight another day', permanently destroyed his credibility.

The arrival of Tebbit has put a different complexion on things, though of course this has nothing to do with his eminently resistable personality. His Act is, and is intended to be, thoroughly obnoxious to the unions. It attacks the closed shop by specifying that it must be periodically re-balloted for and makes unions liable for damages in the event of support for certain secondary actions.

In terms of presentation for popular consumption the Act is extremely cunning. Designed to appeal to widely-held prejudice and ignorance, and clothed in libertarian rhetoric there can be little doubt of its popularity. It especially touches a chord with respect to the closed shop. It seems likely that, in the *abstract* many feel the compulsion to become a union member is tyrannical, even though in *practice* only derisory numbers are likely to feel that way.

The cunning of the Act with respect to the closed shop consists in this: it touches that nerve of 'philosophical anarchism' which runs so strongly in the British working class wherein all forms of compulsion are deeply resented; it comes at a particular point in history when just about every institution has lost its legitimacy. In the context of this political sentiment the Act can be presented as libertarian while its *intent* is authoritarian. The Act is nothing if not part of a wider attempt to roll back advances made by labour with a democratising *potential*, and to re-assert 'chiefs and indians' patterns of authority. From the point of view of the long-term interests of individual and collective capital this is quite logical, for it is indisputable that labour, albeit unwittingly, has shown itself capable of thwarting capital. All of this is well-understood by the more sophisticated of industry's 'commanders'. But, while they savour the long-term promise, they have been less certain about short term costs that might be incurred. In December 1981, the UK chairman of International Harvesters mounted a swingeing attack on what was then the Tebbit *Bill*. The gist of this was that given the recession, industry had quite enough on its hands without being plunged into industrial relations problems that new legislation might provoke.

Thoughtful industrialists feel themselves trapped. On the one hand they yearn for the command structures and disciplines of an army, and on the other there are the political realities of the shop-floor which can only be managed with consent and cooperation. At least in most of the larger companies the exigencies of practice have tended to take precedence over ideological reveries.

It is true that the prospect of a second term for Thatcher has stiffened some of the more timid spirits in the boardrooms. It is true also that the industrial relations professionals feel themselves on the defensive. Nevertheless, 'big capital' remains cautious. Naturally on specific issues concerning everyday operations positions of advantage are being ruthlessly pressed, but on the major question of trade union recognition caution is much in evidence. Indeed in many cases, far from taking the recession as an opportunity to be thoroughly unpleasant, the 'official' company line seems to be one of studied 'moderation' wherein management pleads for 'cooperation' in order to see a way out the crisis. Participation is the order of the day, both in the pages of *Management Today* and at the CBI. The CBI's 1981 pre-budget manifesto contained a list of 'Fifty Action Points': twenty-eight of them indicated the need for trade union co-operation.[22]

In the same month the British Institute of Management issued a press release which began: 'British management is actively encouraging employee participation. Nine out of ten companies who have so far responded to a survey by the BIM have set up or are setting up some form of participation scheme.'[23] This kind of practice is dear to the hearts of One Nation Tories and received the active support of James Prior. With Prior at the Department of Employment it seemed that the Tory strategy was to be one of conciliation toward labour once the 1980 Act was on the books. That One Nation attempt at diverting the right-populists by negotiating a new consensus slightly to the right of Heath-Callaghan has now been torpedoed.

As Andrew Gamble has pointed out, while the One Nation group are still lodged in the cabinet none of its members, with the exception of Patrick Jenkin at Industry, have any purchase on economic policy. Tebbit's promotion heralded a new legal onslaught on labour.[24] This second round appears to be tactical and strategic. Tactically, the government has needed to divert attention from its economic failures. Strategically the government has privately disavowed its absurd public propaganda about the 'new mood of cooperation on the shop-floor'. Evidently, and intelligently from its perspective, the right-populists have decided that labour is merely keeping its head down and could well put its boots back on again when unemployment stops rising. The new measures are therefore designed for future developments. It is exactly this which worries the Tory constituency in industry.

While the closed-shop bestows on industry what it would rather be without — trade unionism — it does have the everyday virtue of establishing orderly and predictable procedures. Periodic ballots for the closed shop have at least the potential for disruption. Ballots would not only generate electioneering which could disrupt production; they could also produce variable results as between different sections and over a period of time. All of these things, one way or another, would have the inevitable result of intensifying shop-floor union activity. No sensible manager is likely to view this with equanimity. Neither are managers likely to be enthusiastic about resorting to the courts to claim damages from the unions. As we have seen, the industrial relations professionals greatly prize their network of personal union contacts. These could hardly survive a legal contest.

Although all except maverick managements will tread very warily, the fact still remains that the new Act marks an extremely significant Tory departure. *Symbolically* it represents the right-populists' desire to exterminate effective trade unionism. Furthermore, even though most firms will be cautious, it does give them a new reserve weapon with which to *threaten* labour. If the Labour Party is decisively defeated at the next election then threats might be realised.

So what, briefly, of the likely trade union response? The TUC has already said that it will fight this Bill as it fought the 1972 Act. This is most unlikely and Tebbit, we can be sure, has come to a similar conclusion. The people on the TUC's General Council are as demoralised as shop-floor activists. Funds are seriously depleted and many a well-organised local union base has been closed. Union treasurers and others responsible for keeping the books are in the ascendant and these are conservative voices. For them solvency takes priority over politics and this is the crux of the problem.

The unions are faced with a political attack while their organisations at all levels are geared up to economism. The unions, as usual, are deeply reluctant to take politics to the shop-floor. But if they do not do so they will be driven from one defensive position to another, and each will be less tenable than the last. As never so intensively before, the Tories are fighting an ideological battle and on *that* terrain they have secured much high ground. Before the unions can start a programme of recovery they will have to regain legitimacy in their own constituency. There are precious few in the ranks who show any sign of possessing the necessary political imagination to accomplish that task.

Notes

My analysis of the Tory Party has drawn extensively on Andrew Gamble's *The Conservative Nation*, 1974 and Michael Moran's, 'The Conservative Party and the Trade Unions Since 1974', *Political Studies*, Vol. XXVII No. 1, 1979.

[1] Quoted in T. Lane, *The Union Makes Us Strong*, 1974, p. 226.
[2] B. Tuchman, *The Proud Tower*, 1967, p. 58.
[3] F.A. Hayek, *A Tiger by the Tail*, 1978, p. 67.
[4] ibid., p. 68.
[5] ibid., p. 69.
[6] ibid., p. 70.
[7] ibid., p. 75.

[8] *Royal Commission on Trade Unions and Employers Associations*, Cmnd. 3623, 1968, p. 101.

[9] C.T.B. Smith et al, *Strikes in Britain*, Department of Employment Manpower Paper No. 15, 1978, Table 31.

[10] *The Times 1000*, 1978-79.

[11] A. Gamble, op. cit., pp. 151-2.

[12] R. Taylor, 'Why Workers Weaken Output', *Management Today*, November 1980, p. 96.

[13] See pages 39, 46, 52-3, 59, 126, 204, 258-9, 260.

[14] Michael Frayn, 'A Perfect Strike' in R. Blackburn and A. Cockburn, eds., *The Incompatibles: Trade Union Militancy and the Consensus*, 1967, p. 160.

[15] On page 69 of *A Tiger by the Tail* a footnote produces a string of supporting references, many of which come from such stables as the Washington Chamber of Commerce, The American Enterprise Association and an employers' front organisation, the Foundation for Economic Education.

[16] It is instructive that combinations of employers only achieve the status of an aside.

[17] S. Brittan, *Participation without Politics*, 1975, p. 115.

[18] *Management Today*, March 1980, p. 133.

[19] BIM Press Release, undated, 1980.

[20] Paul Johns, 'How to Relate Industrially', *Management Today*, January 1981, p. 68.

[21] *The TUC Case Against the Employment Bill*, 1980, p. 3.

[22] See *The Financial Times*, 6 March 1981.

[23] BIM Press Release, 4 March 1981.

[24] See Andrew Gamble, 'Mrs Thatcher's Bunker', *Marxism Today*, November 1981.

Jean Gardiner

Women, Recession and the Tories

Mass unemployment and the right-wing policies of the Thatcher government are having major effects on the relationship between men and women at work, in the house and in the labour movement. Much of the progress made by women in recent years is now threatened. The opportunity this poses for the left to set about winning the political support of masses of women in this country has, in large part, been missed. Instead many women on the left have felt pressure being brought to bear on them to drop their feminist demands in face of the common threat posed by Thatcherism. A united opposition to the Tories cannot be built by ignoring the very different ways in which men and women have experienced recession and Tory rule. Still less can such an approach result in broadening the base of support for the left and the Labour Party amongst women. The emergence of the SDP-Liberal Alliance must make this doubly apparent.

There were a number of important changes in women's lives in the twenty years after the second world war, including the expansion of job opportunities for women. These changes gave rise to growing aspirations amongst women and increasing awareness of the limits of advances that had been made. This new consciousness was voiced most clearly by the Women's Liberation Movement but has also been reflected throughout labour movement and women's organisations in the 1970s. Its impact was felt in a number of social reforms. Yet within the last few years the progress made by women has appeared increasingly limited and vulnerable. Steadily rising unemployment culminating in the present deep recession poses a special threat both to women's jobs and to women's expectations more generally. This threat has been reinforced by the economic and political philosophy of the Thatcher government and the attacks on women that this has produced. In many respects women are in a stronger position to resist these attacks than was the case in the comparable period of the 1930s. However weaknesses in the women's movement, in the relationship between the women's movement and the labour movement and in the left's alternative strategy all work against the development of an effective resistance.

The Forward March of Women?

The economic and welfare reforms implemented in Britain in the period after the second world war had contradictory effects for women. Women were to benefit from the increase in job opportunities associated with a commitment to full employment, from the expansion of education, and from the collective provision of a fange of welfare services. Yet none of these changes challenged the traditional assumption that the majority of women would continue to be primarily housewives and mothers dependent on marriage rather than employment. The commitment to full employment did not entail ensuring that all women with children who desired to work had the opportunity to do so. The expansion in welfare services did not include nursery provision. Vocational training and promotion ladders remained geared to male working lives. Sex stereotyping continued to be reinforced by the education system. Sexual inequality was built into tax and social security legislation. Growing numbers of women, particularly married women, were drawn into a narrow range of relatively low paid jobs, consistent with traditional notions of women's work. Women were expected to retain responsibility for the care of home and family in line with their continued economic dependence on marriage and a male breadwinner.

By the end of the 1960s the aspirations which welfare capitalism had awakened and failed to satisfy were being voiced as demands for equal pay and equal opportunities at work. Many further demands followed in the 1970s, with the development of the Women's Liberation Movement, which emphasised the ways in which the existing welfare state reinforced the traditional sexual division of labour and women's oppression. Their criticisms of existing state services often led feminists to opt for the establishment of self help alternative services outside the framework of existing welfare provision, e.g. community nurseries, women's aid refuges and pregnancy-testing services. Whilst those self-help groups which survived were generally forced to negotiate a relationship with the state in order to gain access to financial resources their development highlights the ways in which feminism in the 1970s rejected an uncritical support for state provision *per se*. Since women are disproportionately the recipients (and providers) of welfare services given their traditional role in caring for the young, the sick and the elderly, the criticisms voiced by the Women's Liberation Movement can be seen as an important part of the groundswell of popular dissatisfaction with state services which the Tory government has sought to exploit in its attacks on the public sector.[1]

Pressure from the Women's Liberation Movement and other women's and labour movement organisations resulted in progressive social legislation in the seventies concerned with sexual inequality (the Equal Pay Act 1970, the Sex Discrimination Act 1975, the Employment Protection Act 1975, amended in 1978, and the Social Security Pensions Act 1975). However there were serious limits in the changes required by this legislation. Moreover even the limited scope for action to improve women's opportunities at work which the new laws provided was quickly undermined by the deteriorating economic climate and rising unemployment.

The Impact of the Recession

Since 1974 in the capitalist world there has been lower economic growth and higher unemployment than at any time since the second world war. The recession of 1974-5 was followed by a brief boom in 1976-8. Since 1979 a new and deeper phase of recession has been entered. Britain has suffered more than most industrial capitalist countries from the effects of the recession because of its relative industrial weakness and decline. Moreover since 1978 the British government has been particularly committed to sharply deflationary policies. For both reasons unemployment has risen more quickly and to higher levels in Britain than in most other industrialised capitalist economies.

There are a number of ways in which a recession such as the present one undermines the limited progress women have made.

Because women are a particularly vulnerable group within the labour market their jobs are more readily threatened and their unemployment less visible than men's. High levels of unemployment greatly reduce training and job opportunities that make it possible for women to enter traditionally male-dominated fields. Moreover the divisive attitudes that unemployment gives rise to can undermine the past progress women have made. In addition the relative pay of women tends to deteriorate in a recession. Finally, cuts in public services associated with the recession both reduce employment opportunities for women and increase the burden on women in the home.

Women, particularly married women and part-time workers, can be used as a more flexible reserve army of labour than men, being drawn in and out of employment in accordance with the demand for labour. Women move in and out of the labour force more than men because of the birth of children or the need to care for children, sick or elderly relatives. Female employment can therefore often be reduced rapidly by means of natural wastage and without the need to make redundancies. Part-time workers (2/5 of all women employed) are particularly vulnerable because they lack many of the minimum legal rights of full-time workers and have lower levels of unionisation.[2] Firms in many industries have used part-time employment as a temporary and cheap means of meeting demand. For example firms have rarely found difficulty in recruiting or laying off workers for the twilight evening shift, popular with married women who have children.

Men and women are of course mainly concentrated in different jobs and this occupational segregation has not diminished as a result of the growth in the female labour force in the last thirty years.[3] The increase in employment opportunities for women that took place was the result of a growth in demand for labour in typically female occupations, especially in the expanding service sector. The relative vulnerability of women and men therefore also depends on the extent to which different jobs are at risk in the recession. Because women tend to be concentrated in relatively unskilled jobs they are again more vulnerable than men. Offsetting this to some extent is the concentration of women's jobs in service industries, e.g. finance, distribution and catering, which in the past have tended not to be so adversely affected by recession as the production industries in which men's jobs are concentrated.[4]

However the introduction of new technology has begun to have a major impact on women's jobs in the service sector. This has led to job losses in many service industries which in the preceding period experienced steady growth, e.g., banking, insurance and finance. Clerical jobs in particular will be adversely affected by the introduction of the new microelectronic technology. It has been estimated that by 1990 17% of the secretarial workforce will be displaced by the new technology.[5]

It is difficult to assess the overall impact of these different tendencies. However, the employment statistics covering 1981 indicate that men's jobs have continued to disappear more rapidly than women's in the economy as a whole. This is mainly due to women's employment being largely concentrated in service industries. Between 1978 and 1981 male employment in Great Britain fell by about 7%, whilst female employment declined by 2%.[6] Part-time female employment actually increased by about 2%. The loss of women's jobs was therefore concentrated amongst full-time workers.

Within manufacturing industries the picture is rather different because women's jobs disappeared at a faster rate than men's. Moreover, part-time women's employment in manufacturing shows a greater reduction (23%) than full-time women's employment (18%). Nevertheless, in all service industries except for public administration and defence, there was a small increase in female employment and most of the increase involved part-time jobs; on the other hand there was a slight loss of men's jobs in the service sector.

Thus, despite the greater vulnerability of women in the labour force, typically male jobs appear to have disappeared more rapidly than typically female jobs, at least until the beginning of the 1980s. However, the continuing trend for part-time employment to increase relative to full-time employment for women confirms a pattern of deteriorating pay and conditions for women in the work force. It is likely that in some circumstances new jobs are created at the expense of some women workers elsewhere whose jobs are disappearing, e.g., staff agencies which substitute casual and unorganised workers for permanent staff.

Female unemployment is less visible than male unemployment. Unemployed women are less likely to register than men because lower national insurance contributions or the need to find part-time employment disqualify them from receiving benefit. In addition, when unemployment is high and job opportunities scarce, many women are discouraged from seeking work and therefore do not even consider themselves as unemployed.

Less Visible

It is, therefore, difficult to estimate the overall impact of unemployment on women. The number of women registering as unemployed has been increasing since the mid-1970s faster than the number of men registered as unemployed. The rise in registered unemployment amongst married women has been particularly rapid. The gap between the official unemployment rates for women and men has therefore been narrowing. In February 1982 the rates were 15% for men and 9% for women.

However, if unregistered unemployment is taken into account, the gap is reduced. About 28% of all unemployed women and 43% of all unemployed married women do not register, as compared with 11% of unemployed men.[7] The actual unemployment rates are therefore about 18% for men and 12% for women.

Finally, we should add to the unemployed those who give up seeking work and drop out of the labour force altogether when jobs are scarce; there are twice as many women as men in this category, most of whom are married.[8] After a steady rise in the labour force participation rates of women for some thirty years there has been an abrupt reversal recently. About half a million women dropped out of the labour force between 1977 and 1980, discouraged by the lack of job opportunities.[9]

A recession affects not only the total number of jobs but the availability of training opportunities and access of women to traditionally male occupations. As firms cut back on training and men's jobs are threatened there are fewer and fewer opportunities for women to acquire new skills. Divisive attitudes, as illustrated by the following example, are on the the increase:

I believe a vociferous and militant minority is fostering the

discontent among women about equal pay and jobs. A woman
wants her man to be in work, not unemployed. Jobs should be first
and foremost for him not her. A woman can and should get
fulfillment from having and bringing up children.[10]

The restriction in women's access to skilled employment
together with the trend for casual and unorganised female labour
to be substituted for stable and better paid women workers both
necessarily have adverse effects on women's relative pay. In
addition, the weakening in the overall bargaining position of
labour has tended to make men within the unions fight more
fiercely for male interests and the preservation of differentials.
For the most part unions have acquiesced in this backlash in the
absence of any effective campaign against it by the left.[11] It is
therefore not surprising that limited progress they made in
narrowing the differential between men's and women's pay after
the introduction of the Equal Pay Act has been halted and even
reversed since 1977. Women's average hourly earnings rose
from 63.1% of men's in 1970 to 75.5% in 1977. Since then there
has been a slight decline to 73.9% in 1982. Any widening of the
still considerable gap in pay between men and women creates
further pressure on women to accept that their jobs are
secondary.

Since 1976 rising unemployment in Britain has been
associated with cuts in public expenditure and services. These
have meant not only reduced employment opportunities, mostly
for women, in the public sector but also additional burdens on
women in the home. And the more responsibility women have
for caring for children, the sick and the elderly, the more difficult
it is for women to seek paid work.

Thatcherism and Women

All the adverse effects of the recession on women discussed
above have been intensified in two ways by the Thatcher
Government. The sharp rise since 1980 in the rate at which jobs
have been disappearing is largely the result of the intensely
deflationary monetarist policies the government has pursued.
Moreover the Thatcher philosophy attempts to provide an
ideological legitimation for both the attacks on women that
result from the recession and for policies that take those attacks
even further.

It has already been pointed out that a recession encourages the development of a right-wing anti-feminist revival. The idea that women should accept their place in society is to be at home caring for their family appears to make sense to more and more people when jobs are scarce. It is therefore not surprising that these ideas were regaining some popularity in the late 1970s and beginning to be expressed all the more vociferously in response to the impact feminism appeared to be having on society. At that time the major campaign to attract the support of those opposed to the advances women had won was the anti-abortion campaign. Many of the anti-abortion lobby would not, of course, be opposed to other aspects of women's rights. However the more generalised anti-feminist stance of many of its constituents is a clear and important aspect of the shift to the right in British politics that the Thatcher government reflects.

An example of the way in which this government is acting to reinforce already existing trends in the recession is the pilot scheme introduced in 1982 to limit further the numbers of people entitled to unemployment benefit. Forms issued to claimants include more detailed questions than before, such as 'Would you take any full-time job which you can do? Do you have any children or anyone else who needs your care during working hours? Will you do night-work/shift work?' The question on child care is particularly insidious for women. Parents may even be asked to supply evidence from a 'responsible' person that their children will be cared for.

However, when it comes to the place of women in their philosophy, the path the Tories have to tread is a delicate one, not necessarily helped by blatant anti-feminist outbursts like the notorious Patrick Jenkin quote: 'If the Good Lord had intended us to have equal rights to go out to work, he wouldn't have created man and woman.'[12]

Tory Ambiguities

It is important to remember that appealing to women in the electorate continues to be a part of the Tory political appeal which must therefore recognise those changes in women's lives and aspirations which are irreversible as a result of experiences in the last thirty years. Moreover the Tories' position on women is not explicit or united as their approach to some other issues, e.g.

trade unions. Some Tories have campaigned actively for sex equality in some areas. A commitment to women's equal rights can coexist with moral beliefs about the family which give rise to policies that go against women's interests. The Tory government is neither explicit about its attacks on women nor even probably aware that its policies have this effect.

For example, Geoffrey Howe's proposals to introduce greater financial equality and independence for married women by changes in the tax law undoubtedly owe something both to his wife's former connections with the Equal Opportunities Commission and to strong lobbying on the part of the Conservative Women's Advisory Committee. The explicit aim of these proposals is 'to enable women to be treated as independently as they wish to be treated, but at the same time to encourage and support the family'.[13] While appearing to remove overt discrimination between the sexes these proposals could encourage married women, with or without children, to stay out of the labour market.[14] One proposal involves abolishing the married man's allowance and giving men and women a higher single person's allowance with the possibility of transferring the tax allowance if one partner is not in paid work. Thus two breadwinner families would no longer receive a higher tax allowance than single breadwinner families. It would be theoretically possible under such a scheme, as it is already within existing tax law, for a wife to be the breadwinner and a husband to stay at home. However role reversal of this kind is unlikely given the differences in pay and access to jobs between the sexes. Moreover such a scheme would intensify family poverty and favour the relatively affluent. High income husbands with dependent wives would benefit. Low income two breadwinner families with children would be worse off.

Thus the Tory government can appear to be making a stand on sex equality by advocating policies which are likely to have adverse effects on the majority of women. This has added to the general shock and confusion feminists and the left in general have experienced as our opposition to the status quo has been eclipsed by the radical right, personified by the country's first woman prime minister.

Tories and the Family

The role of the family and traditional values have been given much more emphasis in Tory philosophy and policies than equal rights. The philosophy stresses the need to return responsibilities and choice to the family, both of which it claims have been eroded by the growth of the welfare state.

It is a philosophy that seeks to legitimise savage attacks on the social services and welfare benefits upon which women and children particularly depend. The Tories have allowed the value of those payments to the family which directly benefit women and children i.e. child benefits, to be eroded. Policies which claim to favour the family as a unit gloss over the structural inequality within it. For example the Tory objective of switching from direct taxation to indirect taxation works against women and children in families where income is not equally shared. This objective has not been achieved in practice however since the deflationary policies pursued by the government have entailed rises in direct as well as indirect taxes.

The cuts in public services which had begun as a regrettable expedient under the previous Labour administration have been pursued with vigour and ideological commitment by the Thatcher Government. As well as withholding cash from the public sector the government has carried through legislation reducing local authority obligations.

What was previously a very weak statutory requirement on the part of local authorities to provide nursery education has now been removed altogether by the 1980 Education Act. In a context of massive cuts in local government expenditure this will ensure a further deterioration in the existing totally inadequate provision. The Government's own White Paper forecasts a drop in the proportion of under-fives receiving nursery education from 40% in 1980-81 to 33% in 1984-85. The attack on the school meals service involves another reduction of mostly female paid labour at the expense of female unpaid labour in the home. Where the school meals service has been retained there has also been a trend towards replacing local authority staff with private contractors employing women on inferior wages and conditions. One local authority, Dorset, has even been considering introducing Continental-style shorter opening hours for schools.

Such cuts in services for children have the direct effect in most cases of tying women further to the home, and of further reducing their opportunity and availability for paid work except for very short hours and very low pay. All these pressures have been reinforced by the policy of restricting maternity rights which was incorporated in the 1980 Employment Act.

Are We Going Back to the 1930s?

Whilst mass unemployment and the beginnings of a reaction against women's right to work revive memories of the 1930s there are many ways in which British capitalism in general and the position of women in particular have changed over the last 50 years.

The British economy is now a lot weaker relative to the rest of the capitalist world than it was in the 1930s. The effects of the recession are therefore felt more sharply in Britain than in many of the other capitalist industrial countries. British industry in the 1930s was more shielded than it is today by imperial markets and protection of industries supplying the home market. Pressures to restructure the economy and the workforce are therefore more intense today.

The economy now depends on female employment, and particularly the employment of married women and mothers to a much greater extent than was the case fifty years ago. Also because of the continuing occupational segregation of men and women, and the fact that women are concentrated in the lowest paid, least skilled jobs which it would be difficult to persuade most men to accept, an increase in the ratio of women to men in employment is difficult to reverse unless the predominantly female jobs are the ones that are disappearing.

The underlying changes

It is also important to take account of the social and political changes which will influence future outcomes for women. There have been a number of major social developments affecting women which are very unlikely to be reversed.

Whilst attempts have been made to whittle away advances in women's control of their fertility and further advances, e.g., in safe contraception or early abortion may seem unlikely at present, a complete reversal to the position of fifty years ago cannot be imagined. The Women's Liberation Movement has rightly stressed how central control of fertility is in shaping women's opportunities in all other fields.

Secondly, while educational opportunities remain unequal between the sexes, in many respects the overall growth in education that has taken place since the Second World War has encouraged new aspirations amongst women in all areas of their lives.

Thirdly, demographic changes and the growth of female employment have made women's financial contributions to family support increasingly important. Within the labour force nearly as many women as men have children to support. About 40% of male workers and 38% of women workers now have dependent children. Only 18% of men in the labour force now provide sole financial support for a wife and dependent child or children.[15] Fewer than one in five male workers therefore now conform to the traditional stereotype of the family breadwinner. The number of two-parent families living in poverty would quadruple without the contribution of a mother's wages. Thus female employment increasingly leads to families dropping below the poverty line.

Moreover liberalisation of divorce laws has reinforced a growing tendency towards marital breakdown. Increasing numbers of women have opted to end marriages which fail to satisfy new aspirations. One in three marriages can now be expected to break down. This has led to an enormous increase in the number of single parent families, mostly headed by a woman. In 1979 12% of all dependent children were in single parent families. Most single parent families have been forced to live in poverty as supplementary benefit claimants. However, because of the cost this imposes on the state there has been growing pressure on non-married mothers to get paid employment, both in the form of concessions to single parents who work (e.g., the reduction in the minimum hours a single parent must work to 24 in order to claim family income supplement) and in the form of the campaign against 'scroungers'.

Because growing numbers of women in the labour force provide vital financial support for children the traditional justification for regarding women's jobs as of secondary importance becomes increasingly difficult to maintain. Moreover, married women are increasingly concerned about the need to establish their own financial independence. The ideology that women's place is in the home depends on the assumption that marriage lasts for ever and provides an accurate permanent financial support for them and their children.

A fourth major social change is the growth in women's dependence on and expectation of state supported social provision in fields such as health, social services and education. Whilst much has been done, especially by the present government, to create a crisis frame of mind in which people are persuaded that the country cannot afford to maintain social provision at its previous levels many people are increasingly aware that alternative familial and community systems of support generally do not exist and cannot be created without further state expenditure.

Political Contrasts

Finally there are two important political changes if we compare the position of women today with the 1930s. First there is the nature and breadth of the women's movement. The earlier women's movement of the first quarter of the 20th century concentrated its energies on the vote, equal rights and welfare reforms, most of which had been conceded to some extent by the late 1920s. By the 1930s feminism had been quiscent for a number of years. By contrast the feminist movement of the 1970s always emphasised the limited nature of single issue campaigns and legal reforms by comparison with the deep structural and ideological causes of women's oppression. For that reason it has tended to gain strength rather than lose momentum as a result of legal reforms. The Women's Liberation Movement which has inspired most of the diverse sections of the women's movement today still has sufficient dynamism and flexibility to adjust to the changing context within which it finds itself, despite differences that have divided it and its lack of any overall national organisational structure. New groups of women continue to be attracted to feminist ideas as the contradictions women experience become more acute.[16]

The second important political change is the position of women within the trade union movement and the basis this provides for a new and stronger link between the women's movement and the labour movement. Not only has there been a large increase in the female membership of unions but also growing pressure from women members has forced more and more unions to give attention to involving women more actively, and to issues of particular concern to women. Whilst unions still have a long way to go in eradicating both sexist attitudes and male oriented policies and practices, enormous changes have taken place, as clearly demonstrated in the 1979 TUC-supported march against the Corrie Abortion Amendment Bill. The fact that this Bill was later defeated demonstrates the power that the trade union movement in alliance with the women's movement can bring to bear.

Grounds therefore exist for optimism that women are in a much stronger position in the 1980s to resist attacks than was the case in the 1930s. Many of the changes in women's aspirations, including their expectation of greater financial independence, are unlikely to be reversed. However in analysing the position of women it is also important to stress how much has not changed and how vulnerable this makes young women, especially those who have never experienced financial independence or trade union membership. We can expect increasing numbers of young women who remain unemployed after leaving school to marry and have children without any experience of paid employment. This may well lower their expectations both of marriage and of work.

Developing the Resistance

Whilst a complete reversal in women's position may be unlikely the conditions for developing an effective resistance to present attacks do not yet exist. Within the Women's Liberation Movement and on the left there is a real need for an honest appraisal of the weaknesses that hold us back as well as the strengths that can take us forward.

The Women's Liberation Movement has had a very great impact on society, not just through the social reforms it has helped fight for and defend, and the thousands of women who have been directly involved and influenced by it, but also through its influence on the attitudes and consciousness of many more people who would not directly identify with it. People have been forced to think about relationships between men and women to a much greater extent than before and there are now reminders in the language for those who might otherwise forget (sexism, chairperson, etc.).

However, there are also problems which feminists will have to tackle if women's liberation is to be kept alive as a movement and an ideology over the coming years.

From the earliest days of the Women's Liberation Movement there has been a tension between fighting for women's own interests on the one hand, and asserting the needs of mothers and children on the other. Many of the women who started the first feminist women's groups in the early 1970s were in fact mothers. Throughout the history of the Women's Liberation Movement feminists have played a key role in fighting to improve the quality of nursery provision for children, and to place children on the left's political agenda.[17] Feminists have also emphasised the links between women's and children's oppression. If women are unwilling mothers or feel frustrated by the way in which their lives are totally circumscribed by motherhood, children are bound to suffer. The campaign for legal and finaeial independence for women has also stressed the material impoverishment that can arise for families from women's dependence on men.

However, feminists have stressed that the interests of women and children are separate and that women need to be aware of their own interests and be able to assert them. They have fought for a woman's right to choose whether or not to have children and for the right of mothers to decide how their children should be cared for. In this process of asserting women's needs feminists have sometimes failed to project a concern for children and an awareness of the positive role that children play in women's lives, and this failure has led many women to be wary of feminism. It has been exploited by those opposed to feminism, many of whom have demonstrated less concern for children in their own practice than those committed to women's liberation. In the face of a government which claims to support the family whilst implementing policies which go directly against the interest of women and children, feminism will only survive if it is seen to be defending the interests of children as well as women. In this way Tory rhetoric about the family will be exposed and a mass movement of women against government policies can be developed.

Mass Action

A movement's ability to develop forms of mass action is crucial not only because of the power such action can have but also because of the confidence it can generate in the movement itself. Without it demoralisation can easily take over, particularly when the government of the day is set on a course of action in total opposition to the aims of the movement. There must be ways of showing that there is widespread support. One of the problems of the Women's Liberation Movement is that often the knowledge of its influence has been confined to the women directly involved within it. The fact that they have taken many of its ideas and methods into other organisations like trade unions and campaigning groups has not always been apparent.

Where mass action in support of one of the demands of the women's movement, the defence of abortion rights, has been organised it has been successful in both achieving its aims and demonstrating a very wide basis of support in and outside of the labour movement. What is needed now are other initiatives like the Women's Right to Work Festival that can mobilise large numbers of women as well as the labour movement in opposition to the attacks being mounted. Small-scale localised action is no longer sufficient.

The support of the labour movement will only be mobilised if there is an active campaign to oppose divisive and anti-feminist attitudes within it. This will only happen if the Communist Party and more men on the left resist the trend towards seeing feminist demands as expendable in the current difficult period.

A Democratic Alternative

Resisting current attacks, however difficult a task, is not enough on its own and probably will not succeed unless alternative policies that relate to the present and an alternative philosophy that makes sense to masses of women and men can be offered. Whilst the left's alternative economic strategy, as a set of economic policies, is an important advance, the fact that it has nothing directly to say to women is a major weakness. There is as yet no recognition that major structural changes will be necessary for social and economic progress to mean something genuine for women.

The alternative strategy will have to tackle the whole relationship between men's and women's work and between work and home. It is not enough to say that the economy will be reflated and more employment created. Steps must also be taken to equalise employment opportunities for men and women. This will depend ultimately on reducing hours of work to make it possible for the present division between part-time and full-time employment to be gradually eliminated. In the shorter term moves in this direction could be made by reducing the hours that parents (fathers as well as mothers) are required to work as well as introducing parental rights to paid leave for family sickness. Positive discrimination will also be needed to break down the occupational segregation of men and women.

In committing itself to an elimination of some of the gross inequalities in Britain today the left as yet has nothing to say on the inequalities that exist between men and women. Inequality is structured into not only the wage payment system but also into taxation and social security. It is no use responding to these issues by merely pointing out how far removed the left alternative must be from a society in which the Communist principle of 'from each according to his/her ability, to each according to his/her need' can operate. If genuine egalitarianism is our long term aim there must be steps, however small, in the short term that can be taken towards it. If none can be found then doubt will necessarily be cast upon the left's long term aims.

New Priorities

Given the pace at which British industry has been declining any left government that came to power in the future would be likely to inherit an extremely weak industrial base lacking the capacity to expand quickly to provide goods for private consumption. Any reflation that takes place would depend initially to a large extent on expanding public services and the social wage whilst increases in take-home pay would be limited. This would provide the opportunity for expanding many services that would be of particular benefit to women, e.g. nurseries and other forms of child care. It is therefore crucial that the left's plans take account of criticisms of existing services that have been made by feminists, and by workers in the public sector. Alternative plans must be more than a commitment to restore cuts. They must highlight what changes in priorities are required and indicate how services can be democratised.

There are many other issues that a democratic alternative strategy would need to tackle in order to satisfy women's aspirations, many of them concerned with attitudes and values rather than economic changes. The alternative strategy will have to be more than a set of economic policies. It will also need to embody a political philosophy concerned with transforming relationships between men and women at work, in the home and in all democratic organisations. Such a strategy will only emerge if the women's movement is actively involved in its development.

This will only happen if the left can overcome its tendency to see the women's movement as a luxury in the present crisis period. Without the support of the women's movement it will go on failing to reach the mass of women. To get that support will require positive steps to involve women more effectively in decision making and the development of strategy. Equally, without the support on the left and the labour movement, and willingness to examine its own weaknesses, the women's movement will also find itself increasingly isolated and ineffective. If an alliance of this kind can be developed it will represent a powerful political force capable not just of resisting Thatcherism but also of showing masses of women and men that the left has the only credible democratic alternative strategy to put in its place.

Notes

[1] See articles by Peter Leonard and Paul Corrigan in *Marxism Today*, December 1979.

[2] Jennifer Hurstfield, 'Part-Time Pittance' in *Low Pay Review*, No. 1, June 1980.

[3] Catherine Hakim, 'Occupational Segregation', *Department of Employment Research Paper*, No. 9, November 1979.

[4] Peter Elias, 'Labour Supply and Employment Opportunities for Women', in *Economic Change and Employment Policy*, Robert M. Lindley (ed.), 1980.

[5] 'Communication Studies and Planning Ltd, Information technology in

the office: the impact on women's jobs', Equal Opportunities Commission, 1980.

[6] 1981 Census of Employment, *Employment Gazette*, December 1982.

[7] *General Household Survey*, 1980.

[8] Marie McNay and Chris Pond, 'Low Pay and Family Poverty', *Study Commission on the Family*, 1980.

[9] *Cambridge Economic Policy Review*, April 1981, p. 41.

[10] Susan Power, 'Opinion Column', *Sunday Times*, 28 December 1980.

[11] Beatrix Campbell, 'Women: Not What They Bargained For', in *Marxism Today*, March 1982.

[12] *Guardian*, 6 November 1979.

[13] Conservative Women's Advisory Committee Discussion Document, *Women and Tax*, 1979.

[14] Fran Bennett, Rosa Heys and Rosalind Coward, 'The Limits to "Financial and Legal Independence": A Socialist Feminist Perspective on Taxation and Social Security', in *Politics and Power*, No. 1, 1980.

[15] Figures are derived from the *General Household Survey*, 1978, and *Social Trends*, 1981.

[16] Figures are derived from the *General Household Survey*, 1978, and *Social Trends*, 1981.

[16] Beatrix Campbell and Anna Coote, *Sweet Freedom*, 1982.

[17] See, for example, Anna Coote, 'The AES: A New Starting Point', in *New Socialist*, November/December 1981.

Lynne Segal

The Heat in the Kitchen

Women's lives are always changing, but the changes over the last two decades have been particularly significant for women. Most women for most of their lives are no longer full-time housewives: many women never were. But the long hours and inflexible conditions of paid work, as well as the nature of welfare provision and state benefits, still fail to register this fact. The now largely magical belief in the existence of a Cinderella always at the ready at the hearth lives on, though in most households she will not be there for much of the time. But if Cinderella has abandoned her post, surely it is an explicit goal of Thatcherism to return her to it? As the left portrays Thatcherism, we see it stealing from the housewife's shopping bag, as it chains her ever more securely to the kitchen sink. Are not women losing jobs faster than men, and forced by brutal cuts in welfare provision to stay in or return to the home? It is not quite so simple as this.

Certainly many women's lives, both at home and in paid work, are becoming more difficult and demanding today. And the tensions between women's two roles in the home and the workforce can only worsen, as the increasing demands on the servicing work still done largely by women in the home are ignored or exploited by the conditions of women's paid employment. But many women cannot abandon their jobs, even if they wanted to. All of which, as most socialist feminists are asserting ever more forcefully, is likely to place women, as a group, in the forefront of resistance to Thatcherism. But the left and the labour movement remain only vaguely aware of the significance of the problems women face, and still resist feminist strategies for transforming the nature of political struggle.

As Stuart Hall warned us,[1] Thatcherism has succeeded in building an authoritarian populism of the right, drawing upon every mean-minded, nationalistic and anti-collective sentiment —

the sentiments of the frightened bully under attack. Thatcherism, has one clear goal in relation to the working class: to destroy workers' militancy and undermine support for the trade unions. And just as unemployment *has* undermined workers' militancy, so, too, incessant union-bashing from the Tories *has* strengthened public suspicion of the trade unions. But what, exactly, are Thatcher's goals and the effects of her policies, in relation to women as a group? I think they are more contradictory, and that within these contradictions a strong resistance is possible.

According to its rhetoric, the effects of Thatcherism on women should not be contradictory. It aims to protect and improve 'the stability and quality of family life', and to stress the centrality of women's place in the home. As central as nationalism and union-baiting to the rhetoric of Thatcherism is its appeal to the importance of the family. 'Bringing up a family is the most important thing of all', Margaret Thatcher assures all women. She sees herself as appealing to women when she asserts that the family unit must remain 'secure and respected'. Just as she sees family values as essentially women's values. 'Women know that society is founded on dignity, reticence and discipline.'[2] It is women's job to be doing that most important work of caring in the home, 'because women bear the children and create and run the home.'[3]

And yet, it is obviously easy to show that the Tory promise 'to be vigilant' in improving family life, is accompanied by policies which continuously erode any such possibility. Thatcher has pursued policies which make the work of caring for dependents more difficult — if not impossible.

The Tories illustrate their concern for the family by pointing to two things. They have enabled certain families to buy their council flats, thus becoming house owners; and they have assisted tiny numbers of parents to send their children to private schools. That, *in reality*, is all that they can claim to have done. Meanwhile public housing stock has fallen drastically as housing has been the very hardest hit of all public spending cuts. And there has been a serious deterioration in state schools — in buildings, textbooks and other basic supplies, while parents must pay double for school meals and meet other educational costs.

Family rhetoric in Conservative thought is *not* about improving how we are all loved and cared for. Quite the opposite, because it is essentially an appeal to individualism. It is about confirming that we must look after *ourselves* and be self sufficient. We are told we must look after what we can claim as *our own* — our wives, children and other 'possessions'. Because if we don't, nobody else will. As Barrett and McIntosh point out in their book,[4] pro-family rhetoric promotes exclusion and selfishness, in what is presented as inevitably a mean and nasty world. And yet that world would seem less inevitably mean and nasty if a greater public and *collective* responsibility were assumed for meeting people's personal needs, rather than confining them to what is seen as the private world of the family. Were it not generally accepted that 'the family', and the family alone, is the only proper place for loving, caring and sharing, the barbarism of the Tory attack on welfare would surely seem unthinkable.

It is only because of the persisting belief in a 'natural' division of labour rooted in our idea of 'family life', that family rhetoric can lend itself so readily to a Tory rationalisation of cuts. Tory ministers like Patrick Jenkin tell us that the family must be the front line of defence when Gran needs help. They mean of course that female relatives must take full responsibility for caring for the elderly at home. They thereby conveniently ignore both that female relatives frequently have jobs, and that a third of the elderly today have no living relatives, and that when they do they will often live far away from Gran. A little family rhetoric is a dangerous thing. And digging deeper into the realities of family life would uncover just how much the set of ideologies which form our notion of the family serve always to obscure the multitude of inadequate ways in which most people's needs are met, as well as obscure what actually goes on in households. Only one in ten of households conform to the family ideal of male breadwinner, full-time housewife and dependent children. Yet in nearly all households women shoulder grossly unfair burdens of domestic work, and countless frustrations as they attempt largely unaided to fulfil what is seen as 'their' task as sole providers of emotional and physical care for dependent and needy relatives. This government has recently decided, despite evidence of the desperate plight of those caring for elderly relatives, that married women, simply because they are married, are *still* to be denied access to the Invalidity Care Allowance.

In hiding what are the *real* effects of Thatcherism on families with children and other dependents, Tories must conceal a very great deal. For such families have become in every way worse off under Thatcherism. Child benefit has fallen since 1979, and in 1982 was worth less in purchasing power than in 1946. Changes in tax laws have been to the detriment of families with children compared to those without, while low paid parents pay disproportionately more tax than parents with high incomes. The value of maternity benefits, already amongst the lowest in Europe, was cut by the Tories. And they have now come up with the extraordinary idea of taxing even this pittance! All this accompanies cuts in the value of unemployment, sickness and invalidity benefit. Single parents, over 90% female and now one in three of households with children in inner London, are the hardest hit of all. It has even become almost impossible for them to claim for 'extras', like children's shoes, clothing, or for fuel.

All capital expenditure on nurseries has been cut, and Boyson has repeated that the Thatcher government had no intention of increasing under-fives provision, because mothers with young children should stay at home. Personal social services for the elderly have been cut, as the government squeeze on local authorities has led to cuts in domiciliary services, home help services, meals on wheels and day-care facilities.

But has this squeeze on welfare provision been forcing women back into the home to meet the otherwise neglected needs of the young, the old, the sick and disabled? It certainly has meant that the work women do in the home has become more and more of a burden. Despite the fact that more husbands and wives now believe that men and women *should* share household chores, surveys have shown repeatedly that the bulk of housework is still done by women, even in households where women and men work equal hours outside the home, or where men and older sons are unemployed. Husbands of working wives do almost as little housework as husbands of full time housewives.[5] And housing shortages mean that women find it more difficult to leave violent and loveless marriages, while economic hardship makes family life grim and depressing. But, perhaps surprisingly, it is not clear that Thatcher's policies will inevitably drive increasing numbers of women out of waged work into full time housework. What they have succeeded in doing is further denying women any possibility of *choice* – choices over whether and how to engage in waged work, and over how to combine waged work with domestic work.

For under Thatcherism jobs are determined not by any Tory family rhetoric on women's place, but are left to market forces in an economic climate of industrial decline, re-structuring and deflationary policies. At first it did look as though women workers, frequently part-time and the least secure and protected by their unions, were losing jobs at twice the rate of men. Many women did lose jobs. But overall, in a situation in which manufacturing jobs are declining faster than service jobs and the effects of new technology are unclear, women do not seem to be any longer losing jobs faster than men. For instance, as Gwyn Williams has pointed out,[6] in Wales it is predicted that within the next ten years women will outnumber men in the workforce, due to changes in employment patterns. And while certain women's jobs, like mechanical office jobs are disappearing, there is also a trend in some technologies, as in computer technology, towards making more and more jobs home workers' jobs. These are the jobs traditionally done by women who have to stay home with young children.

Moreover, the expansion of part-time and 'job-splitting' opportunities, which Thatcherism is supporting, make it possible for women to do paid work on top of heavy domestic burdens. Since January 1983 there have been grants for firms offering job-splitting schemes. This suits many employers, as women part-time workers are the most highly exploited. On top of missing out on various workers' rights, their average hourly earnings in April 1981 were only 58% of those of full-time male workers.[7] Now, ironically, an expansion of part-time work (but at decent rates, and in suitable conditions) has been pushed by certain socialist feminists, like Jean Gardiner and Sheila Smith,[8] as part of their strategy to enable the sharing of domestic work between men and women, especially, the care of young children. Clearly, however, it is very far from this government's intentions to promote greater choice and sharing between men and women in the home. Nor in general have they, for women are deprived of choice.

For example, many women in jobs are likely to fear leaving them to have children, because of the threat of permanent unemployment. The 1980 Employment Act means employers can now more easily refuse a woman her job back after maternity leave. So women are less free to choose to give up work to have a child, as well as knowing that nursery cuts mean that they are also less likely to be able to return to paid work, even were it available. Meanwhile, male unemployment and declining living standards will force many women to take on paid work – however exploited and unpopular, and whatever her domestic burdens.

Other women, however, and in particular very young women, who can find no jobs, may feel forced into motherhood, as the only role available to them. With no other identification with an adult role, it is not surprising to hear young women say, as I heard on a television programme on teenage pregnancy, 'You feel a lot older if you've got a baby. People don't look down on you like if you're unemployed.' Having a baby can give unemployed women a reason for living (as well as a home away from their parents). Though trying to survive as a single parent on the pitiful allowance of about £30 a week she and her baby will receive, will most likely mean a miserable life for them both.

So women who may wish to leave jobs will be forced to retain them while others who would like jobs will be forced to stay at home. Some feminists have perhaps too readily accepted the *rhetoric* of Thatcherism, believing that women will be – or could be – forced back into the home. But one thing is certain, that the tensions inside the home, and the tensions between men and women can only increase. Tensions and stress will increase not just from greater poverty and poorer services, but because women's special exploitation both at home and at work will be experienced ever more sharply. Women will continue to face unequal domestic burdens on top of paid work, while unemployed husbands and sons have been found to add to rather than decrease the work in the home. Pay and conditions in women's jobs will continue to deteriorate, as trade union power still remains overwhelmingly in the hands of men, who have up until now paid little attention to part-time women workers, or to how trade union priorities might begin to integrate the conflicting demands of home and work.

In this situation the labour movement and the left will simply fail to connect up with the now obvious militancy and imagination of women in struggle unless they can abandon long traditions of Labourism which see 'the worker' as essentially male (and preferably skilled and white). It is not the time for them simply to bemoan the loss of manufacturing jobs, nor the demoralisation of the old male vanguards of the working class, now, like the miners, understandably unwilling to take on this government. It is the time for them to adopt genuine *socialist feminist perspectives*, which not only make the links between home and work, but also recognise the power relations of conflict between women and men in both spheres. It is not enough therefore for the left to demand a woman's right to jobs, nor even to demand improved contraception and abortion, nursery and maternity provision, as the Labour Party and the TUC now do – at least in principle. Socialist feminist strategies also raise other questions. First of all, the question of sharing housework and child-care (and hence demanding shorter and flexible hours in paid work: and paternity leave). Secondly, it raises the question of job training and sex segregation at work (which remains as strong as it had ever been; indeed women are today even more ghettoised into low paid, low status jobs). And thirdly, it raises the question of greatly expanded childcare provision, centres for the elderly, and other public resources. All these schemes would create vast numbers of new jobs, hopefully for both woman *and men*. As centrally however, socialist feminist strategies would seek to find *effective* ways, through positive discrimination, consciousness raising, and women's collective confrontation with men, of challenging the full and threatening complexity of sexist ideology and social relations which maintain male privilege and power, whether in the workplace, the home, the left or the labour movement.

Unlike the Moral Majority

Moreover, it is *not* unrealistic to stress as crucial, the mobilising power of socialist-feminist strategies in this period. For either Thatcherism remains ambivalent, or it has been less than successful, in mounting an overall attack on women's rights. I suspect both factors are operating together. In this respect, it is *unlike* the moral right in the USA, supported by Reaganism, which is directly anti-feminist, explicitly against abortion and equal rights for women, as well as anti-gay. The American new right has now successfully undermined the equal rights legislation feminists fought for, as well as attacking abortion rights and removing state funding for abortions. Its proposed

Family Protection Act, supported by the tirelessly active Moral Majority and National Pro-Family Coalition, aims to strengthen parental authority and in particular paternal authority, while attacking legal funding for divorce, homosexual rights and abortion. In Britain though, the Tory Party and Thatcher's cabinet proclaim an officially 'neutral' policy on abortion, divorce and homosexual rights.

Despite a surreptitious attempt to remove non-medical reasons for abortion on forms for surgeons in March 1981 (which was successfully flouted by gynaecologist Peter Huntingford), the Minister of Health has denied having any plans to restrict abortion services. It seems more likely that the Tories are more interested in promoting private abortion facilities, in line with their general support for privatisation. Nor have the main right wing pressure groups in Britain, SPUC and LIFE, had any particular success lately, though we might expect Thatcherism to provide a suitable political terrain for them. In 1982 LIFE lost its prosecution of Dr Arthur for failing to preserve the life of a severely handicapped baby against the wishes of its parents, although it did manage to obtain some funding for its anti-abortion services from the Department of the Environment, and has applied for further funding.

The anti-feminist right in this country has been weakened by the continual success and vigour of feminism in mobilising support for women's rights and equality. Contrary to popular, typically misogynist myth, it was not women, as a group, who switched their votes to Thatcher in the last elections. The highest shift in support was from skilled, white workers from the South of England.[9] I see it as a possible weak link in Thatcherism that it has not successfully crushed a feminist consciousness which is aware of the oppression of women's lives as vulnerable and exploited workers and as hopelessly overburdened housewives, mothers and daughters. It is an oppression which Thatcher's policies can be seen to exacerbate. Mobilising on a feminist platform, which embodies quite new ways of working, caring for and supporting each other will be central to any movement which hopes to defeat and replace the ideas of Thatcherism.

Notes

¹ S. Hall, 'The Great Moving Right Show', in this volume.

² M. Thatcher, 'Women in a Changing World', Press Office, Downing Street, July 1982.

³ *Ibid.*

⁴ M. Barrett and M. McIntosh, *The Anti Social Family*, London 1982.

⁵ See A. Oakley, *Subject Woman*, Martin Robertson 1981, pp. 250-251.

⁶ G. Williams, 'Land of our Fathers', *Marxism Today*, August 1982.

⁷ *Ibid* p. 24.

⁸ J. Gardiner and S. Smith, 'Feminism and Alternative Economic Strategy', *Socialist Economic Review*, 1982.

⁹ It is interesting that at the moment in the USA, voting trends indicate that it is women who are in the forefront of opposition to Reagan – to the extent that there is said to be a 'yawning gulf' between the way the two sexes are voting. C. Reed, *Guardian*, 4 November 1982.

Martin Kettle

The Drift to Law and Order

'People have asked me whether I am going to make the fight against crime an issue at the next election. No, I am not going to make it an issue. It is the people of Britain who are going to make it an issue.'

The words belong to Margaret Thatcher, spoken at the 1977 Conservative Party conference. They echo dozens of similar remarks from senior Conservative politicians and Fleet Street editorials over the past decade. For they all agree that once again in the late 1970s, as a decade earlier, 'law and order' had become a deep popular worry, that this was why it then became a central plank in the radical platform put forward by Margaret Thatcher's wing of the Tory Party, and remained a spicy ingredient of the party's revival at the end of the decade.

Many would argue, quite specifically, that 'law and order' was one of the key election issues in May 1979. The echoes of the Selsdon Toryism of 1970 had never died away, though it was now refocused. The assassination of Airey Neave MP and major street confrontations involving National Front election meetings pitchforked the subject back into centre stage during the campaign itself. The Police Federation, which represents all police officers up to chief inspector rank, stirred the pot with an unprecedented 'law and order' manifesto which appeared as an advert in almost every daily paper. The former Metropolitan Commissioner, Sir Robert Mark, hit the front pages with an outspoken attack on the trade unions. And Margaret Thatcher went out of her way to stress her keenness to give parliament a quick opportunity to bring back the death penalty, while making no secret of her personal support for the return of hanging.

There is no doubt that large numbers of people *do* worry deeply about something called 'law and order'. A recent survey of post-war opinion polls on the subject concluded: 'the trend of public concern over law and order is unmistakeable'.[1] The polls show that three-quarters of us want the death penalty back, that 93% of us want heavier sentences imposed for violence and vandalism, and that only 25% of us have ever felt uneasy about anything the police have done. And in a period when corruption in their ranks has rarely been out of the news, the police's reputation for honesty and ethical standards remains five times higher than that of trade union officials.

Perhaps we may suspect the value of such surveys, but no amount of monkeying about with figures can disguise the fact that the overall serious crime rate has quadrupled over the last quarter century and that one's chances of being a victim of violent assault have increased in the same period.

However, 'law and order' isn't that simple. It is a subject which stirs strong feelings and, often, strong prejudices. As a result, most discussions on the subject generate heat rather than light. Think of the public attitude to any mention of Brady and Hindley, the 'moors murderers', for instance, or to Peter Sutcliffe and the 'Ripper' murders. In the rush, vital facts are frequently overlooked.

> Seen objectively against the background and problems of 50 million people, crime is not even among the more serious of our difficulties ... In 1976, there were only 565 homicides in England and Wales, including deaths from terrorism, and 548 of these led to arrests.[2]

This is the judgment not of some devil-may-care libertarian 'do-gooder' but of Sir Robert Mark, who is certainly no law and order dove.

It is vital to get the crime question into perspective. International comparisons show how lucky this country remains. The murder rate in England and Wales, for example, remains significantly lower than that in the city of Detroit alone. Indeed, Britain's overall reported crime rate (a problematic but emotive index) actually went down in both 1978 and 1979, though it began to rise again in 1980 and 1981. The police remain markedly less powerful, violent and, indeed, less corrupt than in many other advanced capitalist and socialist societies. The courts are under heavy pressure to avoid sending offenders to prison. And, by no means least, the liberal legislation of the 1960s (on abortion, homosexuality, hanging, censorship and so on) has so far stood very firm against repeated and well-marshalled assaults to which, in what some have called a 'law and order society', it might have been expected to succumb rather easily.

So what is meant by 'law and order'? First, it is a policy area covering crime and justice. Within this, it is also a group of big state-run 'agencies' – like the police, courts and prisons. It is also some specialised agencies, like the immigration control and security services. In England and Wales, at any rate, it is therefore the part of the state which is administered by the Home Office.

But, second, it is a much broader idea or attitude – even a sanction. It is a belief in and practice of *discipline* in attitudes, behaviour and choices in the home, the streets and the workplace. Stuart Hall and others have described the way that the first has broadened into the second as 'legitimating the recourse to law, to constraint and statutory power' under which society is 'toned up and groomed' for the 'routinisation of control'.[3] To support this thesis, they point especially to the use of legal constraints on the labour movement and, in particular, to the Heath Government's Industrial Relations Act, 1971.

The problem with this analysis, it seems to me, is that while it rightly defines 'law and order' in terms outside the narrow limits of crime and justice policy, it pays insufficient attention to the concrete changes within that crime and justice field. These changes, which mainly concern the autonomous development of the 'agencies', and their readiness, willingness and ability to dictate what is and isn't 'law and order', provide the chief thrust of the growing intervention in political and social events.

This article will therefore try to show how it is inadequate to speak of 'law and order' in purely crime and justice terms (and will analyse the specifics of the Tory and Labour records in government). But it will also show how internally-generated changes within the 'agencies' largely define the scope of the disciplinary sanctions invoked against wider society.

Law and Order: the Tory and Labour Records

There were four specific 'law and order' commitments in the

1979 Conservative manifesto. They may have been vote winners, but their real combined effect would always have been limited and was, in several cases, moderated in practice after the election.

(1) The commitment to a free parliamentary vote on hanging at an early point in the new session was always carefully hedged. It was nothing more than a pledge to test the parliamentary temperature. And when the test was taken, on 19 July 1979, there was a majority of 119 against reintroduction (one of the largest majorities in recent times). In spite of Thatcher's personal support for it, 94 Conservatives voted against hanging, led into the lobbies by the Home Secretary himself, William Whitelaw.

(2) The commitment to a tougher regime in detention centres for young offenders – the headline-grabbing 'short sharp shock' – was a pledge merely to introduce an *experimental* tough regime. It is now being tried out, at four detention centres, and it remains very doubtful whether it will ever be extended wholesale. Apart from anything else, it is an experiment whose success or failure is very difficult to assess either quickly or at all. And, in addition, the scheme has little support within the Home Office or among the people responsible for supervising it.

(3) The commitment to a wider range of sentences for offenders – especially for young offenders – certainly sounded tough. In reality, there was only one specific pledge, to change the Criminal Justice Act, 1961, to allow the courts to send young offenders to prison for less than three years. For the most part, though, the Government's sentencing policies have centred consistently on urging courts to impose non-custodial sentences (i.e., not sending people to prison), suspended sentences (i.e., not sending them to prison unless they reoffend), or, if prison sentences must be given, to make them shorter. 'Would such a change really create so much difficulty?' Whitelaw asked in July 1980.[4] The entire thrust of his sentencing policy is directed to keeping prison numbers down. Many of these measures were included in the Criminal Justice Act, passed by Parliament in 1982. On reflection, it would have been far more threatening if the manifesto had pledged a *narrower* range of sentencing.

(4) The commitment to tighten the immigration rules probably affected the lives of more people than any of the proposals. Even so, because of the strictness of the controls already in operation,

the maximum numbers whose chance of entry into the UK would have been lost under the new proposals would have been 4,000 a year. Even so, significant parts of the package were dropped after the election. The plan for a register of dependants and for annual quotas (measures long advocated by Enoch Powell) were abandoned after civil service pressure. However, the controversial 'foreign husbands' rule was slackened – albeit in a more racist way, and after concessions were made to conservative right-wingers.

It makes good headlines to label the Conservatives as the 'hang 'em and flog 'em party' – and undoubtedly the Party contains more hangers and floggers than other parties. But it is also worth stressing how few of the traditional 'backwoods' demands ever formed or yet form part of the Government's plans. No moves to bring back corporal punishment (abolished in 1948). No moves towards the bill of rights so often demanded by the Tory right and by Lord Hailsham (who as Lord Chancellor is certainly in a position to do something about it). No moves to abolish the Commission for Racial Equality or the Equal Opportunities Commission. No moves to introduce repatriation of immigrants.

Although it would still be foolish not to expect something more dramatic during the lifetime of the administration, its record so far is undeniably modest. Judged by what it has done, and by what it has said it will do, as well as by what it has not done, the Thatcher government has not even attempted a shake-up in the Home Office to match its aggressive attitude in other areas of government.

Indeed, the dominant feature of narrow Conservative 'law and order' policy is its basic continuity with the policies of the last Labour Government, even while masquerading as a tough new broom. The first action of the Conservatives after the election provided a classic example. With great theatricality, they awarded a pay increase to the police. It seemed to show the new regime's priorities and Whitelaw naturally made a proud boast of it at that autumn's party conference. It called forth great indignation from the unions and from the left. And yet, all that the Conservatives had done was to bring forward by a couple a months a pay award which had been already agreed by their Labour predecessors.

The absence of a real break between the two governments

also shows in more substantive matters. The Criminal Justice (Scotland) Act, 1980, which (among many other things) strengthens police powers by legalising the practice of detention for questioning, may seem like a trial run for similar changes in England and Wales and like proof of a 'pro-police' policy. Both are true, but Labour introduced an almost identical Bill at the back end of its term of office, which only fell because the general election was called.

Moreover, the Conservative Government was also faced with making similar changes south of the border as well, following the publication in January 1981 of the report of the Royal Commission on Criminal Procedure. These changes will cover police powers to search, detain and question. It is the most significant legislation in this field in modern times. But it would be very misleading to see it as 'a Tory Bill'.

The changes proposed in the Police and Criminal Evidence Bill are based, albeit loosely, on the conclusions of a Royal Commission set up by James Callaghan and, although a Labour Government might not (as it claims in opposition) legislate in exactly the same way as the as yet unknown Conservative proposals, it would undoubtedly legislate on the issues in some way. There would, obviously, be important differences of emphasis in a Labour Government measure on these subjects. However, the substance of such differences cannot be allowed to obscure the important element of bi-partisan policy-making continuity in the criminal policy field.

This is because the Home Office (in the person of its civil servants) has *its own line*, quite independent of any party line, even that of the Conservatives. This line is largely dictated by its need and desire to sustain the agencies which it, nominally, controls. But, of course, it is heavily dictated to by the agencies themselves. And if *they* put their foot down, then so will the civil servants and so too (as their records show) will the Home Secretaries who, again nominally, run the department.

Inside the prison system, recent restructuring of management and administration announced by Whitelaw was wholly based upon the proposals of the May Committee of Inquiry set up in 1978 by Labour's Merlyn Rees. And the Government's 1980 White Paper on the reduction of pressure on the prison system gives just as little ground on internal reform as did the Home Office under Rees when the Select Committee report to which the new White Paper is a response was first published in 1977. In both cases, it is the *Home Office's own view* which has prevailed, not any *party view*.

Where the traditional running or self-interest of one of its agencies or departments is at stake, the Home Office's dead bat is well-nigh unbeatable. The reluctance to respond positively to the 1977 select committee on prisons is of a piece with the way the Home Office refused to accept the 1980 all-party Select Committee call for the abolition of the 'sus' law. In this case, the interests of the police department and of the Metropolitan Police ensured that abolition would be compensated by new powers contained in the 1981 Criminal Attempts Act, and in the Police and Criminal Evidence Bill. (The Home Office is profoundly resistant to changes which are forced upon it from outside. But this doesn't mean that it opposes any change. The new 'liberalism' in sentencing policies referred to earlier is a major shift in thinking, not to be underestimated. But it is an internally conceived change, responding to departmental needs — in this case the financial and managerial imperatives of an overcrowded prison system and the unavailability of major capital investment for new buildings or wholesale renovations.)

Labour's record, too, is littered with the corpses of forgotten radical reports. It was Labour which capitulated to the furious front-page denunciations of the *Sun* and buried the 1978 report of the Advisory Council on the Penal System (now cut down in the quango cull) which called for wholesale shortening of prison sentences. It was Labour which failed to legislate on the basis of the Devlin committee on identification evidence. It was Labour which came to power in 1974 committed to reform of the Official Secrets Act and then dropped the idea because of Home Office opposition, and Labour which later failed to introduce safeguards on personal information called for by the Lindop report on data protection.

In the 1960s, it was perhaps possible to draw real distinction of substance between Conservative and Labour Home Office policy — distinctions which were personified in the contrast between Henry Brooke's inhumanity and Roy Jenkins's liberalism. By the 1970s, these distinctions had beyond question been reduced to mere matters of degree. Jenkins's second term at the Home Office (1974-6) was far less innovative than his first; its main legacy, ironically, being the 'temporary' Prevention of Terrorism Act, brought in after the Birmingham bomb atrocities in November 1974. His two successors, Merlyn Rees and William Whitelaw, share a personal friendship and a schooling in consensus administration at the Northern Ireland Office. Now they have brought these traditions to the Home Office, too.

Since Roy Hattersley replaced Rees as shadow Home Secretary at the end of 1980, there have been signs of a departure from this tradition. Hattersley has been more outspoken than Rees would have been – notably on nationality law and on criminal procedure. But it is far too early to judge the long-term significance of these events. Just as I have argued that the real test of the Conservatives is in what they do rather than what they say, so the same applies to Labour. The real proof lies in a party's actions in government, not in its statements in opposition.

One major reason for the consensus and continuity between Conservatives and Labour in office is the absence of a living alternative libertarian tradition in the modern Labour Party and in the labour movement generally. E.P. Thompson has suggested that this absence is due in part to a 'profoundly pessimistic determinism' within the left about law and the state. Crudely put, it is based on the simplistic notion that the *sole* function of the state under capitalism is to defend the capitalist system and that any attempts to reform it are mere glosses. It sanctions the notion, as Thompson puts it, that 'If *all* law and *all* police are utterly abhorrent, then it cannot matter much what *kind* of law or *what* place the police are held within'.[5]

For the most part, the Home Office has also been regarded by the Labour Party at best as a wholly marginal department to the economic and spending departments, at worst as a ministry which seems to be doing a necessary job. The only break in this pattern came in Jenkins's first term (1965-7) and was influenced by a group of articulate professionals (mainly liberal lawyers) outside the mainstream of the movement.

The result has been that the central policy areas in the Home Office – policing, prisons, criminal procedure and (to the left's shame) immigration – have been allowed to develop autonomously. They are treated as administrative areas, within which substantive political disagreement is not only unlikely but also even undesirable.

In part, this stems from a worthy, and almost Enlightenment notion that the workings of a fair system of legal procedures should be free from executive or 'political' interference. But it also reveals a black hole in the theory of the peaceful transformation of the state. And it has allowed the state agencies which operate these policy areas to develop and expand their own definitions of the proper boundaries of their work and to lay down a deep-rooted autonomy within these boundaries. This process lies at the heart of the 'drift into a law and order society' under which law and order takes on its wider meaning and begins to involve every one of us.[6]

Law and Order and the State Agencies

The autonomy of agencies is especially marked within the prison system. Here there has been, for several years, a massive crisis of internal conditions – largely created by ever-rising numbers having to be housed in a finite number of inadequate buildings. There is, too, a crisis of regimes, created by the officially acknowledged failure of the 'treatment' model of imprisonment (which claimed that prisons should aim to make prisoners into nice citizens) – now to be superseded by 'positive custody'.[7] Above all, there is a crisis of control, as the courts on the one hand, and the prison administrators on the other, manoeuvre against the militant, hard-line prison officers.

Occasionally, as during the prison officers' work to rule in the autumn and winter of 1980/81, this conflict becomes newsworthy. For the most part, though, these continuing crises fester behind locked doors, both literally and metaphorically. This is partly because the law gives so much administrative licence to the department. The courts are unwilling, and to some extent, unable to intervene. As a result, British prison practice has to be challenged further afield, by using the European Convention on Human Rights. Parliament consistently fails to make good the courts' reluctance. Informal attempts to exercise some control from outside have been tried – by local authorities, by prisoners' relatives and support groups, sometimes even by lay workers in the prisons, like teachers and probation officers. But all are met with deep and, so far, effective antagonism from the two warring factions. Like the police, the prisons are able to rely upon and exploit a tradition of non-interference given sanction by the laissez-faire approach to the doctrine of law and order.

The same goes for the immigration process. Here, too, the system is closely controlled by a department within the Home Office. The courts are content to endorse and extend the administrative autonomy of the Secretary of State (and hence of immigration officers). The day to day practise of immigration control at ports of entry is jealousy screened from independent supervision.

But with immigration, autonomy is not the only important issue. Sanctioned by the all-party consensus on illegal immigration (a term that has been greatly widened by the courts), and bolstered by periodic bouts of hysteria about 'swamping', the immigration service and the police with whom they work enforce a system of checks which relegates all non-whites to the margins of the law and order society. Immigration practice, and the ideology which underpins it, place all black people at risk by constantly questioning their right to be in this country.

In so doing, immigration control consistently negates and frustrates the aims of race relations legislation. The same goes for the new nationality law passed by parliament in 1981. This is not the view of both the major parties, however, who still assert that firm control provides the atmosphere of reassurance to the white population that will enable good race relations to prosper. In fact, the reverse is the case. Even the government-backed Commission for Racial Equality has tried to mount a major inquiry into the government's own immigration department – an inquiry bitterly opposed by the Home Office.

Thus law and order grinds into everyday life. The immigration system provides a classic example – though by no means the only one – of the process by which these unsupervised agencies have been able to tighten the social disciplinary screw by extending their regulatory powers into speculative surveillance over much larger groups than they were originally set up to control.

Far and away the most powerful engine in this movement is the police force. The police have never been solely concerned with catching criminals. As every speech and publication in

1979 celebrating the 150th anniversary of the police pointed out, they see their major task as *prevention* – creating the conditions in which crime will not take place. But as Robert Peel's original instruction to the Metropolitan Police in 1829 pointed out, their goals are not merely the prevention of crime, but also the prevention of *disorder*.

Thus, from the first, the police have been involved in social conflict as well as crime. The process has ebbed and flowed through the past century and a half but there is no doubt that the past two decades have witnessed a renewed expansion of these terms. In particular, with the growth of the modern state, a range of social problems have been redefined in policing terms. One example would be the Notting Hill Carvival – a community even now redefined as a big policing 'problem'.

Robert Mark is rightly most associated with this process, but he has left a widespread legacy. Sir James Crane, the Chief Inspector of Constabulary for England and Wales, sums up the current official assessment in a recent annual report: '1979 ... heralded the end of a decade of unprecendented economic and social problems and technological change, with accepted standards and values of behaviour being strongly questioned and severely tested by some sections of society'.[8]

In terms of 'prevention', these lessons have led the police in different directions. On the one hand, there is the 'proactive' community policing advocated by the eloquent John Alderson, former Chief Constable of Devon and Cornwall. This concentrates on evolving a common strategy among social services, community groups and voluntary organisation – all coordinated by the police – to identify and carry out crime prevention needs at grassroots level. This form of policing 'reaches out to penetrate the community in a multitude of ways ... It seeks to reinforce social discipline and mutual trust in communities'.[9]

On the other hand, there is the highly technologised political surveillance side of prevention. This is notably associated with James Anderton, the hard-line Chief Constable of Greater Manchester, who informed TV viewers in 1979: 'I think that from the police point of view that my task in future, in the ten to fifteen years from now, the period during which I shall continue to serve, that basic crime as such – theft, burglary, even violent crime – will not be the predominant police feature. What will be the matter of greatest concern to me will be the covert and ultimately overt attempts to overthrow democracy, to subvert the authority of the state and, in fact, to involve themselves in acts of sedition designed to destroy our parliamentary system and the democratic government in this country'.[10]

Even in the traditional areas of policing, criminal catching, the preventive principle is being invoked to justify the extension of boundaries. The proposals made by Sir David McNee, the Metropolitan Commissioner, to the Royal Commission on Criminal Procedure in 1978 would make it easier for the police to question and search suspects at an earlier stage of their inquiries. They would allow the police to have access to information on more members of the public through banks and fingerprint checks. A more speculative approach to policing would be legitimised, and all in the name of the great god, prevention.

The contrast between the Alderson and Anderton approaches is frequently made. In fact, the two are different sides of the preventive coin, as Anderton has acknowledged in a recent annual report when he observed that 'neither is complete, sufficient nor appropriate in itself and both complement the middle ground'.[11]

It is also recognised by Alderson who, although he has frequently and bravely criticised the seduction of police thinking by the 'quasi-military reactive concept', still presides over a force which contains all the specialist reactive squads – like the Special Patrol Groups and Police Support Units – more associated with the Anderton approach.

The elision between crime and disorder is fundamental to an understanding of the spread of the preventive policing concept and, indeed, to the whole festering power of 'law and order' ideology. It isn't confined to Britain, of course. Spiro Agnew once said: 'When I talk about troublemakers, I'm talking about muggers and criminals in the streets, assassins of political leaders, draft evaders and flag burners, campus militants, hecklers and demonstrators against candidates for public office and looters and burners of cities'.[12] The law and order creed embodied in this bracketing of killers and demonstrators is a feature of all western countries.

British politicians and police are just as practised as Agnew. A 1977 police 'field manual' by a senior London officer advises new recruits to watch out for people who 'although not dishonest in the ordinary sense, may, owing to extreme political views, intend to harm the community you have sworn to protect,' and continues: 'While there are subtle differences between these types of extremists and thieves, it is difficult to put one's finger on material distinction'.[13]

These attitudes are institutionalised by a variety of routine police practices. Almost every aspect of police work is subjected to a routine – an important point to remember when occasional repressive practices come to light. The most important general practice is the centralisation within each police force of local intelligence through the collator system. Collators maintain personal files on people of interest to the police, and are not restricted to those who have been charged or convicted. The computer records of one force – Thames Valley – are computerised in a Home Office experiment which may be extended nationally – though if it is, the decision to do so will be taken without advance parliamentary discussion. The sort of material held in these records is frequently trivial and unsubstantiated, as well as irrelevant to any conceivable crime-fighting police – like whether a person lives in a squat, for instance.[14]

Police records are like a giant sponge, gradually soaking up all sorts of information. But it is information for action. In the case of the Special Branches, it is political information, collected both for the use of the security services (MI5) and for the police operational use against demonstrations and strikes. The SB has quadrupled in size in the last decade and is now 1,600 strong, maintaining files on over $1\frac{1}{4}$ million people. Each of the country's 52 regional police forces has its own SB. One of their acknowledged targets is 'subversion' – and government admissions have now confirmed what most of us assumed anyway, that this label applies to socialist and industrial activists and others who are also engaged in completely legal oppositional activity.

Some police will assert that this whole marginalisation and delegitimation of sections of the community has been forced upon them by the growth of terrorism. There is no denying that there is some truth in the claim. Terrorist actions in Britain have compelled a trained police response, some of which, had it not been for terrorism, would not have been developed otherwise.

However, there is no real doubt that the response penetrates far beyond the threat, that it was developed well before the threat materialised in the early 1970s and that the marginalisation process has, in any case, many causes, such as immigration control, in addition to terrorism.

Since 1968, the year in which street demonstrations against the Vietnam war reached their peak, the police have engaged in a long-term attempt to destroy the legitimacy of public protest. They have been at the forefront of the attempts to impose legally binding advance notice conditions on marches, and to extend other legal curbs over large crowds. This drive has not been based upon any fear of excessive violence. It rests upon the police's growing opposition to demonstrations as such.

The Association of Chief Police Officers (ACPO) – the chief constables' 'union' – has said, for example: 'Today the right to demonstrate is widely exploited and marching is the most chosen form of demonstration adopted by protesters. *Irrespective of the peaceful nature of the processions,* the numbers involved bring town centres to a halt, business is severely disrupted and the public bus services thrown out of schedule. In short, a general annoyance is created to *the normal process of daily life*'[15] (my italics).

The police use any violence which does occur on demonstrations to back their campaign – though, in doing so, they arbitrarily single out this aspect of the danger of the officer's job. They constantly harp on about the alleged financial cost of their public order policing – often with highly dubious figures. And on the streets themselves, tactics such as mass policing, the use of the Police Support Units and SPGs, unnecessary cordoning off of routes, surveillance from rooftops and helicopters all help them to draw more firmly the frontier between 'the normal process of daily life' and political protest.

In 1981, the police took the process a stage further. Reversing their traditional policy of protecting racist marches on the streets, the police successfully applied for a series of local bans not only on racist marches but also, effectively, on all political marches as well. However welcome such bans may appear to be in terms of racial tension, their effect is a further undermining of the legitimacy of political protest.

It is less clear that the police play such a crucial leading role in policy-making for the handling of industrial public order. To some extent, this is due to sleight of hand. In several recent submissions to government they have tried to redefine mass picketing as 'assemblies', in an attempt to differentiate it from the limited peaceful picketing defined in the new Employment Act. There is no doubt that the police seek to delegitimate mass picketing and that this is broadly in line with their campaign against marches.

However, in the industrial field, police leaders seem anxious not to be drawn into the strict regulation of any and every picket line. They have also taken steps recently to adopt a conciliatory line towards trade union leaders; Len Murray, for example, has been invited to address police cadets – a notable break with tradition, especially in a management still edgy over demands for police unionisation and the right to strike.

A former ACPO president, Alan Goodson, has taken a cautious view of the Government's code of conduct on picketing. He has claimed that the police need no new powers. Sir David McNee has made it clear that the police will not get involved in identifying outsider pickets against whom employers may be contemplating civil action under the Employment Act. And the former head of the Police Staff College, Gerald Lamford, has spoken out in favour of James Prior's cautious approach to industrial relations law. 'There is no way in this country in which legislation which does not command general support from the people can be enforced,' he told a meeting of the Industrial Society.[16]

But if the police are wary of confronting the labour movement when it is exercising one of its basic weapons – picketing – there are other areas where fewer scruples exist and where the police knowingly and explicitly function in a non-consensual framework.

The police's involvement in the emergency planning network compels them to act in this way. As a result of changes introduced in the early 1970s, the police themselves have now been given the role of summoning military aid in civil emergencies. In principle, these powers are for use in time of flood, disaster or war. In practice, though, in the last decade, the emergency powers have been invoked in the context of industrial disputes and the police's preventive public order powers. Since 1977, the police themselves have acted in a strike-breaking role during the firemen's strike (1977-78), the ambulance drivers' strike (1979) and the social workers' strike (1979). A detailed study has concluded that, in constitutional terms, 'there are no limits whatsoever placed on the employment of police officers replacing striking workers.' As a result, the study said, the only problem facing either government or chief constables wishing to extend the role is 'a question of legitimation'.[17] It is hard to believe that in the recession, with over three million unemployed, that they will fail to find a way of providing that legitimation.

There are several other important examples of this law and order imperialism under which social and political movements are redefined in policing terms. In Europe, nuclear energy has been one such and some illustration of how this may also happen in Britain can be found in the remarkable powers given to the UK Atomic Energy Authority police in 1976, and in the vetting and security measures which now surround the industry.

Cultural events have not been immune from the process ever since the 'moral panics' of the late 1960s. Rock festivals have often been unnecessarily and aggressively over-policed – notably in Windsor Great Park in 1971. Explicitly political musical festivals organised by Rock Against Racism have been regarded by the police with great suspicion.

Nationalist movements are given special attention. This has long been true of the Irish, of course; the Special Branch itself was first set up as long ago as 1883 to penetrate Irish nationalist sympathiser groups. But few people realise that the SB and MI5 have long been equally interested in Welsh and Scottish nationalism – as part of their brief to defend the unity of the state – the United Kingdom. The police treatment of Welsh language militants would seem inexplicably and ridiculously fierce were it not for this factor. It helps to explain the harassment of language activists in the wake of the second-homes arson campaign in Wales. As experience of the Prevention of Terrorism Act has shown, the original aim of catching those responsible for specific crimes soon degenerated into wholesale monitoring of the movements and activities of entire communities.

Above all, though, it is in relations with the black community that the traditional notion of policing with the consent of the public has broken down. There are many long-term and many immediate causes of this situation: the disproportionate use of stop and search powers, the use of immigration and passport checks, raids on black clubs, treatment of carnivals and other cultural events as public order threats, crude 'crime prevention' operations by elite groups like the SPG, neglect of black grievances against the police, the apparent readiness to protect racist activities in black areas. In 1981, these antagonisms provoked the uprising by black youth against the police in Brixton – an event which was the most important challenge so far to British policing in the post-war era.

At the same time as the state agencies extend their spheres of influence under the sanction of law and order, they have resisted every single outside attempt to control them. Thus the osmosis of law and order works all the while against democracy, because its inherently authoritarian character is incompatible with debate, discussion, participation or accountability. At local and national level, in the prisons, the immigration service, the courts and the police, the resistance to control has been consistent.

Law and order ideology drives this determination. It encourages the police and their like to condemn every criticism of them as both politically motivated (left-wing) and 'anti-police'. Whoever criticises them is, by definition, anti-law and order and hence not a part of that 'society' from which the police claim their authority. Margaret Thatcher herself gave the clearest possible proof of this process when, in a short, sharp remark following criticisms of police attitudes to the National Front by Lewisham councillors in April 1980, she ordered that what the police need 'is support and not criticism'.[18]

The Labour Movement Response

The police are most effective at encouraging the press to take up this attitude. When criticisms were mounted over deaths in police custody and the Blair Peach murder, an article immediately appeared in the *Daily Mail* entitled 'This sinister plot to knock our police'.[19] The Labour Party has done little to distance itself from the authoritarian backlash. A hawkish motion on law and order was pushed through the 1978 Party Conference at James Callaghan's instigation, to ensure that Labour couldn't be accused of being soft on law and order in the coming election. And six right-wing Labour MPs' response to the criticisms of the police was to put down an early-day motion 'abhorring political propaganda from any source designed to weaken and discredit the police'.

But there are now slight indications that the tide is turning. Groups like the Labour Campaign for Criminal Justice, chaired by former Home Office minister, Alex Lyon, have been formed to counteract the hawkish response on policing, prisons and sentencing which all too often comes from the Party. Several Labour parties have begun to tackle the question of police accountability and in London the Labour Party came to power in the 1981 GLC elections pledged to a measure of local control over the Metropolitan Police. The Labour national executive has set up a study group on the security services, the Special Branch and surveillance techniques such as telephone tapping. Moreover, as mentioned earlier, the new shadow Home Secretary has taken up a more radical stance than his predecessors.

None of this constitutes a reform movement on the scale, or of the significance, of police reform movements in some other countries, notably Italy's 'Nuova Polizia'. It has made no inroads into the police themselves, nor even managed to legitimate a real dialogue with the police or other agencies. But it must be the shape of things to come, and it must be a process in which the whole of the left – the Labour Party, the Communist Party and others – is involved, to which it must now, address itself seriously, basing its views on the growing body of serious socialist writing on these subjects. If it does not do so, the dramatic force of the autonomous development of the law and order agencies can only gather further momentum during the recession.

[1] *New Society*, 12 June 1980.

[2] Robert Mark, *In the Office of Constable*, p.255.

[3] Stuart Hall, Chas Critcher, Tony Jefferson, John Clarke, Brian Roberts, *Policing the Crisis*, 1978, p. 278.

[4] Speech to NACRO conference, 15 July 1980.

[5] E.P Thompson 'The Secret State' in *Writing by Candlelight*, 1980.

[6] Stuart Hall, *Drifting into the Law and Order Society*, 1980.

[7] *Committee of Inquiry into the United Kingdom Prison Services*, Cmnd 7673 October 1979.

[8] *Report of Her Majesty's Chief Inspector of Constabulary 1979* Cmnd 725 July 1980 p.3.

[9] John Alderson, *Communal Policing* 1978.

[10] BBC-1 'Question Time', 16 October, 1979.

[11] *The Times*, 13 May 1980.

[12] *The Internationalist*, March 1979.

[13] David Powis, *The Signs of Crime*, p.12.

[14] See 'Society under surveillance' by Duncan Campbell in *Policing the Police Vol 2* (ed Peter Hain) and David Leigh, *The Frontiers of Secrecy*.

[15] *Home Affairs Committee: Law relating to public order,* HC 384-iii, February 1980.

[16] *Daily Mirror*, 28 February 1980, *Daily Telegraph*, 21 February 1980. *The Times* 26 February 1980, *Guardian*, 21 July 1980.

[17] *State Research*, Bulletin 14, October-November 1979.

[18] *The Times*, 18 April 1980.

[19] *Daily Mail*, 22 February 1980.

Steve Iliffe

Dismantling the Health Service

If the NHS is the 'jewel in Labour's Crown' it is also the great test of Conservatism. Should the National Health Service be dismantled and replaced by some sort of market-oriented medicine, the Conservatives will have achieved two things: the destruction of the most politically important of all the institutions of the welfare state; and convincing proof of the labour movement's fundamental inability to dominate social development.

The present Conservative government may well fail this test, but there is no guarantee of this, nor any reason why a successor might not pass. The politics of health may be a relatively unknown field to Conservatism, but the labour movement which created the present NHS has little understanding of the issues either. However guarded the Cabinet may be about its capacity to dismantle socialised medicine, its immediate opponents are so weakened by reformist and Fabian thought and practice that the political initiative still lies firmly with the right. Our fortune is that the right does not know how to proceed, is unsure of its ground, and fears an overwhelmingly hostile response to any attempt to destroy the National Health Service. By force of circumstance, rather than force of opposition, the Government must move slowly and quietly if it wants to replace our present system of health care with some variety of private medicine.

The goal of the present Government is clear; they wish to see market forces dominate the development of health care as far as possible. Within the ideology of Conservatism, responsibility for health is to become personal rather than social.[1,2]

Such a grand design must overcome substantial obstacles: the small size of the existing private medical sector, and its financial instability; the scope of the service provided by the NHS, and the pervasiveness of its institutions; the size of the NHS labour force and its influence. The factors favouring the Conservative attack are less impressive: the presence of a willing ally in a section (potentially a majority) of the medical profession; the deterioration in the standards of care given by the NHS; and the precedent created by the long-tolerated parasitism practised by the drugs industry.

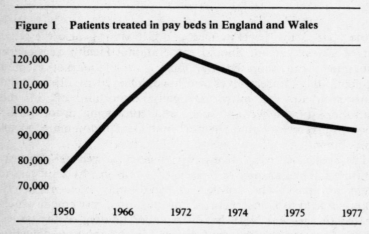

Figure 1   Patients treated in pay beds in England and Wales

Source: Michael Lee, *Private and National Health Services*, London Policy Studies Institute, 1978.

The Conservative strategy is directed at stabilising the private sector, diminishing the scope of NHS activity through cuts and cash limits, and shifting certain (profitable) areas of health care into the private sector. The Government will take a 'firm line' on industrial relations within the NHS, aiming to weaken trade unionism and solidarity generally by limiting trade union rights and turning one group of health workers against another. The medical profession (and professions like nursing) will be given more influence in planning development and allocating resources, and doctors will be encouraged to act as the link between private and public services. Finally, declining standards in NHS care that have been caused by cuts imposed by this (and previous) governments will be used as evidence of the failure of state intervention and the superiority of private enterprise.

The Obstacles to Conservative Strategy

There is no part of the welfare state that reaches more people of such varied ages, races and social classes within British society than the health service. The client-groups for public housing, public education, personal social services, welfare benefits, and even public transport are restricted by comparison with the population in contact with the health service. Each day of the year an average of 100,000 people attend hospital accident and emergency departments. Each year there are about nine million *new* attendances at out-patient clinics. Each year each person makes an average of three visits to their general practitioner.[3] Those people exclude the contacts people have with maternity services, health visitors, district nurses and clinic doctors. In terms of volume of contact between people and institutions, the NHS is a pervasive and enormous influence. Its provision of services free at the time of need (even when limited by charges), of a comprehensive range of services (however badly distributed), and of its continuity of care (however inefficient) make it a living and accepted example of a socialist institution.

An important aspect of the acceptability of socialised health care to a wide cross-section of social classes is that it is an open-access system, with no financial barrier to consultation with a health worker (whether the worker be doctor, nurse, health visitor, midwife) although there may be such a barrier to treatment (e.g. prescription charges).[4] Such open access is crucial when the whole realm of illness and health is such a mystery, such an unknown issue, for everyone. The inability of an individual accurately and realistically to predict his/her future needs for medical care makes insurance-based health services very inadequate. None of the private medical insurance schemes[5] can ensure against all eventualities; a health service financed out of general taxation and catering for the whole population can cope with almost all medical requirements, even if it cannot always accommodate the scale of need.[6] All systems of health care that depend on individuals making decisions about how to use their personal resources fail because an informed decision about future need is impossible.[7]

Finally, the rivals of socialised health care are unimpressive. Strictly private medicine, in the form of private hospitals and pay beds in NHS hospitals has been small scale since the

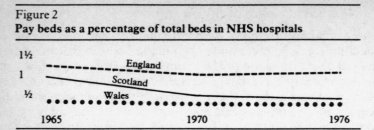

Figure 2
Pay beds as a percentage of total beds in NHS hospitals

Source: Report of the Royal Commission on the NHS, 1979.

formation of the NHS (Figures 1 and 2).

Not only has the scale of private hospital in-patient care been small, but its scope has been narrow and largely restricted to non-urgent surgery and investigation of non-urgent problems. There is little financial gain to be made from long-term care, particularly when it involves those whose income is reduced by their disability (the mentally ill and the elderly). Even the chain of privately run nursing homes for the elderly depend on an NHS subsidy, with more than 40% of the 27,000 nursing home places being occupied by people referred from and paid for by the NHS.[8]

Private medicine conducted outside hospitals, in consulting rooms and GPs' surgeries, is on a larger scale, yet still cannot match the enormous scale and range of NHS-population contact. The financial rewards of private medicine are so small that it has remained a tiny proportion of general practitioners' incomes,[9] whilst the private practice enjoyed by London specialists in Harley and Wimpole Streets has depended on a massive influx of overseas patients to compensate for a decline in the local market in the mid-seventies.[10] The early 1970s demonstrated the vulnerability of private medicine to general economic change. As personal incomes were squeezed, at the beginning of the economic crisis, the number of individual subscribers to private medical insurance fell. Doctors in private practice responded by cultivating an overseas clientele. The insurance schemes turned to group enrolment as an answer, presenting private medical insurance as a fringe benefit for companies to give their middle-management personnel or offer to their workforce as a part of wage negotiations. The overseas market proved unreliable, as the oil-producing states that sent their citizens to London for medical attention were found to be quick to complain about poor service, and slow to pay. On the other hand the group enrolment schemes of the insurance schemes were effective, producing a 25% increase in subscription between 1971 and 1979, despite the slump in membership in the early seventies. Although the private medical sector recovered from this period of shrinking markets, the instability it demonstrated still haunts the insurance schemes. Nothing since Thatcher's victory has fully dispelled this fear of instability, even though recruitment to private health insurance has sky-rocketed. The number of subscribers to health insurance schemes increased by 25% in 1980, but fell to 13% in 1981 and was forecast at 8% for 1982. The demand from new subscribers was so great that in 1981 BUPA went into the red, as benefits were claimed faster than assets increased through new recruitment. BUPA was able to bail itself out by using reserves, but their surprise loss has had longer-term effects. Premiums have been increased, particularly in the group enrolment schemes so carefully negotiated with unions like the EEPTU, and this has prompted subscribers to transfer to cheaper rivals, like Private Patient Plan (PPP). BUPA also criticised the profit-making (usually US owned) private hospitals for overcharging patients, and prompted a vicious public exchange of accusation and counter-accusation that boiled on throughout 1982.

Conservative Advantages

The greatest Tory ally in any strategy to promote private medicine at the expense of public services is the medical profession. Whilst only a section of the profession is openly in favour of a partly or totally private health service, and the majority of doctors probably accept the value of the present NHS, the whole definition and conduct of professionalism in medicine leans towards paying for health care. The organisation of the medical profession has evolved from a marketplace transaction between patient and doctor over a package of commodities — medical advice and medical treatment. The relationship between doctor and patient, provider and customer, is the central feature of the 'liberal professionalism' of medicine. All the other elements of medical professionalism flow from this source: 'clinical freedom'; 'the doctor-patient relationship'; 'confidentiality'; consultant power over the distribution and provision of services, and the 'individual contractor status' of general practitioners. The right to charge a fee for services (or to waive that fee if so desired) is only one part of the ideology of medicine. State intervention in health care has altered this ideology to some extent by making hospital doctors salaried staff and by bringing general practitioners into a contractual relationship with the NHS. The significance of private practice has become marginal because of this intervention, but the ideology remains intact. Private medicine is *defended as a principle* because of its overall significance to medical professionalism, not because of its actual relevance to the work of the majority of doctors. With such a profession at the centre of power in health care, any government actively supporting the growth of private medicine would be acting within the existing ideological framework of medicine. Even if only a minority of the profession actively support the resurgence of private practice, the majority will find that resurgence compatible with their conception of medicine, even if not desirable. This is the Government's greatest asset.

The individuality within medical professionalism has serious consequences for health service activity. Distribution of services and facilities may be determined according to the needs of doctors rather than the requirements of the population, with the most needy areas, classes and individuals getting the least.[11] Medical care may be poorly co-ordinated and unplanned (particularly in general practice), with consequent wastage of time, money and resources. And consumer demand may be allowed to take priority over forward planning and analysis of needs. These are the consequences of the market-orientation of the medical profession, even seventy years after the 1911 Insurance Act initiated state intervention in health care. The promotion of private medicine will lead to the amplification of all these complementary problems.

This does not make a case for an anti-professional attitude to health care. There is no doubt that medical professionalism as it now stands is important to medical care, and relevant to the future. The nature of personal contacts between health workers (not just doctors) and people consulting them is crucial to the maintenance of health and the management of illness. Some system of decision-making involving those with practical experience is essential, but the balance of clinical, planning, service and consumer views and skills is not going to be found in the present combination of professionals and businessmen[12] on health authorities. An alternative view of medicine – as an applied social science dealing with definable problems within a whole population – exists within much of the activity of the NHS, amongst planners and managers as much as amongst doctors, but it has not yet evolved its own ethic or its own political institutions. The powerful conservative wing of the medical profession will do much to prevent such evolution, for 'liberal professionalism', itself a special form of conservative 'freedom', is the jewel in medicine's crown.

Private medicine, if it is to grow further will need opportunities to expand and justifications for doing so. The successive waves of cuts and cash-limits applied to NHS spending by both Labour and Conservative governments have meant a reduction in services, facilities and staff, and compensatory attempts to increase efficiency and 'productivity' by demanding more of staff and patients alike. The extension of waiting lists for surgery, and waiting times for out-patient appointments, plus the limitations on time for communication and explanation of problems and solutions, are propaganda for the private sector, which can step in and offer its own solutions at a price. As the economic decline proceeds and problems of housing, transport and employment increase, we can expect an increase in the incidence of major physical and mental disorders and a consequent increase in the demands made on health services. There is some evidence that the level of employment has a *direct* effect on patterns of heart disease, overall death rates, admissions to mental hospitals, infant mortality and suicide rates.[13] And there is little doubt that unemployment and housing difficulties are major contributors to serious and widespread psychological disturbance.[14][15]

Of course the population that bears the full burden of the crisis will not be in much of a position to take up private medical services, for low income will be one of its major problems. Any expansion of the private sector will come because the increasing demand on the NHS will preoccupy the service, particularly as cuts in expenditure reduce the service capacity to respond to demand. The pressure on staff will increase, and the temptations of opting out of the NHS and into the private sector (already noticeable amongst nurses working part-time) will grow. The deterioration in standards and speed of care will also act as an incentive for those not hit hard by the economic crisis to seek alternative forms of health care. In the cities, where health services are costly to run and subject to pruning, hospital closures will deprive local populations of small, nearby (if outdated) District General Hospitals and concentrate facilities on larger, often Teaching, Hospitals.[16] As a result both buildings and staff previously available to the NHS will come onto the market. Over a period of time the private sector may obtain a larger potential clientele,[17] trained staff of all categories, and even ready-made facilities.[18]

The full impact of the budget restrictions in the NHS hit the headlines in September 1982, when Oxford Regional Health Authority officials launched a public consultation document that described their Region's financial problems and the difficult choices the Health Authority had to face. The document, produced in the middle of the Tory Party conference, was partly designed for its embarrassing effect, but it reflected the problems of the Region with the best track-record for planning and the efficient use of resources. Oxford's long-term plan, aimed at improving and expanding priority services over a twenty year period, had to be abandoned because of budget limits. Worse, to stay within its projected budget, the RHA would need to cut back on existing services as well as on planned ones, and the cuts would have to be massive. Amongst the options discussed were maximum use of day-care surgery (instead of in-patient care), the transfer of non-urgent surgery and family planning services to the private sector, and the imposition of 'residence qualifications' (of unspecified time) within the Region before free NHS care could be obtained. Even allowing for deliberate exaggeration in the Oxford document, the Region's financial difficulties clearly favour the growth of the private sector in the four counties covered by the Regional Health Authority.

The role of market forces in determining the development of health care is already well-established in Britain outside the private medicine field. The pharmaceutical industries have an influence over medical practice that distorts medicine by blatantly presenting chemical 'solutions' to social problems, encourages over-prescribing and multiple prescribing with the attendant risks of potentially dangerous drug combinations, and divert finance from other areas of health care.[19] [20] Massive advertising campaigns directed at doctors who insist that they know exactly what they are doing ('clinical freedom'), despite evidence to the contrary, set patterns of drug use in the population that are as much a reflection of profit needs of a monopoly industry as they are of the medical needs of the ill. Postgraduate education of doctors, particularly general practitioners, is heavily dependent on the drug companies, through their visiting representatives, while their advertising revenue keeps medical journals going, and major subsidies are given for conferences and meetings. This cooperation between the profession and one facet of monopoly capitalism, despite the evident disadvantages of it to the population and the health service, is a warning that a similar relationship — between doctors and large private medical corporations — would have a precedent.

Conservative Tactics and Strategy

Thatcher's Cabinet does not have one single tactical line for shifting medical care back into the market. On the contrary, it has three tactics that may be pursued in isolation or independently, according to circumstances. The first tactic is to aim for minimal change by encouraging individual consultants to undertake private practice inside the NHS and letting the private insurance schemes look after themselves without too much assistance from the government. The second tactic leads to the creation of two health services, one public and one private, working in parallel and in conjunction and finding their own balance of influence and responsibility for provision of care. The third tactic aims for maximum change — replacement of the National Health Service with an insurance-based system like those operating in the USA or in parts of West Europe.

The tactic of minimum change has almost been achieved already, with the abolition of the Health Services Board that phased out pay beds under Labour, and the suggestion that a limited re-investment of paybeds was possible in certain areas.[21] Consultant contracts have been revised to permit all consultants in the NHS to undertake private practice, not just those consultants with part-time contracts as now. The general character of this Government's commitment to restructuring the whole of society and removing the features of socialism introduced by Labour governments suggest that they will want more than the first tactic can give. Nor will the medical insurance schemes happily abandon their chances of supported growth, as they made clear in talking of the need to 're-educate' Conservative politicians about private medicine in an internal discussion document leaked by the Communist Party in 1979.[22]

The tactic of maximum change is a big step, even for the radical right, for it could antagonise many Conservative voters aware of the NHS's value and fearful of the financial implications of private care *imposed* upon them rather than chosen. It would also embroil the Government in conflicts with the million strong workforce of the NHS whose jobs could be threatened by such an enormous change in health care, including the medical lobby that wants to keep private medicine under its control, inside the NHS. Finally, it would mean the creation of a service that would probably be more bureaucratic and more expensive (or rather, less cost effective) than the public service. Worse still, it would demand direct government subsidy, since a proportion of the population would not be able to afford medical insurance, either through poverty or through disability that was uninsurable. This group of people would need some kind of provision, however shoddy, and the cost of that would have to be borne primarily by government (although charities could be recruited to obtain some of the revenue). The most important point about medical insurance systems is that they *must* exclude a proportion of the population; an insurance system that included everybody would just be a form of specially-earmarked tax on income, and new (and cumbersome) forms of taxation are not a part of the Government's plans.[23] [24] To adopt an insurance system, therefore, would mean that the Conservatives were prepared for a short-term political conflict and in the long-term were prepared to accept the social and economic consequences of excluding a section of the population from health care. The Cabinet has always been aware that such an approach would produce the kinds of problems now experienced in the American health system, but nevertheless prompted a DHSS feasibility study of insurance-based health care. This study, although completed, has not been made public, probably because it spelt-out uncomfortable home truths about the economic efficiency of the NHS compared with insurance-based health services. Instrumental in the suppression of plans to convert to an insurance-based service was the BMA's own rejection of the idea, in a policy document produced in 1981. The subject has become so embarrassing to the Thatcher government that when far right 'Think Tank' proposals for conversion to insurance funding resurfaced at the 1982 Tory Party conference they had to be sternly dismissed by Cabinet Ministers and Thatcher herself.

The tactic of parallel health services is the Government's tactic of choice. It runs contrary to Conservative thinking in some senses, for it implies a long-term subsidy from the public sector to the private sector (which can only provide a marginal service from its own resources, to the eternal shame of the advocates of private enterprise). Equally, Government boasts about direct, honest and fearless policies could not be applied to an approach that is piecemeal, pragmatic and sometimes covert. Such objections are unlikely to worry the Cabinet, however, when the prize is Labour's jewel.

The mechanics of this are three-fold. Firstly, the cuts in expenditure and the imposition of cash limits on health authorities that were begun by Labour governments are being continued, and intensified, to force a 'rationalisation' of health services. As outlined above this will have consequences for the extent and quality of medical care that in turn will tip the balance in favour of private services, both from the point of view of the consumer and the service workers. Secondly, the structure of the NHS has been reorganised to push responsibility for provision of services away from central authorities (like the DHSS and planners and administrators at Regional and Area level) towards the 'grass roots'. Management methods are also being reorganised so that personal accountability of administrators can replace the collective responsibility of the present complex committee structure.

These structural reforms, presented in a consultation document called *Patients First*, and enacted in April 1982, will have dramatic effects on the NHS. The decentralisation of responsibility is dressed up as being democratic, yet is the opposite. The proposed new District Health Authorities have fewer representatives from local government (or any other lay source), and fewer non-professional staff representatives than the previous Area Health Authorities. They probably have more medical representatives, however, reversing the trend towards displacement of medical influence that the 1974 reorganisation began. The new Authorities are based upon existing hospitals (themselves distributed in an unplanned way) and community-based services will be organised around them, threatening the intended community orientation of health service growth that has been aimed for over the last decade. The very title *Patients First* expresses a vision of health care as dealing with *patients* almost exclusively, and not with *people* seeking to maintain health. This vision is essentially a doctor's vision of disease, and the idea of shifting influence further back towards the medical profession and concentrating it on hospitals confirms the one-sidedness of Conservative thinking about health care. Even the new management proposals contribute to this narrowing of NHS functions, for consensus management based on consultation with staff (however inadequate in method and uninspiring in practice) is more democratic than the command structure of the old Hospital Management Boards and Hospital Secretaries that the Conservatives seek to recreate under new names. Planning future development is going to become the responsibility of administrators primarily concerned with day-to-day organisation and increasingly influenced by the reinforced medical voices on the management committees.

The role of the medical profession in controlling health services will become increasingly important. This is the overall objective for the Government precisely because the medical profession has a complex and traditional relationship with private medicine in particular and monopoly capitalism in general. As a supplementary objective the Government is intervening in industrial relations with new provision for dealing with disputes in the NHS. These provisions include organisation of voluntary labour and use of outside services (catering, laundry and laboratory facilities) if NHS services are disrupted by industrial action.[26]

The Government's perspective for change was outlined in a letter from Health Minister Gerard Vaughan to the Secretary of the British Medical Association in July 1979. The letter described the cooperative growth of private and public hospital facilities at a local level, listing a number of practical steps that could be taken:

1. Advance notification of all significant private hospital development plans should be made to the relevant NHS Health Authority.

2. Local consultation between Health Authorities and private medical interests to ensure orderly and effective development of health services. Disagreements would be settled by the Secretary of State for Health and Social Services.

3. Increased use of contractual arrangements (working in both directions) for the joint provision of services, sharing of some staff, collaboration in research and in staff training.

The letter pointed out that most of these suggestions could be implemented without legislative provision, but that extra powers would be needed to permit private hospitals to provide services for the NHS and to take part in collaborative projects. Enabling legislation that gives such powers now exists under the Health Services Act.

The end result of such changes will depend upon future expenditure on public health services. If the erosion of the NHS is halted and increased funding provided, a parallel structure of private services would lose its opportunities for growth and face genuine competition. On past evidence it would not be able to compete and would maintain its marginal position, but would achieve the minimum option described above. If, on the other hand, public expenditure on health is further reduced, and the demand for private medicine increases enough to warrant large-scale capital investment in new facilities, the private sector could grow in areas where substantial affluence persists despite the economic crisis. Under these circumstances the maximum option – largely insurance-based health care – may evolve in some parts of the country whilst public services predominate in others. At present the distribution of private medical practice is the same as the distribution of wealth, both socially and geographically, and we may see a phase in the development of health care when the South East has a different system of health service provision than, say, North East or North West England. The prospects of such growth clearly excite the medical insurance schemes. The Chief Executive of BUPA, Derek Dammerel, wrote an article in a medical newspaper that expressed this excitement directly:

In the Republic of Ireland they have an NHS, but quite deliberately in recent years have encouraged the growth of voluntary health insurance. When I say encouraged they have given tax concessions, subsidise those who go into private or semi-private beds and indeed, encourage a private facility to be built alongside the state system and to share in the expensive equipment in every way possible.[27]

The prospect of parallel health services, then, is an attractive one for the vested interests concerned. In the short term it will subsidise the private sector. And in the long term, it could provide the springboard for replacement of the National Health Service by an insurance-based system.

The Conservative victory over the NHS trades unions in 1982 may have tipped the balance in favour of the private sector, by weakening trades union resistance to privatization. The unprecedented unity of health workers in the 12% pay campaign seemed unbreakable, but Government ministers had to resist it if they were to demoralise and divide health service workers. New DHSS Circulars on privatisation of catering, laundry and cleaning services inside the NHS were rumoured to be ready for distribution during the health workers dispute, but were withheld because of the negative impact they would have for the Government. Once privatization had begun in these areas, redirection of clinical work to the private sector would face less trades union resistance from within the NHS.

The Left and the Politics of Health

At first glance the left and the labour movement generally have become increasingly concerned about political issues arising from health care over the last decade. The unionisation of health workers, the shift of professional organisations towards or even into the trade union movement, the disputes around pay beds, the resistance to the cuts, the development of a health students' movement, the appearance of agitational magazines and newspapers in hospitals and amongst unionists, the flurry of pamphlets and books, all of these suggest an intense interest and response to the politics of health. The impression is false, just as the measurement of an organisation's activity in terms of leaflets distributed or meetings held gives a false impression of its impact.

If we look at the results of this activity the picture (apart from improvements in wages and salaries) is not impressive:

1. Trade union involvement in management of health services has developed up to a point, but persistent conflicts with professional organisations plus lack of trained cadres prevent full penetration of trade unionists into the administration of a public industry with more than a million employees.

2. Community-based organisations concerned with health issues have arisen from outside the labour movement more often than not. Trades councils with health subcommittees are the exception, not the rule, and the whole range of single-issue voluntary organisations like MIND (mental health), the Spastics Society, Age Concern and so on are outside the influence of the labour movement. Community Health Councils have shown themselves to be effective organisers of resistance to cuts as well as careful assessors of the standards of service in many areas, but trade union input into them is patchy and the only political party that has shown serious interest in them is the Conservative Party — which wants them abolished. The happy exception to this pattern is the relationship between the labour movement and the campaigns to defend the 1967 Abortion Law.

3. The level of analysis of specific problems — like what to do with the pharmaceutical companies — is low, with Labour Party policy being caught (still) in mixed-economy ideas and partial reforms of price structure and advertising restrictions. Issues of management, administration and planning are outside the left's sphere of politics, and there is a general feeling (most marked on the far left) that issues like private practice and prescription charges are worth more attention than the more protracted struggle within the institutions of health care.

As a consequence the labour movement does not have a perspective for the development of health care, even though individuals within the movement do (or think they do). The slogan 'Defend and extend the NHS' fails because neither adequate defence nor practical extension are possible for a movement that has left all such complexities to 'experts' without watching carefully what they do, and interfering in their activity when necessary.

When the opportunity arose for Labour to counter-attack during the 1982 health workers pay campaign, it was missed. The dispute elicited enough trades union and general public support for it to have been turned into a political conflict rather than simply a wages struggle, had the Labour Party seized the chance. Instead the whole dispute was conducted in trades union terms, and inevitably the campaign faltered as Government intransigence bolstered Right wing opinion within the unions. Apart from initiating Parliamentary debates, Labour's leaders did little to mobilise opinion in defence of both the health workers and the Health Service.

Two Key Problems

If the labour movement is to stop the Conservatives achieving their goal of restructuring the NHS, two problems have to be dealt with. The first entails bringing the politics of health into the mainstream of labour movement activity, by using organisations like the Socialist Medical Association (SMA) and the Medical Practitioners Union (MPU) more as autonomous campaigning bodies and less as specialist adjuncts to the broader movement. The second requires the right issues to be selected and campaigned around, through appropriate forms of organisation. Both problems will be difficult to solve, given that in the post-war retreat of socialist ideas and organisations, the labour movement surrendered its weakest areas first. Health care was, and still is, one of those weak areas. Paradoxically the most significant creation of post-war social democracy is also its area of greatest ideological and organisational weakness. The effect of reformism has been to deny that the NHS is an area of class conflict, choosing instead to pose efficient administration against professional influence. The political significance of the medical profession, the nature of its 'professionalism', and the need to organise politically within it, have all been underestimated and neglected. Concern over policy issues has been presented as a special matter and taken out of the normal range of labour movement consideration. The political dominance of the right in the Labour Party has inflicted this on the movement as a whole, and a Communist Party pushed to the margins of politics has had little choice but to accept this.

The first problem is potentially soluble. Renewal of the Socialist Medical Association, reorganisation of its branches and a return to active campaigning within the labour movement, are all occurring. Whether the SMA can ultimately coordinate

NHS trade unionists, Constituency Labour Parties, Community Health Councils, trades councils and socialist and radical professionals remains to be seen. But given careful attention by the left there is no reason why it should not do so.

Taking the politics of the labour movement into the medical profession's structure is a more difficult problem. The Medical Practitioners Union is the only vehicle available to the movement, but receives insufficient priority within trade unionism and is short of resources. Given adequate support it could take a spectrum of labour movement policies into the organisations of the medical profession and engage the right on its own ground. To do that the MPU has to be free from a form of left sectarianism that is prevalent within the labour movement. The assessment of doctors as a group being 'the class enemy' means that organisations like the MPU are seen as havens for 'class traitors' from medicine who can be drawn towards the labour movement. There is no conception of mass organisations that could drive a wedge into the medical profession. Combating this approach requires conscious effort in trade unions and political parties from the top levels of leadership down to cadre level – the kind of effort where Communist Party initiatives may be decisive.

The problem of selecting priority issues in health care and campaigning around them is a lesser one for the labour movement. The wide range of single-issue and broad initiatives by small, local organisations gives scope for labour movement action, even though most of these campaigns have arisen outside the traditional working-class organisation. The prospect of winning new services or improving existing ones suggests that campaigns around community-based and preventative medical services should be pursued: in defence of existing child care clinics and screening programmes, and for their extension to areas lacking them; to establish well-woman clinics and day-care abortion units; and for experimental salaried general practitioner services in the cities. The pressure in favour of private medical insurance is so great that a labour movement' campaign against insurance schemes is imperative. In the first instance such a campaign must be aimed at the most vulnerable sections of the working population, to whom insurance schemes may appear attractive. In the longer term, the attack on private medicine needs projecting into the NHS structure (to minimise or undermine local relationships with private medicine) and the medical profession (to neutralise the Tory's major ally, if at all possible). Finally, the extension of trade union and community opinion into NHS administration at all levels is a high priority. Correction of the imbalance between professional interests on the one hand and non-professional and lay views on the other could tip the balance of power at local level, in favour of rational planning to meet local needs. Co-ordinated intervention in the day-to-day activity of the NHS by progressive professionals, trade unionists and community organisations could have an increasing impact on Health Authority functioning. Such intervention is feasible now in some areas where the component forces already exist (if only in embryo) in anti-cut campaigns and health-service sub-committees of trades councils, and could be extended to other, mainly industrial, areas where organisation has a strong basis.

If this counter-attack can be launched, it could halt Conservative plans to dismantle the NHS, if only by drawing-out the political conflicts that the Government already fears could be unduly prolonged. Could a stalemate over health service reform throw wider policy issues into question, and blunt the Tory ideological offensive? And could a socialist renewal, even if a decade or more distant, spring from the campaigns to preserve the National Health Service? How ironic it would be if the left found the spearhead of anti-Conservatism through the hesitations and reservations of an otherwise strident Government, and not through its own 'scientific' analyses!

[1] Jenkin's interview with the magazine *Director*, 1980.

[2] Vaughan's letter to the BMA, July 1979.

[3] Royal Commission on the NHS Report, pp125-126.

[4] There are some financial barriers to consultation where consultation almost invariably leads to treatment – chiropody and dentistry are examples. The Government intended to introduce charges for eye testing despite the opposition of the opticians, but was forced by strong pressure to remove this proposal from the Health Services Bill.

[5] The major organisations are British United Provident Association (BUPA), with 73% of the privately insured, and Private Patients Plan (PPP) which has 24%. Nine other small schemes cover the remainder. A detailed

account of how the insurance schemes work can be found in *In Defence of the NHS*, Radical Statistics Pamphlet, pp.21-2.

[6] An example is renal dialysis; facilities are currently insufficient to meet need, but technically need can be met.

[7] B. Abel Smith, *Value for money in health services,* 1976.

[8] *Observer*, 8 July, 1979.

[9] Taking the GP population as a whole; some are very involved in private medicine, particularly in inner London.

[10] Ilman, *General Practitioner*, 15 December 1978.

[11] J. Tudor Hart, 'Inverse Care Law', *Lancet*, 1971.

[12] J. Robson, 'NHS Inc?', *International Journal of Health Services*, 1974.

[13] Harvey Brenner, 'Mortality and the National Economy, *Lancet*, 1979, pp.568-73.

[14] Len Fagin, 'The psychology of unemployment', *Medicine in Society*, Vol 3, No 1, 1978.

[15] G. Brown and T. Harris, *The Social Origins of Depression*, Tavistock, 1979.

[16] J. Yudkin, *British Medical Journal*, Vol.2, p.1212, 1978.

[17] BUPA estimates 8 million potential subscribers and actually has about 2 million.

[18] Witness the proposals to save London's Elizabeth Garrett Anderson Hospital for Women through private involvement.

[19] *The Pharmaceutical Industry: a discussion document for the labour movement,* Labour Party, 1976.

[20] J. Robson, *Take a Pill: the drug industry private or public,* Communist Party pamphlet, 1974.

[21] See note 2.

[22] 'Private medical insurance in a changing political environment', *Medicine in Society*, Vol.4, No.4, 1979.

[23] See note 7.

[24] P. Torrins, *Lancet,* 5 January 1980.

[25] *Hansard,* 23 January 1980.

[26] DHSS Circular, December 1979, HC (79) 20.

[27] *Pulse*, 27 January 1979.

III   The Falklands Factor

Eric Hobsbawm

Falklands Fallout

More has been talked about the Falklands than about any other recent issue in British and international politics and more people lost their bearings on this issue than almost any other. I don't mean the great bulk of the people, whose reactions were probably considerably less passionate or hysterical than those whose business it is to write, and formulate opinions.

I want to say very little indeed about the origins of the Falklands war because that war actually had very little to do with the Falklands. Hardly anybody knew about the Falklands. The number of people in this country who had any personal relations with the Falklands or even knew anybody who had been there, is minimal.

The 1800 natives of these Islands were very nearly the only people who took an urgent interest in the Falklands, apart of course from the Falkland Islands Company, which owns a good deal of it, ornithologists and the Scott Polar Research Institute, since the islands are the basis of all the research activities in the Antarctic. They were never very important, or at least they haven't been since World War I or perhaps just the beginning of World War II.

They were so insignificant and so much out of the centre of interest, that Parliament let the running be made by about a dozen MPs, the Falklands lobby, which was politically a very, very mixed lot. They were allowed to stymie all the not very urgent efforts of the Foreign Office to settle the problem of the islands' future. Since the government and everybody else found the Falklands totally without interest, the fact that they were of urgent interest in Argentina, and to some extent in Latin America as a whole was overlooked. They were indeed far from insignificant to the Argentines. They were a symbol of Argentine nationalism, especially since Peron. We could put the Falklands problem off for ever, or we thought we could, but not the Argentinians.

I am not judging the validity of the Argentine claim. Like so many nationalist claims it cannot bear much investigation. Essentially it is based on what you might call 'secondary school geography' – anything that belongs to the continental shelf ought to belong to the nearest country – in spite of the fact that no Argentines had ever actually lived there. Nevertheless we are bound to say that the Argentine claim is almost certainly rather stronger than the British claim and has internationally been regarded as rather stronger. The Americans for instance never accepted the British claim, whose official justification changed from time to time. But the point is not to decide which claim is stronger. The point is that, for the British government, the Falklands were about as low as they could be on its list of priorities. And it was totally ignorant of Argentine and Latin American views, which are not merely those of the junta but of all Latin America.

As a result it managed, by withdrawing the one armed ship, *The Endurance*, which had always been there symbolically indicating that the Falklands could not be taken over, to suggest to the Argentinian junta that the UK would not resist. The Argentine generals, who were patently crazy and inefficient as well as nasty, decided to go ahead with the invasion. But for mismanagement by the UK government, the Argentine government would pretty certainly not have decided to invade. They miscalculated and they should never have invaded but it is perfectly clear that the British government actually precipitated the situation, even though it did not mean to. And so, on 3 April 1982 the British people discovered that the Falklands had been invaded and occupied. The Government should have known that an invasion was imminent, but claimed it didn't, or at any rate if it did know it took no action. This, of course, is the subject of the Franks Commission's report.

But what was the situation in Britain when war broke out and during the war itself? Let me try and summarise it fairly briefly. The first thing that happened was an almost universal sense of outrage among a lot of people, the idea that you couldn't simply accept this, something had to be done. This was a sentiment which was felt at all levels right down to the grass roots and it was unpolitical in the sense that it went through all parties and was not confined to the right or to the left. I know of lots of people of the left within the movement, even on the extreme left, who had the same reaction as people on the right. It was this general sense of outrage and humiliation which was expressed on that first day in Parliament when the pressure for action actually came not from Thatcher and the Government, but from all sides, the ultra-right in the Conservative Party, the Liberals and Labour, with only the rarest of exceptions. This I think was a public sentiment which could actually be felt. Anybody who had any kind of sensitivity to political atmosphere knew that this was going on, and anyone on the left who was not aware of this grass roots feeling, and that it was not a creation of the media, at least, not at this stage, but genuinely a sense of outrage and humiliation, ought seriously to reconsider his or her capacity to assess politics. It may not be a particularly desirable sentiment, but to claim that it did not exist is quite unrealistic.

Now this upsurge of feeling had nothing to do with the Falklands as such. We have seen that the Falklands were simply a far-away territory swathed in mists off Cape Horn, about which we knew nothing and cared less. It has everything to do with the history of this country since 1945 and the visible acceleration of the crisis of British capitalism since the late 1960s and in particular the slump of the late 70s and early 80s. So long as the great international boom of Western capitalism persisted in the 50s and 60s even the relatively weak Britain was to some extent gently borne upwards by the current which pushed other capitalist economies forward even more rapidly. Things were clearly getting better and we did not have to worry too much although there was obviously a certain amount of nostalgia in the air.

And yet at a certain stage it became evident that the decline and crisis of the British economy were getting much more dramatic. The slump in the 70s intensified this feeling and of course since 1979 the real depression, the deindustrialisation of the Thatcher period and mass unemployment, have underlined the critical condition of Britain.

So the gut reaction that a lot of people felt at the news that Argentina had simply invaded and occupied a bit of British territory could have been put into the following words: 'Ours is a country which has been going downhill for decades, the foreigners have been getting richer and more advanced than we are, everybody's looking down on us and if anything pitying us, we can't even beat the Argentinians or anybody else at football any more, everything's going wrong in Britain, nobody really quite knows what to do about it and how to put it right. But now it's got to the point where some bunch of foreigners think they can simply march some troops onto British territory, occupy it and take it over, and they think the British are so far gone that nobody's going to do anything about it, nothing's going to be done. Well, this is the straw that breaks the camel's back, something's got to be done. By God we'll have to show them that we're not really just there to be walked over.' Once again, I'm not judging the validity of this point of view but I think this is roughly what a lot of the people who didn't try and formulate it in words felt at that moment.

Now in fact, we on the left had always predicted that Britain's loss of Empire, and general decline would lead to some dramatic reaction sooner or later in British politics. We had not envisaged this particular reaction but there is no question that this was a reaction to the decline of the British Empire such as we had predicted for so long. And that is why it had such very wide backing. In itself it was not simply jingoism. But, though this feeling of national humiliation went far beyond the range of simple jingoism, it was easily seized by the right and it was taken over in what I think was politically a very brilliant operation by Mrs Thatcher and the Thatcherites. Let me quote her in the classic statement of what she thought the Falklands war proved: 'When we started out there were the waverers and the faint-hearts, the people who thought we could no longer do the great things we once did, those who believed our decline was irreversible, that we could never again be what we were, that Britain was no longer the nation that had built an empire and ruled a quarter of the world. Well they were wrong.'

In fact the war was purely symbolic, it didn't prove anything of the kind. But here you see the combination of somebody catching a certain popular mood, and turning it in a right wing (I hesitate, but only just, to say a semi-fascist direction). That is why from the right wing point of view it was essential not simply to get the Argentinians out of the Falklands, which would have been perfectly practicable by a show of force plus negotiation, but to wage a dramatic victorious war. That is why the war was provoked by the British side whatever the Argentine attitude. There is little doubt that the Argentinians, as soon as they discovered that this was the British attitude, were looking for a way out of an intolerable situation. Thatcher was not prepared to let them because the whole object of the exercise was not to settle the matter now but to prove that Britain was still great, if only in a symbolic fashion. At virtually every stage the policy of the British government in and out of the United Nations was one of total intransigence. I am not saying that the junta made it easy to come to a settlement but I think historians will conclude that a negotiated withdrawal of the Argentinians was certainly not out of the question. It was not seriously tried.

This provocative policy had a double advantage. Internationally, it gave Britain a chance to demonstrate her hardware, her determination and her military power. Domestically, it allowed the Thatcherites to seize the initiative from other political forces within and outside the Conservative Party. It enabled a sort of take-over by the Thatcherites not only of the Conservative camp but of a great area of British politics. In a curious way the nearest parallel to the Thatcherite policy during the Falklands war is the Peronist policy which, on the other side, had first launched the Falklands into the centre of Argentine politics. Peron, like Mrs Thatcher and her little group, tried to speak directly to the masses using the mass media, over the heads of the establishment. In our case that included the Conservative establishment as well as the Opposition. She insisted on running her own war. It was not a war run by Parliament. It was not even run by the Cabinet; it was a war conducted by Mrs Thatcher and a small War Cabinet, including the chairman of the Conservative Party. At the same time she established direct lateral relations, which I hope will not have long term political effects, with the military. And it is this combination of a direct demagogic approach to the masses, by-passing the political processes and the establishment, and the forging of direct lateral contact with the military and the defence bureaucracy, that is characteristic of the war.

Neither costs nor objectives counted, least of all of course the Falklands, except as symbolic proof of British virility, something which could be put into headlines. This was the kind of war which existed in order to produce victory parades. That is why all the symbolically powerful resources of war and Empire were mobilised on a miniature scale. The role of the navy was paramount anyway, but traditionally public opinion has invested a lot of emotional capital in it. The forces sent to the Falklands were a mini-museum of everything which could give the Union Jack particular resonance – the Guards, the new technological strong men, the SAS, the paras; all were represented down to those little old Gurkhas. They weren't necessarily needed but you had to have them just because this was, as it were, a recreation of something like the old Imperial durbars, or the procession at the death or coronation of British sovereigns.

We cannot in this instance quote Karl Marx's famous phrase about history repeating itself, the first time as tragedy, the second time as farce, because no war is a farce. Even a little war in which 250 Britons and 2,000 Argentinians get killed is not a matter for jokes. But for foreigners who did not realise the crucial role of the Falklands war in British *domestic* politics, the war certainly seemed an absolutely incomprehensible exercise. *Le Monde* in France called it a Clochemerle of the South Atlantic. You may remember that famous novel in which the right and the left in a small French town come to enormous blows over the question of where to situate a public convenience. Most Europeans simply could not understand what all the fuss was about. What they did not appreciate was that the whole thing was not about the Falklands at all and not about the right of self-determination. It was an operation concerned basically with British politics and with the British political mood.

Having said that let me just say very firmly that the alternative was not between doing nothing and Thatcher's war. I think it was politically absolutely impossible at this stage for any British government not to do anything. The alternatives were not simply to accept the Argentine occupation by passing the buck to the United Nations, which would have adopted empty resolutions, or on the other hand, Mrs Thatcher's intended replay of Kitchener's victory over the Sudanese at Omdurman. The pacifist line was that of a small and isolated minority, if indeed a minority with a respectable tradition in the labour movement. That line was simply politically not on. The very feebleness of the demonstrations which were being organised at the time showed this. The people who said the war was pointless, and should never have been started, have been proved right in the abstract, but they themselves have not benefited politically and aren't likely to benefit from having been proved right.

The next point to note is more positive. Thatcher's capture of the war with the aid of the *Sun* produced a profound split in public opinion, but not a political split along party lines. Broadly it divided the 80% who were swept by a sort of instinctive patriotic reaction and who therefore identified with the war effort, though probably not in as strident a manner as the *Sun* headlines, from the minority which recognised that, in terms of the actual global politics concerned, what Thatcher was doing made no sense at all. That minority included people of all parties and none, and many who were not against sending a Task Force as such. I hesitate to say that it was a split of the educated against the uneducated; although it is a fact that the major hold-outs against Thatcherism were to be found in the quality press, plus of course the *Morning Star*. The *Financial Times*, the *Guardian* and the *Observer* maintained a steady note of scepticism about the whole business. I think it is safe to say that almost every single political correspondent in the country, and that goes from the Tory ones right down to the left, thought the whole thing was loony. Those were the 'faint-hearts' against whom Mrs Thatcher railed. The fact that there was a certain polarisation but that the opposition, though it remained quite a small minority, was not weakened, even in the course of a brief and, in technical terms, brilliantly successful war, is significant.

Nevertheless, the war was won, fortunately for Mrs Thatcher very quickly and at a modest cost in British lives, and with it came an immediate and vast pay-off in popularity. The grip of Thatcher and the Thatcherites, of the ultra-right, on the Tory Party unquestionably increased enormously as a consequence. Mrs Thatcher in the meantime was on cloud nine and imagined herself as a reincarnation of the Duke of Wellington, but without that Irish realism which the Iron Duke never lost, and of Winston Churchill but without the cigars and, at least one hopes, without the brandy.

Now let me deal with the effects of the war. I shall here only mention briefly the short term effects, that is between now and the general election. The first of these is likely to concern the debate on whose fault it is. The Franks Commission has inquired into this, and produced a report which fails to lay the blame at Thatcher's door. The second issue is the cost of the operation and the subsequent and continuing expense of maintaining the British presence in the Falklands. The official statement is that it is going to be about £700 millions so far, but my own guess is that it almost certainly will run into thousands of millions. Accountancy is, as is well known, a form of creative writing, so exactly how you calculate the cost of a particular operation of this kind is optional, but whatever it is, it will turn out to be very, very, expensive. Certainly the left will press this issue and they ought to. However, unfortunately, the sums are so large as to be meaningless to most people. So while the figures will go on being much quoted in political debate, I suspect this issue will not be very prominent or politically very effective.

The third issue is the bearing of the Falklands on British war policy, or defence policy as everybody now likes to call it. The Falklands war will certainly intensify the savage internal warfare among admirals, air marshals, generals and the Ministry of Defence which has already led to one post-Falklands casualty, the Minister of Defence himself, Nott. There is very little doubt that the admirals used the Falklands affair to prove that a large navy, capable of operating right across the globe, was absolutely essential to Great Britain – whereas everybody else knows that we cannot afford it and that it just is not worth keeping a navy of that size in order to be able to supply Port Stanley. These discussions will certainly raise the question of whether Britain can afford both a global navy and Trident missiles, and what exactly the role and importance of independent British nuclear weapons is. So to this extent, they can play in the development of the campaign for nuclear disarmament a part which should not be underestimated.

Next, the future of the Falkland Islands themselves. This, once again, is likely to be of little general interest since the islands will cease to be of any serious interest to most Britons again. But it will be an enormous headache for civil servants, for the Foreign Office and for anybody else involved because we have no policy for the future. It wasn't the object of the war to solve the problem of the Falkland Islands. We are simply back to square one, or rather back to square minus one, and something will sooner or later have to be done to find a permanent solution for this problem unless British governments are simply content to keep an enormously expensive commitment going for ever, for no good purpose whatever, way down there by the South Pole.

Finally, let me deal with the more serious question of the long term effects. The war demonstrated the strength and the political potential of patriotism, in this case in its jingo form. This should not perhaps surprise us, but marxists haven't found it easy to come to terms with working class patriotism in general and English or British patriotism in particular. British here means where the patriotism of the non-English peoples happens to coincide with that of the English; where it doesn't coincide, as is sometimes the case in Scotland and Wales, marxists have been more aware of the importance of nationalist or patriotic sentiment. Incidentally, I suspect that while the Scots felt rather British over the Falklands, the Welsh did not. The only parliamentary party which, as a party, opposed the war from the start was Plaid Cymru and of course, as far as the Welsh are concerned, 'our lads' and 'our kith and kin' are not in the Falklands, but in Argentina. They are the Patagonian Welsh who send a delegation every year to the National Eisteddfodd in order to demonstrate that you can still live at the other end of the globe and be Welsh. So as far as the Welsh are concerned the reaction, the Thatcherite appeal on the Falklands, the 'kith and kin' argument, probably fell by the wayside.

Now there are various reasons why the left and particularly the marxist left has not really liked to come to terms with the question of patriotism in this country. There is a particular historical conception of internationalism which tends to exclude national patriotism. We should also bear in mind the strength of the liberal-radical, anti-war and pacifist tradition which is very strong, and which certainly has passed to some extent into the labour movement. Hence there is a feeling that patriotism somehow conflicts with class consciousness, as indeed it frequently does, and that the ruling and hegemonic classes have an enormous advantage in mobilising it for their purposes, which is also true.

Perhaps there is also the fact that some of the most dramatic and decisive advances of the left in this century were achieved in the fight against World War I, and they were achieved by a working class shaking off the hold of patriotism and jingoism and deciding to opt for class struggle; to follow Lenin by turning their hostility against their own oppressors rather than against foreign countries. After all, what had wrecked the Socialist International in 1914 was precisely the workers failing to do this. What, in a sense, restored the soul of the international labour movement was that after 1917, all over the belligerent countries the workers united to fight against the war, for peace and for the Russian Revolution.

These are some of the reasons why Marxists perhaps failed to pay adequate attention to the problem of patriotism. So let me just emphasise that patriotism cannot be neglected. The British working class has a long tradition of patriotism which was not always considered incompatible with a strong and militant class consciousness. In the history of Chartism and the great radical movements in the early 19th century we tend to stress the class consciousness. But when in the 1860s one of the few British workers actually to write about the working class, Thomas Wright the 'journeyman engineer', wrote a guide to the British working class for middle class readers, because some of these workers were about to be given the vote, he gave an interesting thumbnail sketch of the various generations of workers he had known as a skilled engineer.

When he came to the Chartist generation, the people who had been born in the early 19th century, he noted that they hated anything to do with the upper classes, and would not trust them an inch. They refused to have anything to do with what we would call the class enemy. At the same time he observed that they were strongly patriotic, strongly anti-foreign and particularly anti-French. They were people who had been brought up in their childhood in the anti-Napoleonic wars. Historians tend to stress the Jacobin element in British labour during these wars and not the anti-French element which also had popular roots. I am simply saying you cannot write patriotism out of the scenario even in the most radical period of the English working class.

Throughout the 19th century there was a very general admiration for the navy as a popular institution, much more so than the army. You can still see it in all the public houses named after Lord Nelson, a genuinely popular figure. The navy and our sailors were things that Britons, and certainly English people, took pride in. Incidentally, a good deal of 19th century radicalism was built on an appeal not just to workers and other civilians but to soldiers. *Reynolds News* and the old radical papers of those days were much read by the troops because they systematically took up the discontents of the professional soldiers. I do not know when this stopped, although in the Second World War the *Daily Mirror* succeeded in getting a vast circulation in the army for precisely the same reason. Both the Jacobin tradition and the majority anti-French tradition are thus part of English working class history though labour historians have stressed the one and played down the other.

Again, at the beginning of World War I the mass patriotism of the working class was absolutely genuine. It was not something that was simply being manufactured by the media. It did not exclude respect for the minority within the labour movement who failed to share it. The anti-war elements and the pacifists within the labour movement were not ostracised by the organised workers. In this respect there was a great difference between the attitude of workers and of the petty bourgeois jingoists. Nevertheless, the fact remains that the largest single volunteer mass recruitment into any army ever, was that of British workers who joined up in 1914-1915. The mines would have been empty but for the fact that the government eventually recognised that if it did not have some miners in the mines it would not have any coal. After a couple of years many workers changed their mind about the war, but the initial surge of patriotism is something we have to remember. I am not justifying these things, simply pointing to their existence and indicating that in looking at the history of the British working class and the present reality, we must come to terms with these facts, whether we like them or not.

The dangers of this patriotism always were and still are obvious, not least because it was and is enormously vulnerable to ruling class jingoism, to anti-foreign nationalism, and of course in our days to racism. These dangers are particularly great where patriotism can be separated from the other sentiments and aspirations of the working class, or even where it can be counter-posed to them: where nationalism can be counterposed to social liberation. The reason why nobody pays much attention to the, let's call it, jingoism of the Chartists, is that it was combined with and masked by an enormous militant class consciousness. It is when the two are separated, and they can be easily separated, that the dangers are particularly obvious. Conversely, when the two go together in harness, they multiply not only the force of the working class but its capacity to place itself at the head of a broad coalition for social change and they even give it the possiblity of wresting hegemony from the class enemy.

That was why in the anti-fascist period of the 30s, the Communist International launched the call to wrest away national traditions from the bourgeoisie, to capture the national flag so long waved by the right. So the French left tried to conquer, capture or recapture both the tricolour and Joan of Arc and to some extent it succeeded.

In this country, we did not pursue quite the same object, but we succeeded in doing something more important. As the anti-fascist war showed quite dramatically, the combination of patriotism in a genuine people's war proved to be politically radicalising to an unprecedented degree. At the moment of his greatest triumph, Mrs Thatcher's ancestor, Winston Churchill, the unquestioned leader of a victorious war, and a much greater victorious war than the Falklands, found himself, to his enormous surprise, pushed aside because the people who had fought that war, and fought it patriotically, found themselves radicalised by it. And the combination of a radicalised working class movement and a peoples' movement behind it proved enormously effective and powerful. Michael Foot may be blamed for thinking too much in terms of 'Churchillian' memories – 1940, Britain standing alone, anti-fascist war and all the rest of it and obviously these echoes were there in Labour's reaction to the Falklands. But let us not forget that our 'Churchillian' memories are not just of patriotic glory – but of victory against reaction both abroad and at home: of Labour triumph and the defeat of Churchill. It's difficult to conceive this in the 1980s, but it is something we must remember. It is dangerous to leave patriotism exclusively to the right.

At present it is very difficult for the left to recapture patriotism. One of the most sinister lessons of the Falklands is the ease with which the Thatcherites captured the patriotic upsurge which initially was in no sense confined to political Conservatives, let alone to Thatcherite ones. We recall the ease with which non-jingos could be tagged, if not actually as anti-patriotic, then at least as 'soft on the Argies'; the ease with which the Union Jack could be mobilised against domestic enemies as well as foreign enemies. Remember the photograph of the soldiers coming back on the troopships, with a banner saying 'Call off the rail strike or we'll call an air strike'. Here lies the long term significance of the Falklands in British political affairs.

It is a sign of very great danger. Jingoism today is particularly strong because it acts as a sort of compensation for the feelings of decline, demoralisation and inferiority, which most people in this country feel, including a lot of workers. This feeling is intensified by economic crisis. Symbolically jingoism helps people feel that Britain is not foundering, that it can still do and achieve something, can be taken seriously, can, as they say, be 'Great' Britain. It is symbolic because in fact Thatcherite jingoism hasn't achieved anything practical, and can't achieve anything practical. *Rule Britannia* has once again, and I think for the first time since 1914, become something like a national anthem. It would be worth studying one day why, until the Falklands period, *Rule Britannia* had become a piece of musical archaeology and why it has ceased to be so. At the very moment when Britain patently no longer rules either the waves or an empire, that song has resurfaced and has undoubtedly hit a certain nerve among people who sing it. It is not just because we have won a little war involving few casualties, fought far away against foreigners whom we can no longer even beat at football, and this has cheered people up, as if we had won a World Cup with guns. But has it done anything else in the long run? It is difficult to see that it has, or could have, achieved anything else.

Yet there is a danger. As a boy I lived some formative and very young years in the Weimar Republic, among another people who felt themselves defeated, losing their old certainties and their old moorings, relegated in the international league, pitied by foreigners. Add depression and mass unemployment to that and what you got then was Hitler. Now we shan't get fascism of the old kind. But the danger of a populist, radical right moving even further to the right is patent. That danger is particularly great because the left is today divided and demoralised and above all because vast masses of the British, or anyway the English, have lost hope and confidence in the political processes and in the politicians: any politicians. Mrs Thatcher's main trump card is that people say she isn't like a politician. In 1982 with 3,500,000 unemployed, 45% of the electors at Northfield, 65% of the electors at Peckham, did not bother to vote. In Peckham 41% of the electorate voted for Labour in 1974, 34% in 1979, and 19.1% in 1982. I am not talking of votes cast but of the total number of people in the constituency. In Northfield, which is in the middle of the devastation zone of the British motor industry, 41% voted for Labour in 1974, 32% in 1979 and 20% in 1982.

The main danger lies in this de-politicisation, which reflects a disillusionment with politics born of a sense of impotence. What we see today is not a substantial rise in the support for Thatcher and the Thatcherites. The Falklands episode may have temporarily made a lot of Britons feel better, though the 'Falklands factor' is almost certainly a diminishing asset for the Tories; but it has not made much difference to the basic hopelessness, apathy and defeatism of so many in this country, the feeling that we can't do much about our fate. If the government seems to hold its support better than might be expected, it is because people (quite mistakenly) don't put the blame for the present miserable condition of the country on Thatcher, but, more or less vaguely, on factors beyond her or any government's control. If Labour has not so far regained enough support – though it may still just do so – it is not only because of its internal divisions, but also, largely, because many workers do not really have much belief in any politicians' promises to overcome the slump and the long term crisis of the British economy. So why vote for one lot rather than another? Too many people are losing faith in politics, including their own power to do much about it.

But just suppose a saviour were to appear on a white horse? None is likely to, but just suppose someone were to appeal to the emotions, to get that adrenalin flowing by mobilising against some foreigners outside or inside the country, perhaps by another little war, which might, under present circumstances, find itself turning into a big war, which, as we all know, would be the last of the wars? It is possible. I don't think that saviour is going to be Thatcher, and to that extent I can end on a slightly up-beat note. Free enterprise, to which she is committed, is not a winner, as fascist propaganda recognised in the 1930s. You can't win by saying: 'Let the rich get richer and to hell with the poor.' In 1982 Thatcher's prospects were less good than Hitler's were; for three years after he had come to power there was not much unemployment left in Germany, whereas three years after Thatcher came to power unemployment was higher than ever before and likely to go on climbing. She was whistling in the dark. She could still be defeated. But patriotism and jingoism have been used once to change the political situation in her favour and can be used again. We must be on the look-out. Desperate governments of the right will try anything.

Robert Gray

The Falklands Factor

The Argentine occupation of the Falklands/Malvinas represents one of those historic moments when the capacity to respond to unexpected events can decisively strengthen or weaken political forces. In this case the effect was to strengthen the right, and specifically the Thatcherite right. Not only did this greatly improve Thatcher's chances of electoral success and a renewed mandate, it also threatened, and still threatens, to roll back the advances made by widespread popular demands for peace and disarmament, by exposing historic weaknesses and dilemmas in the left, and in the peace movement. Thatcher may thus have won some ground from what has perhaps been the most deeply and broadly based area of dissent from her government's policies.

This essay attempts to explore the wider implications of the Falklands adventure for British politics. I shall argue that these events represent a new application of Thatcher's distinct kind of politics, now in the arena of foreign affairs; the appeals of this initiative expose certain weaknesses of other forces – from Tory 'Wets' to the left and the peace movement – which might have resisted it. An effective fight-back requires the left to confront historically awkward issues, so as to redefine the national identities and loyalties which Thatcher has so powerfully mobilised. This is a challenging and daunting task, and one which the left has been reluctant to undertake, but until it is tackled the right will draw a strategic political advantage from its hegemonic definitions of 'national interest' and 'national unity'.

The Thatcherite Initiative

The aggressive military response to the Argentine occupation bears the marks of Thatcherism, extended to foreign affairs. Foreign and defence policy had notoriously been a preserve of Tory 'Wets' in the grand whig tradition, men whose patrician style always co-existed somewhat uneasily with the populist rhetoric of the new-style Tory right. Carrington, a noted exponent of the whig tradition, had argued in a lecture at the Royal Institute of International Affairs that Britain's diminished military strength made diplomacy more, not less vital for the preservation of British interests; a week or two later he resigned at the start of the Falklands crisis. Thatcher's bellicose policy seemed designed to make Carrington eat his eminently reasonable words.

Two features of this policy stand out. First, not only did the Government opt for a military response, but it also chose one of the more extreme possibilities. The task force was despatched, not with diplomatic pretexts about safeguarding lives and properties (the classic formula of gunboat diplomacy), but with declarations of intent to dislodge the Argentinians (even if only temporarily) by any means necessary: 'Failure is a word we do not use'. Most wars since 1945 have begun in a shamefaced way, with growing military entanglements kept secret from both world and domestic opinion; this war began with flags flying, drums beating and cameras rolling, and with the revival of a rhetoric which many people, especially on the left, too easily assumed to be dead. The course pursued may not be that different in content from what other political leaders might have done; but, as so often with Margaret Thatcher, the style and rhetoric were crucial to the political effect.

Second, the sheer audacity of this response, the speed with which events moved, and their relaying to the British public through carefully orchestrated media have muted opposition. Those elements of centre opinion, in all the parliamentary parties, which might have preferred a 'softly softly', if still basically military approach were consistently out-manoeuvred (talk of prolonged blockade, rather than all-out invasion was probably a piece of disinformation put out to keep these elements happy). The response of the parliamentary Labour leadership was despicable, to the point where the Labour party 'appears to be entirely in the train of Mrs Thatcher' (*Le Monde* 28 May 1982); the parliamentary left, with notable exceptions, was stunned, confused and divided. Both the leadership and some left MPs appear to have believed that the Falklands affair would turn into a debacle on which Labour could capitalise. This led to a 'wait and see' attitude, a dangerous political passivity which allowed Thatcher to retain the initiative (quite apart from the odious tendency to play party politics with people's lives). The Labour Party was thus unable to give a lead in opposition to the war. In this situation, the political clarity and mobilising capacity of the Communist Party, together with the courageous stand taken by Tony Benn, Judith Hart and others, made a crucial contribution to the emergence of an anti-war movement.

International pressures were also out-manoeuvred by the speed of events. Britain's allies, the USA and EEC countries, would undoubtedly have preferred some less extreme action, but were likewise stunned and, forced to choose, inevitably chose Britain. The US and the EEC may in the future exert important pressures for British restraint and a negotiated settlement, but they could not stop Thatcher's war.

Once the force was on its way, with support from the majority of the media and a bi-partisan parliamentary consensus, the whole grotesque enterprise took on a life of its own. The formation of a 'war cabinet' reinforced Thatcher's authority. Popular opinion was frightened, but also excited by the creation of a war atmosphere, and the tendency for the control of events to pass a purely military logic (for example, the way that the safety of the troops became a strong reason for getting them ashore as soon as possible, regardless of the progress or otherwise of diplomatic efforts). With the commitment of forces to combat, identification with the men became a compelling motive, even for people who had reservations about the initial despatch of the task force. The *Guardian* and the *Mirror* which, to their credit, had maintained a relatively balanced and critical attitude nevertheless carried reports from the battle-zone written in a stereotyped rhetoric familiar from every war this century (the assault troops waiting patiently, sipping cups of tea, etc). Perhaps most compelling of all were the photos of 'British' children welcoming liberating British soldiers. This atmosphere of national emergency and danger inevitably strengthened the authority of Government; opposition leaders have indicated that their criticisms of Government responsibility for the origins of the situation were merely postponed till after the crisis — by when criticism could well be too late and politically marginalised.

'Victory' and the long drawn out return of ships and men provided the occasion for a seemingly endless prolongation of media exposure. This was in many ways the ideal war – short, sharp, 'successful', directly involving small professional armed forces and their families, but consumed vicariously through press and TV – for cementing a reactionary chauvinist consensus. The bellicose atmosphere was quite quickly and directly projected against such domestic enemies as ASLEF. The euphoria will of course one day die down and the nagging question of 'what next?' will surface, given the apparent difficulty of a continued British presence in the face of an embittered Argentina, or of the cession by negotiation of what has been won with lives.

However it would be a mistake to underestimate the extent to which Thatcher (helped by the passivity of the official oppositions) gained the initiative on this issue, or to assume that the emergence of these problems will automatically discredit her. Even if Thatcher suffers subsequent defeats over the future of the Falklands, the whole issue may by then be quietly marginalised. Its political effect anyhow rests on the graitfying Palmerstonian spectacle of the British lion punishing a Latin despot, rather than on Thatcher's wilder visions of maritime imperial rebirth centred on the South Atlantic.

To say that Thatcher has won an important initiative is not therefore to say that the eventual outcome will be what she would favour. Nor does it imply that she has gained the near-unanimous support portrayed in the more sycophantic elements of the media – there has certainly been more dissent, some of it in unexpected quarters, than the media and parliamentary balance would suggest. But that dissent has been largely isolated and leaderless, in terms of mainstream electoral politics. Tail-ending behind Thatcher's war, the official opposition parties added to her glory, rather than gained any for themselves. Winning the political initiative is reflected in the demoralisation and division of opposing forces – something less tangible than numerical support, but nonetheless real.

Thatcherism and the New Nationalism

Thatcher's seizure of command in any case has consequences that extend beyond the conjunctural strenghtening or weakening of her position, or that of her party. We may be faced with a relatively permanent and organic shift in the political landscape. As is argued elsewhere in this volume, 'Thatcherism' constitutes a shift of this kind, to which the personal fate of Thatcher herself is relatively marginal; whatever happens to her, or the government she leads, she has already done her political work. That work may be characterised as the mobilisation of hitherto subterranean and politically incoherent currents of right-wing populism, in a way that is something of a new departure within the conservative political tradition, to build support for reactionary 'solutions' to Britain's chronic ecnomonic and social crisis. This has succeeded by drawing on popular experience and a pervasive sense of crisis and decline, and articulating them in reactionary decisions. The expression of this in foreign affairs had previously been confined to enthusiastic support for the new cold war and the new arms race, Britain's role as Reagan's best friend, and thumping the table at EEC negotiations. Now, the articulation of a distinctly British nationalism has been added to this.

Like the domestic formula of the 'free market and the strong state', this assertion has drawn on a sense of crisis related to Britain's long decline and articulated it in a reactionary, and very dangerous direction. One striking, and alarming feature of this has been the backward-looking, atavistic rhetoric, the motif of imperial nostalgia. At the crudest level, this appeals as a sign that Britain is still Great, that, despite change and decay we can still, when pushed, get it together. 'Thank God the most professional armed forces in the world are BRITISH', one poster seen in Portsmouth proclaimed (together with 'Britain does not appease dictators' and 'Congratulations to the Royal Navy'). Debate at the parliamentary level at times presented the grotesque spectacle of different protagonists all re-enacting some moment in the national past from which they draw comfort and hope, in a magic ritual to exorcise the facts of twentieth century life, an attempt to 'conjure up the spirits of the past to help them' (Marx, *Eighteenth Brumaire*). Thatcher dons the mask of Churchill or Lord Palmerston, while Foot appears to believe that the Falklands are part of the Sudetenland and that he is about to 'speak for England'.

It is easy enough to laugh at all this, to see it as a wave of hysteria aided by media manipulation. But it has powerful appeals, expressed in varied languages, not all of them as crude as the version propagated by the *Sun*; the resonances are not simply of Victorian 'gunboat diplomacy', but also of the popular experience and memory of the Second World War. Thatcherism benefited from the organisation of all these currents into more or less enthusiastic support for a war that Thatcher made her own.

Atavistic rhetoric makes sense of an experience of crisis, uneasy decline and lack of forward-looking political leadership. The national past, or a selectively mythologised version of it, is a source of identity and hope. Like all such rhetorics this is in reality the creation of something new, since the old cannot in its entirety be restored. The new factor is the clear assertion of distinctly 'British' interests and power in a post-imperial world dominated by the stalemate of the cold war and the 'nuclear balance'. A language of chauvinism that had seemed out of place in this world is thus given renewed credence.

One aspect of this is the re-definition of Britain's relations with the US. Conservative policies since the 1950s have sought to come to terms with the diminished position of British imperialism by asserting Britain's special role as the senior European ally in the Atlantic alliance, but at the same time as a world power with interests transcending the purely regional ones of the NATO pact. These pretensions have at times seemed hollow: at Suez, for instance, the refusal of American support made the British posture untenable. There has always been a residual anti-Americanism on the Tory right, relating to this and other grievances. Now the Suez debacle has been neatly reversed; it is the Americans who have been forced, after a singularly unconvincing attempt at 'mediation', to support British claims, at least for the crucial period of armed confrontation. This had demonstrated the value of the Atlantic alliance (and thus of British hospitality to existing and proposed US nuclear weapons), while at the same time asserting British independence and appealing to residual anti-Americanism of the right. In the same way, EEC sanctions have shown the value of an association that had been questioned, not just by the left but by a nationalist right. Britain, in short, is not just one more European country, but can call the tune for its allies on an issue of extra-regional interest. Apart from its short term effect in helping Thatcher to seize the initiative, this may have a longer term effect on national consciousness and the production of a new nationalism.

This poses dangers and challenges for the left. It can be a potent force in winning renewed support for the cold war and the arms race, as well as the re-assertion of a British imperial role. The Falklands war is likely to reinforce the ideology of war preparation and 'negotiation from strength'. While the failure of a nuclear strategy to protect the Falklands may demonstrate the incoherence of British military doctrines, this can be masked by less discriminating perceptions of the need for military strength. The spectacle of an actual war, and the atmosphere surrounding it, threatens to erode the widespread popular support for peace and disarmament, which has limited enthusiasm for the new cold war and the new arms race. Indeed it is tempting to see the Falklands operation as the real beginning of Nott's celebrated 'spring offensive' against CND.

The Response of the Left

The left may thus be faced, not just with the immediate aftermath of the war, but also with a more permanent shift in opinion. If Thatcherism has generated renewed support for itself on this issue this is partly because the left, for historical and ideological reasons, is ill equipped to respond to the crisis of national consciousness associated with imperial decline. The faltering growth of the organised opposition to the war, the chauvinist opportunism of the Labour front bench, and the confusion and division on the left are symptomatic of this. The ground lost will not be won by narrowly party political approaches, electoral calculation and parliamentary point-scoring, or passively waiting for the Tories' militarism to discredit itself. The left must address itself to transforming the 'common sense' views and assumptions of the British people, creating a new popular consensus around a progressive definition of British interests and policy options. Such a conception is vital in blocking the path to regressive definitions such as we are currently witnessing; it will also be vital in ensuring that a future left government does not become the prisoner of the military and diplomatic establishment.

The left has generally operated with a 'shopping list' of

demands, rather than with a coherent philosophy of Britain's place in the world to which specific demands can be organically related. Responses to events – which no shopping list, however long, can accommodate – have oscillated between an abstract internationalism and capitulation to chauvinist definitions of national interests. The rhetoric of the new Thatcherite nationalism has filled a vacuum. It has been powerful partly because it has addressed issues that the left has ignored (indeed the confusion of the Labour left is part of the price of this neglect). The long crisis of British imperialism is reflected, not simply in economic decline, but also in a crisis of national identity, of the re-definition of Britain's postion and role in the world. This crisis has presented the left with a historic opportunity to challenge the national leadership of the ruling class, but the left has been unable, for a number of reasons, to respond adequately. The space has been filled by spasmodic reassertions of Britain's power and world role, combined with policies of adaptation to the enhanced power of the US and the regional economic bloc represented by the EEC.

This vacuum in the thinking of the left has partly reflected historic difficulties and dilemmas. The long history of the British empire has also, as EP Thompson has pointed out (*Guardian*, 31 May 1982), been the history of large sections of the British people. The ruling class has been very successful – though this success has never been total, or without its contradictions – in organising a sense of national identity around its own political, and often military projects. Despite the long decline of British economic and military power, the establishment has never suffered a defeat of the kind that might discredit its claim to national leadership. It has been difficult, for historical reasons, to define a sense of national identity distanced from the chauvinism of a long imperial tradition. The concept of 'national interest', in both domestic and international affairs, has been the preserve of the right, or at any rate of a consensus stretching from the right of the Tory party to the centre of the Labour party. The left's characteristic response to this has been defensive and oppositional: the very idea of national identity or interest has been denounced as a reactionary illusion, rather than seen as an arena for political intervention and struggle. Yet, in Gramsci's words: 'It is in the concept of hegemony that those exigencies which are national in character are knotted together.'

It is not easy to unpick that knot, with all its nasty twists and all its sticky residues of a past not of our making; but until it is unpicked, and re-tied in a new way the field will be open to interventions of the kind we have recently seen, and the right will retain, and reinforce a strategic political advantage. If the Falklands adventure does indeed represent a rightist transformation of 'common sense' views of national identity this is the price the left will pay for its failure to address such issues. A purely oppositional, campaigning approach to international issues, necessary though it is and will always remain, cannot by itself transform the way British people see themselves, their country and its proper relation to the rest of the world. The politics of protest, and the general values to which everyone on the left subscribes, have to be incorporated into an alternative view of Britain's circumstances and future as a nation-state. The recent discussion around the European dimension of nuclear disarmament, and the challenge posed by national aspirations within the UK are among the elements from which such a conception could be constructed.

The right's solutions — oscillating between integration as a junior partner in the Atlantic alliance and spasmodic reassertions, unsuccessful at Suez, perhaps more successful in the Falklands, of a British world role — have not been without their contradictions. A sense of identity based on an imperial tradition has become more and more disjointed from the realities of a post-imperial and nuclear-armed world. As the economic situation has deteriorated it has become increasingly difficult to keep all the balls in the air; there is a fundamental gulf between British pretensions and British capabilities. This does open spaces for the left to intervene, with a coherent alternative conception.

But the condition of effective intervention, and of blocking the path to future episodes of military adventurism, is that the left must begin to think more concretely and creatively about national identity and national interests. What for example constitute the legitimate interests of a Britain engaged in progressive democratic changes along the road to socialism? What sort of military forces would be needed to protect those interests? In the absence of clear thinking about these issues the left and the labour movement will be unable to win the leadership of society, and the right will continue to paper over the cracks and to win popular support for regressive and dangerous options of the kind we are witnessing. Above all, the left has to present some hope for the future, an alternative vision which puts forward realistic ways to safeguard national independence and those real interests essential to the well-being of the British people, and hopefully also to contribute modestly to making our planet a safer place. Such a vision might evoke a response from large numbers of people who are demoralised and politically confused, but as yet the left has had little positive to say to such people. If nothing else, Thatcher's war should show us the urgency of remedying that shortcoming.

Tom Nairn

Britain's Living Legacy

The oppressors of yesterday are the saviours of today; right has become wrong and wrong right. Blood appears, indeed, to be a special elixir, for the angel of darkness has become the angel of light, before whom the people lie in the dust and adore. The stigma ... has been washed from his brow, and in its place the halo of glory rings his laurelled head.

Wilhelm Liebknecht, 5 August 1866

Liebknecht's ironic comment was made on the triumph of right wing, military Prussian nationalism. The Liberals and much of the German people had been carried away by the successes of 1864 (against Denmark) and 1866 (against Austria). Blood and iron had trampled constitutionalism underfoot. A protesting minority prophesied that Bismarck might imprint a permanently reactionary character upon the new-born German state. They were ignored.

Over a century later, one is tempted to similar irony over the oldest of bourgeois states. The United Kingdom has plunged into military adventure in its dotage. Today's Liberals, the British Labour party, have been unable to resist the fever and protest only that there must not be *too much* blood. Our female Bismarck has drummed up the national soul not to found an empire, but to bury one. As if in the grip of a death-wish, her legions pursue the spectre of 'national honour' into the Antarctic winter and a war where real victory is inconceivable.

Most detached observers have sensed something bizarre and puzzling about the spectacle. What has happened to the familiar pragmatism, the hypocritical subtlety of Britain's foreign policy? Why has Dr Jekyll vanished so utterly before this demented Mr Hyde? What reactionary disintegration of the ruling class has allowed such a perilous change — and what will the change portend for the subsequent evolution of the state? Not since the

Suez expedition of twenty-six years ago have these questions been posed; but there is little doubt that the South Atlantic War will prove more serious in its effects than the events of 1956.

The problem is to locate the adventure correctly in the old story of British decline. Libraries have been written on the latter theme. Everybody is familiar in outline with this tale of imperialists reduced to the dole queue. However, it has appeared principally as a history of graduated decay, relatively unmarked by trauma. This has been particularly true of the generation since 1945. Easy de-colonisation and the postwar boom furnished the conditions for genteel subsidence, rather than collapse or crisis: the contrast with France's torments in Algeria, Portugal in Africa, and the United States in Vietnam was obvious.

Yet there was a deceptive aspect to this transition. It distracted attention from the dark but persistent underside of British civilisation. The amusing archaic liberal-conservative regime endured all right, bringing something of the 18th century into the 20th. Apologists ascribe this to a kind of special political magic: the soul-secret of the Westminster Constitution. More realistically, one must emphasise that survival was due very largely to successful warfare. Britain's imperialism had its own peculiar formula; and within that formula, a special place – far more substantial than the regime's ideology conceded – for military and naval force.

The underpinning of British conquest consisted, above all, of naval power. Land armies were traditionally small (by continental standards) and often dispersed across the globe in a variety of minor conflicts. Hence, though the sum total of such military action was great it made little impact on metropolitan society. Was this not the essence of *la perfide Albion*, as the French saw with both exasperation and envy? The dominant empire could send its pirates anywhere, yet remain immune from militarism at home; its bourgeoisie would fight six wars at once without questioning its deeply civil ideology, or doubting that wealth was a merit-award from God.

The militaristic 'other self' was normally distanced from English civil society. At bottom such distancing corresponded to the curious, outward-directed structure of its capitalism. Originally built up through maritime plunder, this system hugely intensified its overseas investment in the later 19th century;

industry gave way to finance, as the controlling nerve of the state. The largest of navies was the outward armour of its form of accumulation, ideologised as 'Pax Britannica'. Foreigners had repeatedly to be disciplined when their egotism upset the tranquil, civilised conditions required for reliable trading.

British imperialism was directly threatened, of course, during the two world wars. However, these threats produced remarkable efforts of total socio-economic mobilisation. British government was unhindered by the stultifying military gerontocracies of the European mainland. It proved able to improvise a mass army and rapidly forge a war economy — more successfully than its main enemy Germany. The great efforts were temporary, but effective.

Great Britain was not in fact victorious in both wars because of its own mobilisation. It won through its alliances, and through its exploitation of imperial resources. But the national *myth* that has sustained Britain in the 1980s makes no such fine distinctions. It represents a psychology of undefeated superiority — a quiet, quasi-racial sense of fighting confidence. This un-militarised society has an innocent, total trust in armed force. Its army and navy are like very large pet guard dogs: normally no threat to anyone at home (indeed something of a joke) they can be relied on to eviscerate any intruder. Only by evaluating the strength of such underlying reflexes can the bewildering transformation of early April 1982 be understood: a murderous armada at sea within three days, a parliament choking with splenetic patriotism, a nation in solid support — because thrown back by the event upon a deeply familiar range of instictive attitudes.

'Decline' vanished on April 3, psychologically speaking. The obsessive problems of Britain's economic feebleness ceased to exist. The scent of righteous blood turned the most unpopular government since 1939 into a nationalist saviour, the redeemer of the British soul. Churchill's mantle has been taken from the cupboard and dusted down. Mrs Thatcher's elected *junta* of landowners, property speculators and *nouveaux philosophes* can scarcely believe its luck. Their three years of assault on the working class so easily forgiven! And American support as well! Can this be — at last — the elixir of eternal, reactionary life and power?

As well as the persistent, undamaged substratum of

imperialist ideology one must remember more recent developments. Britain's military *alter ego* has been nourished and strengthened by them. During the inexorable decline of the last forty years, an extraordinary proportion of spending has been maintained on defence. As British state power dwindled, external alliances became even more vital. They were indispensable to a capitalism so uniquely external in its interests so dependent upon a favourable trading environment. One way of securing that environment was constant over-investment in arms. Great Britain chose to be the 'good boy' of the American empire and NATO. Astronomical expenditure on the 'independent' nuclear deterrent, the British army in Germany, and the fleet served to foster a climate of suitable obligation among the allies. They were constrained to keep up in return the economic world which the City of London demanded.

Until the later 1960s the burden of this capitalist exchange of gifts was mainly economic. Mr Hyde grew in size and had plenty of toys; but by and large he stayed in his kennel to play with them. Then came Ireland. By 1970 militarism had entered the house and appropriated a guest bedroom. Anti-guerrilla warfare became permanent in Ulster. The public grew habituated to the daily diet of terror and reprisal and the exploits of 'our boys'. A monstrous apparatus of military-police surveillance and control acquired legitimacy, next door to the metropolitan territory itself.

On the left, more alert observers grew disquieted in the 1970s. Though parliamentary in outward form, the British state was also extremely secretive and unbound by any modern, formal constitution. Might not this apparatus of repression be imported from Ireland and used against civil disturbances? British socialists had been traditionally friendly to the state. They saw it as the dispenser of social services, a potential tool of anti-capitalist reforms. Rather belatedly another scenario suggested itself: the *actual* state might destroy unwelcome opposition without too much fuss and legitimise military-police tactics against 'extremism'.

Admittedly, there was often a strain of paranoia here. It was easy to say that the British ruling class possessed a powerful mode of political and cultural hegemony, and had no particular need for force. It played by Gramscian rules, so to speak — why should it abandon them now, after so much success? Only political crisis would provoke such a change, surely? The argument was a strong and reassuring one for a long time. By 1980, however, its time was up.

For 'political crisis' is exactly what began to manifest itself between 1979 and the sudden outbreak of war. Mrs Thatcher's ultra-right regime was intended as a bitter purgative for the British Disease. What it achieved was the collapse of the old political system. In the hands of her patrician clique the Conservative Party plunged into Friedmanite lunacy, determined to 'cure inflation' at the cost of any number of unemployed and any amount of bankruptcy. At the same moment an analogous movement occurred inside Labourism. Responding both to the reactionary offensive and to the shame of Labour's record in office from 1974 to 1979, the socialist left went on a determined counter-attack. Internal struggles paralysed the Labour Party for two years, and a major scission appeared. A new right wing Social Democratic Party was born with amazing speed, advertising itself as the saviour of the nation from 'extremists of both Right and Left'.

On the eve of war, everyone had become resigned to years of crisis. Polarisation seemed on the point of liquidating the ancient, leaden stability of Britain's 'two-party system'. The famous liberal-conservative 'middle ground' of consensus had gone. Even if the Social Democrats and their Liberal allies could recreate it, they would do so (as all their propaganda made clear) through drastic changes in the constitution itself. Consensus was to be imposed, in a less dramatic, civil equivalent to the reforms of the French Vth Republic. Opinions varied about what would happen after the next election. It was agreed that everything would be different, unpredictable and conflictual — perhaps even dangerously so, since no one could have much idea what would come of attempts to modernise such a venerable, cumulative edifice.

In a few days all this disappeared too — along with Britain's economic problems. Under the din of mobilisation the 'spirit of 1940' called the country to order again. Propagandists have made much of the Argentinian *junta*'s need for a cause to distract the people's attention from crisis. But the politics of distraction are not confined to fascist regimes. Though less overt, brutal and habitual the British 'crisis' is probably deeper than that facing General Galtieri. To see the conflict as one between a democracy and a tyranny is correct, but superficial: democracies too may resort to the angel of darkness and nationalist frenzy, threatening their own freedoms if the stakes are high enough.

In this case, what are they? The official justification of war is the liberty of the Falkland Islanders; restoring their 'right of self-determination' against Argentine aggression.[1] The reality is the restoration of Britain's degenerating conservative state. Such ostentatious fervour for far-away liberties, such clamorous unanimity over fascist misdeeds would in any case have been suspect, emanating from a government hitherto pallid in its endorsement of democratic rights. Their ambiguity leaps to the eye, in the circumstances described. All outside observers have discerned a degree of disproportion in Britain's reaction to the seizure of those remote islands; many dismiss it as post-imperial lunacy. Subjectively, however, the 'madness' has irresistible sense. Only the call to arms will 'pull the nation together again', 'restore the national will', arrest the escalating crisis — and give Mrs Thatcher another five years in power.

The war is a perfect recipe for restored, semi-permanent reaction. It will hammer every radical or revolutionary impulse back into the ghetto. Mr Hyde will return from the Antarctic to plant his military boots under the dining room table, occasionally cracking his whip to remind us that — formalities apart — opposition really *was* treason. The shoddy, hoary values of the old English world will be resanctified in blood. Our old philosophy of state — crowned spiritual imperialism, the exhalation of Public School and City — will be once more unchallengeable, in rough proportion to the casualty lists. Other parts of Europe have shown signs of emergence from the decade of retrogression; Great Britain will now inaugurate a new one. This last true act of empire is intended to rewrite our history, by decreeing *which* birthright will take us into the next century: the dark one of the gentlemen, monarchs and parasites, of the 'officer class' and its massive social retinue.

Genuine victories (like those of Bismarck) change historical conditions permanently for the victor. But the Tory expedition can alter nothing in that sense. Recapture of the islands would merely perpetuate the dilemma causing the conflict: colonially-founded 'sovereignty' over impossibly distant territory on someone else's continental shelf. Argentina would prepare for its

Second Malvinas War. However hostile socialists may be to *this* seizure of the Falklands — one element in the absurd petty-imperialist project of *Argentina mas grande* — they know that there is also an enduring popular nationalist wish for recovery. In the end this will be irresistible.

The point is thus underlined: 'victory' will be illusory in the South Atlantic, but *not at home*. All that matters for the moment is plain, outright resistance to this fact. The official, parliamentary opposition has crumbled into collusion with the Great-British Id: roped to the war chariot they scamper along in the dust crying 'Not so fast, be *careful!*'

Plaid Cymru is the only parliamentary party to have denounced the war from the start. However, significant sections of other parties and groups have joined them in honour, overwhelmingly on the left: Labour, the Communist Party, the SNP's Group 79, the peace and feminist movements and many others. These are the forces which after 1979 moved with increasing hope to forge a new socialist alternative strategy out of the visible crisis of the state. The war is meant to pulverize them. Marxists occasionally try to draw comfort in situations like this from the thought that, at a deeper level, the British post-imperial disease is of course incurable. At other levels, regrettably, the hands of the clock *can* be set back: each day hurls us backwards through the time locks of a decadent constitution and an archaic but virulent culture.

Wars may either conserve or explode a degenerating social order. Our ruling class, fortified by the great conserving triumphs of 1918 and 1945, has undertaken the wild gamble of a salutory repetition of them. However, such 'farces' may endure for a generation or more (as Louis Napoleon's did). The poor actors and their crass show can hold the national audience spellbound long enough. Failure would send them into the night under a hail of beer-cans; but even short-term success might mean an indefinitely long run.

The reason lies in the peculiar susceptibility of England's national idea. Distorted and over-inflated by the long, popular experience of imperialism, this state identity has been neither broken nor replaced. It has been merely wearied and puzzled by a long episode of decline and petty humiliation. Both intellectually and politically, the left has now done some groundwork for a democratic-popular alternative; but few would pretend that this has gone far enough. The malaise and uncertainty of an old order are one thing – its active overthrow by a new national-popular idea is another. In April 1982 it would probably be fair to say that the need for such change was better understood by socialists and many of them were groping towards it, away from the collaborationists of 'British Socialism'.

The *real* England is irredeemably Tory. This is the message of the South Atlantic War. The last scene of the 'Moving Right Show' strikes into the ideological viscera, moving not just the conscious sentiments but the very fundaments of collective personality to the right. So, when the parades are over, Mrs Thatcher's popularity sinks once more, the SDP-Liberal Alliance regains some ground, Labour 'pulls itself together' for the fourth or fifth time, and other signs of normality represent themselves, it will not be to the same people. The centre of gravity will have been shifted. Everything basically hopeless, class-bound, insular, irreformable and non-European about the English will be justified. Churchill, Orwell, Thatcher: these might be the joint heads on the new Falklands war-medal. Whenever political crisis does return, it will be that much more likely to find a right-wing, or at least a right-inclined, solution.

As for the break-up of Britain, the Scots and Welsh will also have much readjustment to make after the shouting. Questions of nationalism apart, no one would claim these were Tory nations. How will they respond to the consequences, should these prove a definitive turning-point – the revelation of an unalterably reactionary course in the metropolitan country? British Union has always depended upon the Whig tradition, transmitted through the Liberals or their right-wing Labour successors. We are not yet sure how much of that was shattered by the Falklands war chariot. As its dust settles the prospects for a continuing united Britain will grow clearer. A die may have been cast for future political geography, as well as for the class struggle.

[1] A number of commentators have underlined the dubious character of these liberties and rights, both in practice and in international law. In another article I suggested that the only tolerable solution to the dilemma is for the Falklands/Malvinas to be placed in suspense for an indefinite period, under a regime of externally-guaranteed autonomy, until Argentina returns to democratic rule. See *Guardian*, 3 May 1982.

IV Response and Realignment

Andrew Gamble

The Impact of the SDP

In 1981 the SDP was breaking records. It began to clear the hurdles which have halted the progress of most third parties in the past, becoming in the process far mightier than its creators. Would Shirley Williams have won Crosby for example if she had been attempting to get back into Parliament as the Labour candidate? Callaghan once dismissed talk of centre parties as 'mere fluff' and many of its opponents believed that something so unnatural and nebulous could have no serious future. SDP support they argued would melt away as quickly as it has come. Events in 1982 appeared to confirm that view.

The main basis for this belief is that, as Chris Husbands has demonstrated so clearly,[1] the vote for the SDP is less a positive vote for the new party, its policies, and its leaders, and more a vote against both the other parties – their record, their leaders, and their mode of operation. But this should give little comfort to the Labour Party. For the Labour Party would still need to ask why it is that this negative vote, on every occasion that it has appeared, should have been at the expense not only of an unpopular Conservative government but also at the expense of the Labour opposition. In periods of Labour government the unpopularity of the government has benefited the main opposition party – the Conservatives. It is a remarkable paradox of the last twenty years that despite all the fiascos of its years in office Labour has often found it harder to maintain and rebuild support when it is in opposition than when it is in government.

Much of the pre-Falklands comment on the SDP naturally concentrated on the impact it has had on the Labour Party. It was bad enough that the major opposition party should fail to benefit from the record of the most unpopular Prime Minster and the most unpopular government since the war, a government which has presided over a doubling of unemployment to three million, an unprecedented slump in manufacturing output, and serious urban riots. It was even worse that it too should be losing support to a third party, and almost in the same proportions as the Conservatives.

The most complacent and ill-founded response on the Left is to dismiss the SDP as a media creation, a conspiracy against Labour designed to avert the danger of the election of a Left Labour government. The Alliance plan to introduce proportional representation is seen as a device to exclude Labour from government permanently. As the old Labour adage puts it 'When the gentlemen of England are losing the game, they change the rules'. The implication of this view is that the SDP represents nothing of importance and that its support is therefore ephemeral. Sooner or later support for Labour will come flooding back; the conspiracy will fail. Behind this notion lies the optimistic faith that nothing can stop forever the advance of Labour and socialism, because politics in Britain is centred around class and the fundamental conflict between capital and labour. It is unthinkable that politics could be organised around anything else.

Such complacency finds little support in recent historical and theoretical analyses of the political position and political prospects of the labour movement. Two major themes in such analyses have been firstly the reasons for the failure of the Labour movement to continue the political advance it achieved in the first half of this century, and secondly the nature of the class stalemate that has prevented governments of any party successfully countering Britain's relative economic decline. The analyses are to some extent complementary, but they differ in this estimate of what is most important. One analyses the problems of Labour from the standpoint of the organisation and representation of interests, the other from the constraints on the formulation and implementation of policy.

Forward March Halted

The first argument has been advanced most forcefully by Eric Hobsbawm.[2] Labour's forward march has been halted, primarily because the movement has not adapted successfully to major historical changes that have occurred in the composition of the working class and the organisation of British capitalism.

These changes have in certain respects increased the organisational strength and the militancy of the trade unions, but there has been no corresponding increase in the political capacity of the labour movement. Indeed Hobsbawm identified popular resentment of wage militancy and union power as a major factor in explaining why support for the Labour Party has declined. The party has failed both to win votes from the one third of manual workers who have never identified with the party of their class, and to win sufficient votes from new white collar and professional groups to offset the losses caused by the shrinking proportion of manual workers in the whole working class. The establishment of the SDP represents from this perspective a further stage in the political decline of the labour movement since it means the loss of an important section of the professional and white collar workers from Labour's coalition, a section which formerly looked to Labour and must be won for Labour again if the forward march of labour is to be resumed. Labour risks becoming a trade union party rather than a broad 'people's party' with which all those who want reforms and progressive change can identify.

The second perspective does not dispute the current political weakness of the labour movement, but argues that it is largely the result of the stalemate between capital and labour which the earlier political and industrial advances of the labour movement created.[3] Labour's failure to make further political advances is paralleled by the failure of capital to reverse the gains embodied in the post-war settlement. The countervailing power which each class has been able to exercise has prevented a government of any party from tackling or successfully overcoming the relative economic decline of the British economy. This failure has caused a polarisation in both major parties and the drawing up of increasingly radical programmes. But neither party in government has yet succeeded in implementing its programme or in permanently altering the balance of class forces which that would entail. One indication of how deadlocked this situation has become is that government has changed hands repeatedly in the last twenty years. The rise of the SDP is explained from this perspective as a direct result of the latest failure – that of the Thatcher government in 1979-81. Thatcher's policies did not work as they were intended to and the Government lost considerable support, but the increasing polarisation between the two main parties was not matched by a similar polarisation in the electorate. Fear of a protracted and possibly unresolved conflict between the two class parties prompted a flight of electoral support to a third force which promises non-ideological policies and was not connected with either organised labour or organised capital. But even if this were to result in an Alliance government it is argued the class stalemate would remain and an Alliance government would be no better equipped to deal with it. Once entrusted with responsibility for policy the hollowness of the SDP's 'rational' alternative would be quickly exposed, and the government might collapse. Then polarisation might begin in earnest, leading fairly quickly to a decisive trial of strength.

Different conclusions can be drawn from these perspectives for the future of the political system. The pessimistic conclusion is that if Labour cannot rebuild its popular coalition, then the rise of the SDP could signal a major change in the axis of the political system, the disappearance of class as the major basis of political alignment, and the banishing of socialist ideas and socialist politics to the sidelines. The optimistic conclusion argues that even if in the short run Labour loses ground to the SDP, the introduction of PR and the destruction of Labourism will present a major opportunity for the development of a mass socialist politics of the Left.

What is coming to be acknowledged in discussion of the SDP is the significance of its emergence. In assessing this significance both the perspectives outlined here have their place, but it is necessary to combine their insights in order to understand the role the SDP is playing and could play in British politics. The debate suffers from viewing the rise of the SDP too exclusively from the standpoint of Labour and the problems of Labour. What needs to be done is to look at the impact of the SDP on the whole political system, and in particular its impact on the Conservative Party.

The SDP and the Tories

There is no doubt that the electoral success of the Alliance in 1981 was staggering. The individual by-election victories at Croydon NW and Crosby and the near miss at Warrington may not have achieved the greatest swings ever recorded, but unlike so many famous by-election victories in the past they were not isolated occurrences but formed part of a distinctive pattern. The Alliance for a period scored over 40% in the opinion polls and achieved that level of support in three very different constituencies, one of them a marginal. Their vote was sometimes dismissed essentially as a protest vote, a vote against the two main parties, their records, their divisions and their policies, but its scale alone made it more than that. The levels of support the Alliance received in 1981 made it a genuine third force and a genuine alternative government.

It is not surprising that the old parties began to display signs of mild hysteria. One helpful computer projection after Crosby suggested that the Conservatives might manage to hold on to one seat at the next general election. The reason why the Conservatives needed to fear the Alliance more than Labour in the short run was because the Conservatives were in government, and at that time the Government and its Prime Minister had become the most unpopular since polling began. Partly also it was because more Conservative than Labour seats appeared vulnerable to the Alliance. The dispute between the partners in the Alliance over the distribution of seats arose because the Liberals wished to contest those seats where they were strongest and had built up a strong local party organisation. Many Liberals would prefer the SDP to contest safe Labour seats where Liberals have made a negligible impact in the past. The implication is that the SDP leadership feared the current poll rating of the Alliance would not be maintained, that the Alliance would as a result capture far more Tory seats than Labour ones at the general election, and that the Liberals if they contested the most 'winnable' Tory seats would emerge as the much larger party. The SDP showed at Warrington, and in numerous local by-elections, that it could make substantial inroads into the Labour vote. But it seemed strangely reluctant to stake its future on it. The prospect of sharing in the pickings from the prospective electoral collapse to which Mrs Thatcher looked like driving the Tory Party was more attractive. The threat to the Conservatives during 1981 was undeniably serious. They had held off third party upsurges before when they were in government – particularly the Liberal revivals of 1962-4 and 1972-4. But great though the support was that the Liberals attracted and spectacular though some of the by-election victories were, the Liberals' fatal handicap was that beyond their

core vote (around 7-10% of the electorate), few voters believed
they could form a government and this both hindered the
attraction of new supporters and encouraged others to drift back
to their original party when the general election came. But the
Alliance was a much more credible alternative government –
Roy Jenkins managed at times to convey the impression that he
was Prime Minister already – so there seemed correspondingly
less reason for voters to return to the Conservatives when the
election came.

There were signs in 1981 that some Conservatives were
beginning to see the Alliance as their main opponent at the next
election. This was a prospect they might have relished for their
class but hardly for their party. For, before the Falklands War
transformed the political landscape, the Alliance would have
been immensely difficult to fight. The Conservatives would have
had to defend the Thatcher government's record. Many sections
of Conservative support in 1979 were plainly disaffected in
1981, not merely those who had suffered redundancy and
unemployment, but those skilled workers who were promised
lower taxes and rising real wages and had experienced exactly
the opposite. Thatcher's reign had created enough bitterness and
resentment to sweep away governments with much bigger
majorities.

The Conservatives' fundamental weakness in the face of the
Alliance's challenge in 1981 was because the Alliance descended
like a swarm of locusts on the Conservatives' traditional sacred
territory – the lush pastures of One Nation. The Alliance
proclaims that it alone is the truly classless party, the party that
puts nation before class, the party that is moderate and
pragmatic in pursuit of the common good, and which has no
association with any sectional interest. The Conservatives'
riposte to these claims was at first remarkably feeble. They
attempted to remind the electorate that Roy Jenkins and Shirley
Williams were really socialists who supported nationalisation
and punitive redistributive taxation when they were in office and
were prepared to protect the legal rights of the trade unions. But
the Conservatives have found it difficult to portray the SDP as
inherently socialist, just as they found it hard to use the
opportunity created by the revival of cold war ideology to brand
them as pro-Communist, hence unpatriotic, and in league with
the enemies of the country. A party which supports NATO and

the EEC as fervently as the SDP can hardly be accused of that.

For sixty years the Conservatives' stance on ideology and policy has been determined primarily by their opposition to socialism and the need to develop a strategy to contain the increasingly assertive Labour movement. The strategy they evolved was based on projecting the party as the party of One Nation, articulating certain recurring and central themes of working class experience which helped substantial sections of the working class to identify more with the Conservative Party than with the institutions and goals of the working class and its Labour movement. The appeal of the Conservatives to the working class and particularly to those sections of the class not in unions, not in work, not in large factories, and not in working class communities, was partly pragmatic — a Conservative society promised greater avenues for individual advancement and secure rewards for individual effort; partly hierarchical — the Conservatives symbolised social privilege and the established institutions of the state; and populist — the Conservative Party expressed certain widespread xenophobic, racist, sexist, and authoritarian attitudes. The party, so it claimed, understood the British people.

The Conservatives also encountered difficulty at first in responding to the SDP because they did not know what kind of party the SDP would in fact become. One wing in the SDP around Stephen Haseler and the Social Democratic Alliance, wanted the party to become a populist working class party. Its heroes are former leaders of the Labour Right, like George Brown, Ray Gunter and Bob Mellish. Such a party would be fiercely anti-intellectual and anti-socialist, and would seek to express directly what it believes is the unrepresented consensus of working class opinion, a consensus which is in favour of collectivist redistributive measures to secure workers' living standards, but strongly opposed to liberal policies on immigration and capital and corporal punishment. All this is combined with an aggressively nationalistic and pro-Western (although not pro-EEC) foreign policy.

Such a party might undermine much of the bedrock on which the Conservative working class vote has been founded and which has been so essential to the party's success. But the SDP has not become such a party. Its leaders and its new members (so many of whom have never belonged to a political party

before) overwhelmingly share the attitudes of the liberal
establishment and the liberal intelligentsia. The SDP is a high-
minded party far more influenced by John Stuart Mill than
Robert Blatchford. This would aid the Conservative Party
except that there is little chance of the Conservative Party
choosing what has for some time been their best vote-maximising
strategy and campaigning wholeheartedly for the anti-immigrant
and pro-hanging vote.[4] The party has toyed with it, and Powell in
his campaign to halt immigration showed the enormous potential
of such an open appeal. But an uninhibited populist campaign on
race and law and order would split the Tory leadership, and would
be hard to mount effectively while the party remains in
government. The Falklands factor in any case is probably more
potent.

In 1981 the Conservatives looked certain to receive a severe
mauling at the hands of the Alliance at the next election. This
opened intriguing possibilities. Most likely the party would have
survived to fight back. They have shown in every period of
opposition since the war that when they are in opposition they
act as a magnet for disaffected groups.

They still possess immense if depleted ideological resources as
the party of the established institutions of the state and civil
society. But there was also speculation that the Conservatives
might have disappeared in their present form due to the
formation of a National government, under cover of which a far-
reaching realignment of political forces would take place. A
large section of the present Conservative Party might then merge
with the SDP to form a new Conservative Party (under whatever
label) opposing the Labour Party. But once the electoral system
had been reformed several small parties on the Centre and the
Right could exist separately, combining to form a coalition
government.

The Threat to Labour

The possibility that such a reorganisation of the political system
might mean an 'American' future for British politics − the
permanent weakening of class as a basis for political alignment
and the permanent exclusion of Labour from government −
is the conclusion most strongly associated with the first

perspective discussed above.

The evidence is contradictory. Despite major social and technological changes the objective strength of the working class in Britain is still overwhelming, and has in some respects been strengthened in the last thirty years. The bulk of the class is composed of second generation workers, mobility into and out of the class is relatively low. Many skills and crafts have been eliminated, much employment in traditional manufacturing has disappeared, but this has been offset by the reduction of skills in many white collar jobs and the growth of unions in these new sectors, particularly the public sector, and amongst women workers. Most striking of all is that although the numerical dominance of the manual working class has declined, the pivotal position of Labour has increased because of the growing centralisation and interdependence of the economy. The comparison between the effect of miners' strikes in the 1920s, when there were four times as many employed in the industry as today, and miners' strikes in the 1970s has often been made. The greatest threat to this great underlying strength of the British labour movement are the twin trends of declining manufacturing output and rising unemployment, which in turn reflect the acceleration of trends towards automation of production in certain sectors and reconstitution of the industrial reserve army of the unemployed.

Politically the labour movement has proved incapable of arresting these trends or significantly influencing their impact. It is true that trade unionism saw a significant expansion in the 1960s and 1970s, which is only now being halted or reversed. It is also true that the organisation of the class remains extremely strong in many sectors; trade union organisation has been weakened but not dismantled by high unemployment. But the political strength of the labour movement in no way matches its industrial strength and importance. The major victories on pay and trade union rights in the early 1970s were not reflected in lasting political gains. The Labour government from 1974 to 1979 was as defensive as its predecessor and in several important respects prepared the ground for Thatcherism. There have been two periods of Labour government since 1951 but neither proved adequate to stop the long-term decline in the party's support. Labour's vote has fallen at every election since 1951 (except in 1966). Individual membership has fallen by at

least half, much of it the 1960s. The labour movement has
become less united than it was. Some of the fastest growing
white collar unions have not affiliated to the Labour Party.

Labour has these problems because it failed to establish itself
as the dominant party of government after 1945. What is now
so often presented as Labour's heroic period between 1945 and
1951 was not perceived in quite so flattering terms at the time,
and it ended with the ceding of the political initiative to Labour's
political opponents. Evelyn Waugh once wrote that between
1945 and 1951 the country felt as though it was under enemy
occupation. In 1951 the siege was very definitely lifted. It is true
the Labour vote remained remarkably loyal between 1945 and
1951 and was actually at its highest level ever in 1951 when
Labour lost office. But it was still below 50%. Labour had failed
to establish a dominant electoral position despite the great leap
in its support which the wartime coalition brought and despite
the mood for far-reaching egalitarian reforms and
reconstruction. Labour tried at that time to become the national
party, redefining the symbols and the goals of the political
nation, but it only had very limited success. The fundamentals of
the old order were untouched.

The penalty for this failure to translate the overwhelming
objective strength of the working class into organisational
strength and political leadership has proved heavy. For the
Conservatives returned to office failed to oblige Labour Party
expectations by cutting back welfare expenditure and
reintroducing policies of sound finance. They also took full
advantage of the great world boom in the 1950s. The Labour
Party was forced on the defensive and became unsure of its
direction. It regarded itself as the main architect of the postwar
reconstruction. This was always double-edged, because
negatively it helped identify Labour as the party of the inefficient
nationalised industries, the bureaucratic welfare services, high
taxes and controls on everything. Above all it reinforced the
party's image as the party of the trade unions. In the 1950s and
1960s Labour organised its national electoral strategy around
two main themes – the defence of the achievements of 1945 and
after 1960 the need for a sweeping programme of
modernisation. But the failure to implement the modernisation
plans has made the last two periods of Labour government most
notable for defensive management of short term crises. At least,

said Labour ministers in 1970, we have got the balance of payments right. It was about all they could say.

Its failures in office do not seem to have harmed the Labour Party too badly – at least, at the time. It is true that during the Labour governments' incompetent handling of the major sterling crises in 1966-7 and 1976 Labour support fell almost as precipitately as confidence in sterling. But in general the Labour Party in government has attracted support to itself as Her Majesty's Government governing prudently in the national interest. It is in opposition that the tension between the party as a party of the state and as a party of the working class reappears, because the balance between the party in parliament and the party in the country and in the unions is different than it is when the party is in office, and the 'anti-national' elements of Labour come to the fore. Labour at these times loses popularity and credibility primarily because the party can be associated with the trade unions and with the left.

The history of Labourism is the history of the rise of a party leadership which has sought to project itself as a national leadership, fit to take over the direction of the state as it is presently organised from the Conservatives. This has entailed the constant curbing of all those activities within the party which have attempted to identify the national interest with the class interests of the working class. The prize of political legitimacy is only conferred on parties which show themselves ready to operate within the constraints imposed by the British constitution which in turn reflects the political and institutional organisation of the British state. Only such parties appear as national parties in the conservative sense in which the political nation and national interests are defined in Britain. Widespread ignorance and passivity about politics in Britain allows ruling definitions about what is 'national' and what is 'legitimate' and what is 'patriotic' to shape popular perceptions of political events and popular ratings of political parties. The Labour Party was established not by the British state but by the trade unions and it has had a strong campaigning tradition in the past. But it has constantly been torn between operating within the state's own definitions of the 'national' and the 'legitimate' and the definitions which have come from working class experience and socialist politics. It has helped modify the former but it has also helped through the style of its politics to reinforce it, and so has been handicapped by the continuing presence of the latter. The result is that in the past fifty years the political space the Labour Party has created for socialist politics in Britain has never been secure and is now under fundamental attack. The failure of the Labour Party to relate more effectively to new social movements is symptomatic of the failure of the party to maintain itself as a radical force in British politics. It is a paradox that so many of the leading polices which the party has put forward command considerable support in the electorate, whereas support for the Labour Party has plummeted because the 'anti-national' elements were seen to be gaining ground at the expense of the 'national' elements (in particular at the Wembley Conference and during the deputy leadership campaign).

The SDP – Organisation and Ideology

The rise of the SDP relates directly to the plight of the Labour Party. All mass parties in Britain must attract working class votes. For the SDP the majority of whose leaders have come out of the Labour Party a politics that does not in some way relate directly to the working class is unthinkable. But for reasons already discussed there is little chance of the SDP emerging as a Mark II Labour Party. The SDP has no ambition whatever to be a trade union party, and no trade unions will be able to affiliate to it even if any wanted to do so. The party as yet has few people from working class origins either as members or leaders. It has attracted far more managerial and professional workers than rank-and-file trade unionists. It has begun to receive support and funds from some sections of business. The ethos of the party is strongly anti-socialist and to a lesser extent anti-collectivist and anti-union. They have had no difficulty in building up the kind of committed and loyal support which the other three parties have. Its main base may well lie among certain managerial and intellectual groups in the public sector and in the advanced technology industries. But how stable this support will prove is uncertain.

One problem for the SDP is that it is not a grass roots party. It has not come about as the expression of some new and insistent social movement. The new politics of the womens' movement, the ecological movement, the anti-nuclear movement, and local communities, are much more firmly rooted in the Liberal Party than they are in the SDP. The main issues which excite the SDP leadership are the EEC, constitutional reform, and economic management of a mixed economy. The focus of the party is on the state and the shortcomings in government policy. It does not spring from social movements outside Parliament and the existing organisation of the state. This is the reason for the now familiar contrast between the 'democratic' and 'radical' Liberal Party and the 'centralist' and 'managerial' SDP. Naturally the policy statements of the SDP leadership do not read like that. They abound with the need to widen democracy and to decentralise decision-making. But there are already considerable tensions between the desire of the leadership to keep control over policy in the hands of the parliamentary party and demands from the membership for more participation. Policies have emerged, but except in a few cases (for example incomes policy) they have been shaped more by the prestigious expert committees the party has established, than by the debates of the rank-and-file membership.

The party also lacks a clear ideological identity. One reviewer thought Shirley Williams' book *Politics for People* should be entitled 'Politics without Pain', so little did it confront the actual choices and dilemmas any SDP government would face. David Owen's book is more substantial but it is flawed by his desire to redraw the Left/Right divide in terms of centralists and decentralisers. It plainly does not work. One of its effects is to make Owen a natural ally of certain currents in the Labour Left, represented by Stuart Holland, Tony Benn, and the Institute for Workers Control, against his former allies in the Labour Right.

It is more fruitful to reflect on the issues that divide the SDP leaders from their former colleagues. Callaghan's 1981 epistle to the electorate in the *Daily Mirror* might after all be mistaken for an SDP policy statement. He expressed support for staying in the EEC, support for NATO, support for the present mixed economy. The national interest as Callaghan and Healey define it is practically identical with the way in which the SDP leadership defines it. But there is one crucial difference: the trade unions. The present leadership of the Labour Party wishes to stay within the Labour Party because it is content that the party should retain its strong links with the trade unions and should continue to protect the corporate privileges of the trade unions. The SDP leaders want a party and a government that is free of all overt entanglements with sectional interests. It wants no special relationship with the trade unions as an organised interest. It wants to project itself as a free-floating party available to serve the national interest without reservation or distraction.

The SDP has thrown off the shackles that have chained Labour to its anti-national, class origins and perspectives. It threatens permanent damage to Labour so long as the Labour Party cannot sort out whether its primary responsibility is to oppose or to sustain the state. Labour's trade union connection and its socialist constituency parties suggest the former. But the policy perspectives and commitments of the majority of its MPs and its Shadow Cabinet point to the latter. Since Labour leaders can no longer harness the two and assert the overriding importance of the party's national strategy, Labourism has been weakened. By adopting certain elements of the Conservatives' One Nation strategy the Alliance is bidding for that part of the working class constituency which the other two parties in 1981 looked like abandoning.

The SDP in Power

The rise of the SDP in 1981 has to be considered as far more than a bubble that burst in 1982. The party is playing and playing very well on one strand of the Conservative One Nation theme which has always been the key to electoral support. The SDP as a centre party is well placed to mobilise the very large numbers of electors who are not strong partisans of either party and who will vote for any party that can credibly promise less social and political conflict and greater economic prosperity. Some kind of SDP participation in government remains a possibility at some point, and its performance in government will be crucial in determining whether it holds its support or not.

If an Alliance government is elected in the next ten years, then to survive for long it must do what none of its predecessors have done; it must find a way of reversing economic decline and overcoming the obstacles to modernisation. The SDP is being careful not to arouse expectations by promising specific tax cuts or spending programmes. But the expectations it has already aroused are nonetheless enormous. What its supporters expect are policies which will reduce conflict and halt the endless crises and cycle of decline.

A fundamental argument of the second perspective, outlined at the beginning, was that the SDP's electoral task is considerably easier than its task in government. There it will find that there are few options open to it. The debate on policy takes place on terrain that Thatcher has marked out, and to which Roy Jenkins, who has some claim to be Britain's first monetarist chancellor, is no stranger. The SDP is a post-Thatcher party and the question it will have to answer is whether there is any significant alternative to the policies Thatcher has pursued. There are the alternative policies canvassed by the Tory critics of the government, but no one suggests that these, if implemented, would be much more than palliatives. They would not be sufficient either to restore full employment, or to make the economy expand again. Since an Alliance government would accept the same foreign policy commitments as the Thatcher government – NATO, EEC, and the liberal world economic order – its options are severely limited. To increase employment and output it must find ways of raising the productivity, efficiency, and profitability of British capital. The labour movement must be either coerced or cajoled into accepting a strategy which lowers wages and living standards, and cuts back all collective state services which are not sold on the market. The prospects are not encouraging. The Manpower Research Group at Warwick concluded in 1981 that there was no mix of policies which could reduce unemployment below $2\frac{1}{2}$ million by 1984. By 1983, with unemployment over 3 million and still rising and manufacturing output lower than at any time since 1967, the prospects look bleaker still. There are two main possibilities for an Alliance government within these constraints. It could pursue a bold market oriented strategy which might carry out some of the reforms to establish a social market economy which loyal Thatcherites have so far only dreamt about. Under this heading come measures not just against trade unions but against many of the social rigidities in Britain that obstruct the working of free markets. They could include action against private education and professional cartels as well as sweeping reforms of the tax system, the transfer of the ownership of all council houses to their tenants, and a change in the funding basis of all the social services, including education and health, from collective taxation to private insurance. An Alliance government might find it easier to do some of these things than a Conservative government ever would.

But the party is more likely to revive a form of modernisation strategy — selective intervention by government to raise efficiency, an incomes policy to restrain costs, and moderate reflation.

Why should such a government prove any more successful than governments which have attempted modernisation in the past? There are two main reasons why it might be. The first is the faith that Alliance supporters have in constitutional changes which the Alliance is proposing (most notably PR), which are intended to end adversary politics and create a stable, more open, and less centralised framework for the formulation and implementation of public policy. The trade unions it is argued will have to accept legislation on the statute book which no government will remove for them; capital will have to accept legislation establishing some form of industrial democracy. Policy making will be more consistent and less short term in orientation and less centralised in the hands of a small group of ministers and top officials. The ambiguity of the intentions of the Labour opposition towards business will be ended. This reduction in political uncertainty, combined with the imposition of permanent legal restraints on trade union activity and the pool of low cost labour power will bring at last the investment boom that has eluded every British government. If the Alliance retained business confidence (which Labour never managed) it might transform industrial relations.

One other ingredient is needed. No recovery is possible unless the world economy starts to improve and that is something beyond the control of any British Government. It depends greatly on the prospects for the American economy and this in turns depends on the success of the Reagan administration in carrying through its plans for increasing spending on defence, cutting spending on welfare, and cutting taxes. If it results in enormous deficits and a stagnant economy which many forecasters were predicting in 1981, then the chances of expansion elsewhere in the world economy will be greatly reduced. Such an outcome would reinforce the strong EEC federalist elements in the SDP who support common European policies to help the EEC become independent of the Americans.

Prospects for the SDP

At the beginning of 1983 support for the Alliance had fallen to 20%. To make a major impact on the next election the Alliance must poll over 30%. If all three parties were to poll over 30% then the result of the election becomes wildly unpredictable. The Swingometer has not been invented which could begin to cope with it. A first pass the post system is always arbitrary and creates anomalies, but these would multiply alarmingly if there were three powerful parties fighting every seat. It is certainly possible as some computer projections have demonstrated, that given the relative distribution of support, Labour could secure the lowest percentage of the vote and still emerge as the strongest party in seats. But really no one knows.

Whatever the outcome of the next election, the prospects for the British economy are bleak and the political consequences of relative decline continue to multiply. It is not easy to foresee when and how the stalemate will be ended. The resilience of the British economy is often underestimated. There is no reason to expect a sudden and terrifying collapse in employment and national income which would bring a decisive contest. There does still exist a space which the SDP can fill provided that world economic trends are relatively favourable. But there will be great difficulties for the SDP's attempt to inaugurate a new era of modernisation.

The Falklands War revived the Conservatives' electoral popularity. It restored some confidence in national leadership and changed many voters' perception of how the Conservatives had handled economic policy. It restored the political initiative to the Conservatives and made an Alliance Government and even Alliance participation in government after the next election much less likely. But the circumstances which gave rise to the SDP and which have threatened the Conservatives in the past have not changed, and the obstacles facing Labour in its bid to reestablish its electoral coalition as a potential national majority look formidable. At some point in the next ten years an Alliance presence in Government is possible. If the policies of such a Government were to fail, or the electoral strength of the centre resulted in deadlocked Parliaments and the paralysis of government, then the rise of the SDP may contribute to the fragmentation of political parties which will weaken political leadership and may speed the drift towards the strong state that will be needed to contain the pressures of several million unemployed and a decaying public sector. The SDP seeks to become the catalyst for significant modernisation of Britain's antiquated institutions and to breathe new life into the economy. After four years of Thatcherism the opportunity for such an alternative still existed. But its prospects of success had dwindled.

[1] Chris Husbands 'The Politics of Confusion', *Marxism Today*, February 1982.

[2] Eric Hobsbawm *The Forward March of Labour Halted?* London, 1981.

[3] One presentation of this perspective can be found in Bob Rowthorn's essay in this volume.

[4] cf Ivor Crewe and Bo Sälvik, 'Popular Attitudes and Electoral Strategy', in Z. Layton-Henry (ed), *Conservative Party Politics* London, 1980.

Stuart Hall

The 'Little Caesars' of Social Democracy

The left has for some time been in some difficulty as to how to explain or respond to the new Social Democratic-Liberal regrouping in 'the Centre'. The formation of the Council for Social Democracy (CSD), then of a Social Democratic bloc in Parliament, and finally of the SDP-Liberal Alliance, was, at one level, such a media-inspired and stimulated phenomenon, that it is hard to know how to make a realistic assessment of its electoral and political prospects. Its pragmatism, soul-searching 'good sense', the eminent 'reasonableness' of its leading figures, the agony of their hesitations, the renunciation of 'doctrinaire extremes', the rhetoric of 'novelty', are all calculated to project just that illusion of a viable centre, free of monetarist and Marxist 'dogma', dear to the centrist instincts of many sections of the press. Commentators like Peter Jenkins of the *Guardian* have been hoping and praying so long for this deliverance from the burden of Socialism, that it is impossible to know any longer whether columns like his represent sober political analyses or just more self-fulfilling prophecies. Pollsters and political analysts have been predicting the 'swing to moderation' for so long, that they might well have simply created Social Democracy themselves, if Mr Jenkins, Dr Owen or Mr Rodgers had hesitated much longer. Rarely in recent memory has a political grouping looked forward with such confidence to becoming the decisive element in a hung Parliament on the basis of so sketchy and gestural a programme. The argument is that there is a vacuum in the centre which has to be filled. The SDP has so far responded to this challenge by being as vacuous as it could possibly be.

Journals like the *Economist*, which abhors a vacuum, did rush in to provide the SDP with the programme which it so conspicuously lacked ('A Policy for Pinks', 14 February 1981). The economic part of the programme included, *inter alia*, a commitment to 'the pursuit of equality' (a fundamental ambition of social democracy) and a wealth tax. Clearly too extreme for Dr Owen, whose own recent writings have avoided the theme of equality like the plague. The polls have had to construct a hypothetical set of policies to provide their interviewees with some credible basis for responding to the question, 'Would you vote for a Social Democratic party – and, if so, why?' The results have simply compounded the confusion. An early *Sunday Times* poll suggested that the Social Democrats would attract support for (among others) the following reasons: they supported (a) more public spending on welfare, and (b) wider worker participation in industry. Neither immediately distinguishes them from their Labour and Liberal rivals. Is Social Democracy, then, just a nine days' wonder, which is not worth discussing seriously? Not necessarily. Though this doesn't mean, either, that we should take it at its own, highly-inflated self-evaluation.

For one thing, it now represents a significant re-grouping of parliamentary forces. Post-war parliamentary politics have been marked by many contradictory cross-currents. But the big parliamentary formations, and the two-party system have, despite several flutters, remained remarkably stable and durable. There have been few significant regroupings. Open splits and group defections from the Labour Party are rare, despite prolonged internecine warfare. It is fifty years since the last one. The left has more often looked like splitting off than the right, which, until recently, has maintained its dominance. Moreover, the departure of the doctrinaire right (for the SDP is nothing if not militant in its 'moderation') marks the isolating out of certain political elements which, up to now, have co-existed with other currents in the unholy mix of 'Labour Socialism'. For years Mr Crosland was the spiritual leader of the group which has now formed the SDP. But Croslandism retained links with more traditional Labour themes (eg, the strong commitment to equality of opportunity), even though he regarded them as old-fashioned. Mr Hattersley is the last representative of this current. The rest have given up on the labour movement. This represents the breaking of certain historic ties. Their appearance as an independent force thus signals a crisis and break in the system of parliamentary representation. And though such breaks do not always mark significant movements (the 'Lib-Lab' pact was more or less pure parliamentary opportunism, marking only the deep degeneration of the Callaghan government in the squalid evening of its rule), they sometimes do — as the break-up of Liberalism at the turn of the century undoubtedly did. It is hard to know, sometimes, just which conjuncture one is in. But, as Gramsci once reminded us, 'crises of representation', when 'social classes become detached from their traditional parties', and organisational forms and leaderships 'who constitute, represent and lead them are no longer recognised ... as their expression' can form part of a more general crisis of ruling class hegemony. The question, then, is whether Social Democracy is simply a new allocation of seating arrangements in the House of Commons, or part of a deeper process of the realignment of political forces. This possibility should not be dismissed as easily as it has been by the left.

Gramsci offered two reasons why such crisis of authority might arise; the most relevant being that 'the ruling class has failed in some major political undertaking for which it has requested or forcibly extracted the consent of the broad masses'. In those terms, the 'objective conditions' look remarkably favourable. For such a historic failure — to wit, the task of stemming the precipitate decline of British capitalism — is precisely what is now before us.

Both the major variants within the governing political repertoire are in some degree of trouble. The social-democratic version, in its Mark 1, corporatist form is deeply discredited: there is very little mileage left at present in neo-Keynesian demand management, corporatist bargaining and the disciplining of the working class through incomes policies. Its viability seeped away through two, long, disheartening Labour regimes. The 'radical right' alternative — the restoration of capitalist imperatives through the application of unmodified social market principles — has had many successes. Working class militancy has been dampened down by the spectre of unemployment; the country has swallowed hard and refused to veer sharply to the left at the spectre of growing unemployment; the prerogative of management has been reestablished in many sectors of big industry and savage wounds inflicted on the defensive organizations of the trade unions; anti-trade union legislation is shaping up slowly but nicely; wage settlements are down, the more militant sectors are exposed; and the return of the profitable sectors of public industry to private ownership is proceeding apace. Foreign adventures abroad and social discipline at home have kept the popular credibility of Thatcherism worryingly high.

However, in the one, essential thing that matters – the Great Economic Reversal – things have not gone the Government's way. Inflation is lower, but the dole queues refuse to diminish and the level of economic activity is bumping along the bottom showing no inclination – despite persistent rumours of a last-minute recovery –to make a significant rise.

The brutal imposition of 'cash limits' on local government has done something to save the targets on public spending; the cuts in services have made a significant contribution. Yet the struggle to contain the money supply has failed so far to record a decisive victory. The Thatcher Government thus retains most of its former industrial allies, but they and the government do not always speak with the same accents of self-confidence. The CBI has shown distinct signs of restlessness. Occasionally, those who should be the government's firmest friends – senior backbench influentials like Mr DuCann – have delivered the monetarist orthodoxies some telling body-blows. The apostle of the free market gospel – Sir Keith – has virtually retired into a stunned silence, having given away more public money to prop up failing industries than the last three or four Chancellors put to-gether. Mrs Thatcher has effectively faced-down some serious challenges from the more militant unions. And, of course, she has appeared on foreign shores, draped in the ensign of the British Empire and thereby winning many hearts and minds. But, if economic success is the ultimate test of her governorship, then the auguries remain ambiguous. Her bellicose adventurism on the world stage – exceedingly dangerous as it is in its own terms – cannot be relied on forever to divert public attention from harsh economic realities at home, even though people may be willing to support her punitive regime for the sake of its moral and ideological pay-offs, long after it has ceased to deliver any tangible economic rewards.

'Thatcherism' has certainly already succeeded in shifting the balance of social forces in the country decisively to the right. But it has failed in the second task of the great populist adventure – to flush out the social democratic vestiges within the power bloc and then reconstruct it, so as thereby to restructure society and the economy. 'Thatcherism' may have *already* filled its 'historic mission'. But neither of the major electoral machines now offer themselves as a cred:ble occupant of power at another turn of the electoral wheel. Not only is Thatcher clearly in difficulties but the Tory Party is very divided. Labour is no longer what it was: but what it is, and even more, what it will become as a result of the internal crisis which Thatcherism has provoked within its ranks, is not yet clear. Its political character is highly indeterminate. The signs are therefore well set for the 'recovery' of more centrist ground. If the Social Democrats were prepared, selectively, to reflate; to restore some version of incomes policy; and to mastermind a modest revival by ditching the struggle against inflation and ruthlessly backing private industry against the state sector, they still might not attract popular support; and there is no evidence that they would succeed in the 'historic task' any better than their rivals. But they *could* look like another — the last? — viable political alternative. And they *could* secure powerful support 'from above', amongst all those forces currently detaching themselves from the Thatcher path to the brink. They are British capitalism's last political ditch.

This makes Social Democracy a powerful pole of attraction of a cross-party coalitionist type — the 'exceptional' alternative towards which, since the Lloyd George coalition, the British political system has tended to veer in moments of severe crisis (remember MacDonald, and Mr Heath's 'Grand National Coalition'?). This does not guarantee it popular support. But here there may be other trends which strengthen its case. There is what political scientists have been calling the 'growing electoral volatility' of the British voters. Between 1945 and 1970, each of the two major parties polled over 40% of the votes at general elections. Their electoral base seemed reasonably secure. But in the 1970s, their share of the vote has fallen significantly. Party identification has weakened, votes have become more fluid. No administration has gone its full term and then succeeded in being re-elected. The old rotation of parties in power has continued: but on an increasingly weak base. This now finds supporting evidence in the findings of the polls that a hypothetical Social Democratic-Liberal alliance would attract a significant proportion of 'floating' and fed-up voters in about equal numbers from both Labour and the Conservatives. The scenario then goes, that they would form the decisive bloc in a divided Parliament. Electoral reform would become the principal political bargaining point. Proportional representation would then destroy the hegemony of the two-party system forever, and secure a permanent majority for 'the Centre'.

The trajectory is certainly clear, even if the scenario is less convincing. Mrs Thatcher may make Royal Progresses; but the two-party political *system* is in deep disrepute. Her popularity may well reflect the fact that she appears to transcend it, with her appeal to Nation and People above 'party', and is prepared to destroy it in order to reconstruct it. But people do sense that we are at or near the limit of the present political arrangements and dispositions. Yet the meaning of this phenomenon is hard to interpret. The political scientists and polling fraternity explain it in one way. Here, at last, appears the 'true' voter: less traditional in political alignments, unattached to dogma and doctrine, rationally calculating political choices on a purely pragmatic, non-ideological, non-class basis: 'Economic Man' in the polling booth – the great pluralist dream. It confirms the wished-for break-up of the class structure of British political culture. And it is said to 'prove' that the true heart of the political system and of the 'British voter' lies in the Centre. Rationality and Moderation have fallen into each other's arms.

This is more self-fulfilling prophecy than hard political analysis. The interpretation of a natural gravitation in British politics to 'the Centre', eschewing all extremes, would make more sense if the parties had represented over the decades the spectacle of alternating extremes. But, until recently, judged in terms of real strategies rather than ideological polemics and stage-managed caricatures, both parties have long struggled precisely to occupy this mythical 'middle ground', provided by a capital-led mixed economy, incomes policy, neo-Keynesianism and corporatism. The social-democratic consensus has been the base-line from which *both* sides have attempted to govern, and to which, in the end, even adventurists like Mr Heath (in his 'Selsdon Man' period) were ultimately driven back. It is the failure, precisely, of the *Centre*, old-style, and the steady erosion of its repertoire of crisis-management, which has provoked successive movements in recent years towards more extreme alternatives. It is the collapse and bankruptcy of 'the Centre' which generated increasing pressure towards these extremes. And if the revival of the left within the Labour Party is one way of inheriting this collapse, it has been much more evident on and towards *the Right*. First, the populist undercurrents of 'Powellism'; then Mr Heath's boom-or-bust excursion, before the miners and the U-turn; then the formation of the Keith Joseph 'Adam Smith' kitchen cabinet; finally — as it became clear that the doctrines of Hayek and Friedman would need to connect with the reactionary instincts of the Tory backwoods — the formation, radical offensive and electoral success of the 'Thatcher party'. This progressive abandonment of 'the Centre' has taken place for the best of all possible reasons: it failed. Things got worse, not better, under its increasingly weak and nerveless leadership. This suggests that the increasing volatility of the electorate is best explained, not in terms of the natural and inevitable gravitation of British politics to the 'middle ground', but because of the manifest inability of the two variants of consensus of politics to stem the tide of British economic disintegration and progressive deindustrialisation. 'Because the ruling class has failed in some major political undertaking for which it has requested, or forcibly extracted, the consent of the broad masses ...'

What's more, the evidence from the movement of public opinion suggests, not the permanence and stability of 'centrist' ideas, but a steady gravitation towards the extreme right. An unpublished paper on movements in public opinion by Tony Fitzgerald has shown that, among voters strongly indentifying with Labour, support for more nationalisation, more spending on social services, retaining Labour's links with the trade unions and sympathy with strikers all fell between the 1960s and the 1970s. Support among the same sections for the sale of council houses, keeping the grammar schools, cutting government spending, cutting profits tax, and strengthening law and order and immigration control have all swung significantly in Mrs Thatcher's direction. Manual workers who are also Labour supporters and trade unionists showed markedly higher shifts of opinion — again in this direction, than other groups — long before the very significant swing to the right in 1979 which brought the most radical-right government of the post-war period to office. This is particularly strong in the area of the Thatcherite populist issues — anti-unions, anti-statism, anti-welfare. When these are placed alongside the cluster of issues which Crewe and others have called 'Populist Authoritarian' — the so-called 'moral' issues of race, law and order, private initiative and self-reliance, where even Labour supporters, strongly pro-Labour on other issues, suddenly become explicitly 'Thatcherite' – the evidence of a natural gravitation to centrist politics is thin. The underlying movement is undoubtedly rightwards. Lack of faith in the two major parties may, therefore, draw people in desperation towards a middle-ground alternative. But not because this is where the natural fulcrum of the British voter permanently and inevitably comes to rest. Social Democracy must occupy 'the Centre' because it is *there*. Besides, that is where *they are*. But their strongest card will not be the promise to 'restore the Centre', but the vaguer threat to 'break the political mould'. In so doing, they inherit, not the mantle of Attlee, but the legacy of Mrs Thatcher – for, though they may deflect it in a different direction, that is what she promised too. Whether it is possible to 'break the mould' *and* 'return to the Centre' at the same time is the particular card trick or sleight-of-hand on which the fortunes of Dr Owen, Mr Rodgers, Mrs Williams and Mr Jenkins (a 'breaker of moulds'?) now depend.

What, then, is its real political character and content? The break with 'Labour socialism', however muted in some instances, is real and deep. It is a final break with the historic Labour-trade union connection. This is mounted as firmly on the back of the 'trade-unions-are-too-powerful' crusade as anything in Mrs Thatcher's vocabulary, though it is less virulently put. It is also a break with even a residual connection to working class politics – even the rudimentary form in which this is still acknowledged by the traditional Labour right – 'Labour as the party of the working class in government'. At this level, Social Democracy is thoroughly managerialist in its political style. It will have no organised political base – only the 'detached voter' combined with a power-base in parliamentary rule. It is 'for' democracy – in so far as this highlights the undemocratic nature of British trade unionism; and especially in so far as it means (or meant) 'one-man-one-vote' for the Labour leadership, and the total independence of the parliamentary party from democratic accountability. This is nothing positively new, since for both the press and for Mrs Thatcher, 'democracy' only *works* when it allows the 'silent majority' to out-vote the left. In earlier days, the Social Democrats were the group within the Gaitskell orbit most prepared to put its democratic conscience into permanent cold storage so long as the trade union block vote delivered the right result to the right. It is deeply and passionately hostile to every manifestation of the left. The media have signally failed to bring out that the single, most important factor which precipitated the final break was the very thought that non-Labour trade unionists might somehow be able to exert an indirect influence over the leadership election – and I don't think it was the Federation of Conservative Trade Unionists they had most in mind!

On the economic front, it is the party of 'incomes policy' in the classic sense: i.e., as an instrument with which to discipline the demands of labour and restore them to their rightful position – led by the overriding imperatives of capitalist profitability and competitiveness. Neo-Keynesian in their sympathy for reflation, the Social Democrats are nevertheless as committed as Mrs Thatcher and Sir Keith are to the leadership of big industrial capital and the play of market forces. That is what they mean by a 'mixed economy'. They emerge as the only, true EEC 'party' – not even in the robust sense of Mr Heath, blowing the cold wind of European competition through the cobwebbed boardrooms of British industry: more as an article of faith. The unity through competition of free-market capitalisms is what they mean by 'Internationalism'. 'A socialist who works constructively within the framework of a mixed economy' is the image to which Dr Owen recently aspired. His reference points – Sweden, Austria, West Germany and Holland. His memorable dates – the assimilation of the German SPD to reformism at the Bad Godesberg meeting in 1959, and the overturning of the 1960 Labour Conference decision for unilateralism. Which 'moulds' are likely to be broken by these ancient instruments is something of a mystery.

Despite its cavilling at the cost of Trident, Social Democracy is fervent in its support for NATO and the Western shield. Indeed, in being less committed to the British independent deterrent, it is likely to be more suppliant to Washington's grand Alliance strategy than even its Labour predecessors. The Social Democrats, in the week of the Thatcher-Reagan resumption of the role of world policemen, and amidst the talk of NATO Retaliatory Forces and offensive Cold War postures, did not allow themselves to blink an eye at what precisely this loyal subordination to NATO strategy promises to become under the

Regan-Thatcher hegemony. Instead, they chose to open their parliamentary career by taking Labour to the cleaners about its wobbling indecisiveness over unilateralism.

This may look, when pieced together, like a *very* ancient and familiar concoction. The *novelty* appears to lie in the terminology with which their politics of the Centre is verbally glossed. Despite their commitment to 'the new', the Social Democrats have failed to identify a single new political constituency around a single new issue. Feminism is a good case in point, where a strong, vigorous and radical movement has developed, to which the traditional political cultures of both the established left and the right are deeply inhospitable. If *any* organised force were in a position to disconnect the feminist movement and women from the left, and to articulate a limited version of feminist demands to a 'new' kind of political programme, Social Democracy ought to be. One or two public figures have indeed given this as their principal reason for evacuating the left for centre ground with embarrassing speed. But it must be said that this is more in the eye of the beholders than it is anywhere evident in the political complexion of the new Centre. Apart from offering the person of Mrs Williams to fortune, Social Democracy has not made a single gesture towards attracting this new social force. It gives every appearance of not knowing it exists and of not knowing how or where to identify and address it, if it did. Indeed, despite the promise of nationwide campaigns and local groups, Social Democracy is at present totally devoid of any single vestige of popular politics or popular mobilisation. It is exclusively and doctrinally attached to the prospects of 'politics from above'.

The only single gesture in this direction is in the fulsome talk about 'participatory democracy'. This is Social Democracy's way of attempting to colonise the growth of anti-corporatism, anti-statism which has been one of the principal forms of popular alienation from Labour. Here, like Thatcherism before it, Social Democracy is indeed working on a real contradiction. Labour-in-power became the means, not for generating a decisive shift of wealth and power towards the popular classes, but a mode of representing the popular classes 'in government' — which, in conditions of recession, rapidly became a means of disciplining popular demands from above. The corporatist triangle is now, and rightly, seen as a directive style of political management – directed against the people, while at the same time incorporating them through their representatives. This has consolidated the Big State *over* the people – an identity which Mrs Thatcher was quick to exploit. This is a contradiction within the very heart of Labourism, with its deep parliamentary constitutionalism, its conception of the state as a neutral instrument of reform, its inexplicable belief that Labour governments can *both* 'represent working class interests' *and* manage capitalism without something giving, and, above all, its fear and suspicion of popular democratic politics in any form. Mrs Thatcher exploited this identity between Labour and the state to considerable advantage. By 1979, Labour seemed much the same as Big Brother, much involved in pushing people around to no visible effect; while Mrs Thatcher was the populist champion of 'the people' *against* the power bloc: a pretty remarkable reversal.

Social Democracy is gunning for the same space. But whereas Thatcherism sought to master the antagonism between 'people' and 'power bloc', transforming it, at a critical point, into a populist movement for National Unity around the new social market programme – bearing Mrs Thatcher, at the same time, *into* the power bloc – Social Democracy hopes to exacerbate the contradiction and transform it through the programme of 'participatory democracy', and 'decentralisation'. Dr Owen and Co are doctrinaire 'decentralisers'. This new doctrine circles around the same themes: the 'bureaucratic centralisers, the corporatists who now dominate British socialism, the mood of authoritarianism ... the state ... seen as the main instrument of reform' (David Owen, 'Power To The People', *Sunday Times*, 25 January 1981). It operates on the same dichotomies: liberty versus equality. Like Mrs Thatcher, and against the long socialist tradition, it privileges liberty over equality. In this sense, it belongs firmly within a much longer process – that of bending and articulating liberalism (and liberal political economy) to the conservative rather than the radical pole. Authoritarianism and the state as an instrument of reform, Dr Owen argues, has not been 'counterbalanced' by a 'libertarian streak'. But whereas Thatcherism, detaching 'liberty' and 'equality', connects it with *authority* ('Free Market' – liberty: Strong State – authority); Social Democracy deflects it towards a third pole, in its struggle to win space from the left. Not authority but – Fraternity: 'the sense of fellowship, co-operation, neighbourliness, community and citizenship'. The authentic centrist, cross-class, coalitionist code-words. Participation gives people a feeling of belonging. Decentralisation gives them the illusion of real power. 'Small is beautiful' is a popular slogan in the era of state capitalism. There is no question but that, somewhere in this space, Socialism has long since ceased to operate – to its profound cost. It has deeply lost its popular, anti-power bloc, democratic vision. There is space, after all, here – as the enemies of socialism in both the right and the centre know well.

But 'participation' without democracy, without democratic mobilisation is a fake solution. 'Decentralisation' which creates no authentic, alternative sources of real popular power, which mobilises no one, and which entails no break-up of the existing power centres and no real shift in the balance of power, is an illusion. It is a *transformist* solution. It conflates the unthinkable with the improbable – all the while giving the strong illusion of 'moving forwards'. Transformism is the authentic programme of the moderate left in a period of progressive political polarisation along class lines. Its function is to dismantle the beginnings of popular democratic struggle, to neutralise a popular rupture, and to absorb these elements passively, into a compromise programme. Its true novelty is that it conflates the historic programmes of the classic, fundamental parties of the left and the right. It is the restoration of the old through the appearance of constructing something new: 'revolution' without a revolution. Passive revolution 'from above' (i.e., Parliament). Gramsci noted two aspects of the programme of 'transformism' which are apposite to our case. The moment when 'individual political figures formed by the democratic opposition parties are incorporated individually into the conservative-moderate political class': and the moment when 'entire groups of leftists pass over into the moderate camp'. We are entering the second.

Since the break-up of the great Liberal formation in the early years of this century, the British political system has shown an increasing tendency, in periods of crisis, to turn to Caesarist solution. 'Caesarism' is a type of *compromise* political solution, generated from above, in conditions where the fundamental forces in conflict so nearly balance one another that neither seems able to defeat the other, or to rule and establish a durable hegemony. Gramsci reminds us that 'Caesarist solutions' can exist without 'any great "heroic" and representative personality' – though in the earlier period there were indeed contenders for this role 'above party and class'. But, he adds, 'The parliamentary system has also provided a mechanism for such compromise solutions. The 'Labour' governments of MacDonald were to a certain degree solutions of this kind ... Every coalition government is a first stage of Caesarism ...,' The Social Democrats are our 'little Caesars'.

In a period when the discipline of unemployment is sending a shiver of realism through the labour movement, it may seem over-optimistic to argue that we now confront a situation of stalemate between the fundamental classes. Yet this does once more seem to be the case. Thatcherism lacks the economic space or the political clout to impose a terminal defeat on the labour movement. The working class and its allies are so deep in corporate defensive strength that they continue to provide the limit to Thatcherism despite their current state of disorganisation. Irresistible force meets the immovable object. On the other hand, the labour movement lacks the organisation, strategy, programme or political will to rule. So far it has failed to act as the magnet for new social forces, thereby itself embracing new fronts of struggle and aspiration. It still shows no major sign of reversing its own long decline. Such statements are ready-made for the appearance of grand compromise.

Whether this is a solution which can more than temporarily stem the tide, remains to be seen. Sometimes 'Caesarism' is only a temporary staving off of deeper currents. Sometimes it can lead, through successive variations, to the formation of a new type of state. More often, it is 'an evolution of the same type along unbroken lines'. This is certainly not to say that it cannot temporarily succeed; or that, having succeeded in winning electoral support, it will not (as Thatcherism has done before it) have *real effects* in preventing that reshaping of the left and of socialism which alone can provide a real alternative – permitting, instead, Labour to recompose itself along familiar lines. A Labour government, succeeding to its third rotation in power, under such conditions, would certainly neutralise socialism for a very long time to come. That, after all, maybe be what Social Democracy is *really* about.

Jon Bloomfield

Labour's Long Haul

Introduction

In the last few years tumultuous events have been reshaping the
British left. A combination of strains and contradictions within
the Labour Party's broad church exploded in the aftermath of
Labour's 1979 electoral defeat. Sharp policy differences;
protracted and bitter conflict over internal constitutional
reforms; close contests in the leadership and deputy leadership
elections, and the most significant defections from Labour's
ranks since the party's foundation all indicate the turmoil that
has been affecting the left. In a relatively short period the Social
Democratic Party, in alliance with the Liberals, has emerged to
pose a formidable electoral and political threat to Labour's
prospects of renewed government office. During a period of
harsh Conservative rule, there have been few signs of a halt in
Labour's electoral decline. This article considers how the
different trends in the Labour Party have been responding to this
situation: how they propose to deal with the economic and
social crisis which shapes the political scene; how they viewed
the question of inner-party reform; and most importantly, how
they intend to equip the party to win a political majority in the
country for progressive and leftward advance.

Historical Survey

Historically Labour has never been a socialist party. The
impulse behind the trade unions' decision to establish the
Labour Representation Committee was to obtain a voice for the
interests of organised labour in Parliament. This would help to
fend off the increasing harassment of unions by the courts.
Socialists were in a clear minority in the federation of unions
and political societies which emerged from the founding

conference in 1900. Defence of working class rights, radical liberalism and strict adherence to parliamentary norms were the major features of the new body.

The increased strength and impact of the working class movement before and during the First World War necessitated a revision and modernisation of the Labour Party for it to become a party of government. This came with the new constitution agreed in 1918 and operative until the 1980 Blackpool conference. Influenced heavily by the Webbs, its famous Clause 4 is commonly regarded as the touchstone of the party's socialism. However, the political bargain struck over the constitution was rather different in intention. Its basic structure reinforced the party's parliamentarianism and reformism. The cohesion of the party was achieved by a strict division of labour between the industrial and political wings of the movement, guaranteeing the unions and Parliamentary Labour Party (PLP) autonomy in their own affairs. Individual membership organised into Constituency Labour Parties (CLPs) was adopted, but these were seen as electoral cannon fodder with no influence on policy. As Richard Crossman perceptively expressed it:

> since it could not afford, like its opponents to maintain a large army of paid party workers, the Labour Party required militants – politically conscious socialists – to do the work of organising the constituencies. But since these militants tended to be 'extremists' a constitution was needed which maintained their enthusiasm by apparently creating a full party democracy while excluding them from effective power. Hence the concession in principle of sovereign powers to the delegates at the annual conference and the removal in practice of most of this sovereignty through the trade union block vote on the one hand and the complete independence of the PLP on the other.[1]

This has proved a very durable arrangement. Predictions that the Labour Party would split have been frequently made and just as frequently confounded. It is a measure of the depth of the present crisis that these long-standing agreements and arrangements have been thrown into disarray. Yet the deep bonds which bind the different sections into one party remain. The left and right may feel that the extreme elements of their opponents have no place in the party, but they generally realise that, as a federal party, Labour has always contained a wide range of views within it. For most, this 'broad church' is seen as an asset.[2] What remains uncertain after the recent upheavals is where the centre of gravity in this broad church will lie.

Labour's Crisis

There are three interrelated components to Labour's crisis which are examined here (a fourth, that of finance, will not be investigated). They are: the uncertainty and division over what policies to adopt in the face of the collapse of the post-war Keynesian boom and Britain's precipitate economic and social decline; the widespread demands for an overhaul of the party's constitutional arrangements; and finally the issue of how the party can regain its lost electoral support and become a political force that is attractive to the British people.

Labour's Response to Britain's Crisis

The Labour Party has lost its political direction and moral vision. The image of 1945 briefly flickered with Harold Wilson's promise of 'the white hot heat of the technological revolution' in 1964. The promise faded away with the first signs that the post-war boom was faltering. Servile obedience to the International Monetary Fund and corporate management to smooth out the bumps of Britain's swift industrial and social decline were the remedies offered by the Wilson and Callaghan governments. The bitter confrontation and disillusion expressed in the dispute of the 1978-9 winter were symptomatic of a deeper malaise. The political credibility of Labour's traditional post-war programme — full employment and public expenditure — had been undermined. Thatcherism stepped into the vacuum.

The Labour Party is not finding it easy to come to terms with this failure and to counteract aspects of Thatcherism's populist appeal. Not surprisingly, since it was primarily the failure of their programme, Labour's right and centre-right has found this self-critical appraisal hardest of all.

Certainly, Jim Callaghan when leading Labour's centre-right offered little new. His recipe of a tepid Keynesianism combined with an incomes policy is echoed by Healey, although it should be noted that this marks a shift from their policy in office, when they introduced the monetarist measures now being pursued so vigorously by the Tories. The centre-right look to the trade union leaderships to stave off the left's challenge and reach agreement on economic policy based on traditional lines.

There has hardly been an ideological ferment on basic economic issues in Labour's broad and amorphous centre.

An increased commitment to public intervention in industry combined with varied degrees of import protection and devaluation are inadequate measures to confront the country's catastrophic industrial decline. Peter Shore, Michael Foot and John Silkin are silent on the bureaucratic management of the nationalised industries and welfare services. People's subsequent disenchantment with these has been turned to the Tories' advantage. On this matter, Labour's centre has said nothing of note.

A hankering for a return to the prescriptions of 1945 still dominates their outlook. However, in a number of areas there have been signs of flexibility, innovation and radicalisation. For example, there seems to be a much firmer commitment to combat racism and a more critical attitude towards police behaviour. In this respect Roy Hattersley cuts a very different figure as Shadow Home Secretary from that of Merlyn Rees. Indeed Hattersley is most illustrative of the essentially social democratic Labour politician who has been forced to reassess and redefine his political position by the emergence of the SDP and who has adopted a more radical posture on social issues as a result. Thus it would be rash to presume that Labour's centre and centre-right are incapable of policy renewal. Indeed Foot has made a most significant policy contribution by making nuclear disarmament the central plank of his platform. Whatever contradictions, compromises and confusions exist on the policy, the core of the Labour Party has now adopted a clear stance of opposition to the siting and purchase of a new generation of nuclear missiles in this country. Labour's centre has now associated itself with the growing peace movement. This represents a most significant shift and offers Labour some of its most favourable ground for challenging Thatcherism.

The Labour Left

On the policy and strategy issues the main initiatives have come from the Labour left. They have begun to construct a much more systematic programme, combining immediate alternative policies with socialist vision and threaded by a consistent emphasis on democracy. In contrast to previous movements of the Labour left there has been a welcome, if not universal, tendency to break from rhetoric and woolly generalisation. Much more rigorous analysis is being attempted. This is evident on the economic front where Stuart Holland and others have tried to give a clear focus to the alternative strategy. Robin Cook has done likewise on defence. Aspects of the state apparatus, a notorious achilles heel of the Labour left, have been scrutinised with Michael Meacher raising the issue of police powers and Brian Sedgemore the role of Whitehall and the civil service. Combined with deeper researched, broader and more imaginative perspectives, sections of the Labour left have expressed a firm commitment to extra-parliamentary struggle. Peter Hain and Audrey Wise have declared this most forcibly.[3] This is a departure from the traditional left's parliamentarianism and reflects a growing recognition that policy and campaigning activity are interconnected.

It is because of this that the left are paying more serious attention to organisation. While Tribune groups are being slowly established in some regions, the main initiative has come from the Labour Co-ordinating Committee (LCC). They are emerging as a new left-wing focus, seeking to build a political base in both the constituencies and trade unions. Their readiness to debate and take on the far left in a 'Debate of the Decade' is symptomatic of a growing ideological and political confidence, although with the left's setbacks in 1982 unwelcome and harmful fragmentation and divisions began to occur.

At the centre of these Labour left initiatives is the figure of Tony Benn, a politician whose own experience in the 1964-70 Labour government led him to recognise the inadequacies of traditional social democracy. During the 1970s he emerged as an authentic leader of the left, a role of crystallised and emphasised by the enormous impact of the 1981 Deputy Leadership contest against Dennis Healey.

The renewal of policy being undertaken by the Labour left is very significant, although many weaknesses remain. This is especially true of strategic issues. While Benn expresses the most advanced strands of Labour left thinking, some of his limitations were starkly revealed in his discussion with Eric

Hobsbawm. When pressed, Benn was unable to outline a political strategy for the achievement of democratic socialism, while his grasp of newer democratic movements was patently limited. These are not personal lapses. The concept of the transition to socialism as a revolutionary process, decisively affected by mass popular struggles, is generally absent from Labour left thinking, while the dismissal of social movements or the attempt to reduce them to Labour Party support groups is commonplace. Hence, for example, the widespread incomprehension of the Women's Liberation Movement found among Labour's left. Nowhere have they been able to integrate their perspectives into the kind of strategic programme represented by the *British Road to Socialism*. While the Communist Party is not finding the practical implementation of that strategy easy, it can justly, if modestly, argue that it represents the best overall socialist strategy that has been outlined to date.

By taking the initiative on the policy issues the Labour left has gained increased support, especially among the constituency activists. The extent to which these views are held by the ordinary, individual member is much less certain, a point which the left frequently dismisses of overlooks. A number of large trade unions, notably NUPE and TGWU, have played an important role in these developments encouraging the Labour Party to adopt key aspects of the alternative economic and social strategy.

However, serious shortcomings still exist on all these policy issues. So far the left has made little effort to give a precise democratic and feminist content to the alternative economic and social strategy. Without specific proposals for public ownership and a welfare state 'of a new type' with genuine industrial democracy and consumer participation, the chances of winning popular support are considerably diminished. Similarly, an inability to incorporate a feminist dimension to the strategy will restrict the left's appeal to women. Such a democratic transfusion into the alternative strategy faces the formidable obstacles of trade union ambivalence towards industrial democracy, Labour's traditional preference for bureaucratic collectivism and a deep-rooted sexism.

Support for a genuinely radical alternative strategy still remains to be won in the party as a whole. As the centre-right

counter-offensive got underway from mid-1981, the impetus
behind these policy shifts weakened, aside from the disarmament
issue where the momentum was largely generated outside the
party by the success of CND. The indications are that many
positive elements of the alternative economic and social strategy
will be neutralised prior to the publication of the Labour election
manifesto. While most of the policy initiatives have come from the
left, their inability to win general acceptance throughout the trade
union movement has meant that the centre and centre-right
remain predominant.

Constitutional Reform

While there have been sharp policy disagreements, the terrain on
which political differences have been fought most fiercely since
1979 has been that of constitutional reform. The party's political
crisis brought its constitutional arrangements into question.
There had been an uneasy tension on occasion between the
annual conference and the parliamentary leadership under both
Gaitskell and Wilson. In 1978 Callaghan brought the issue to a
head when he disregarded the conference's rejection of his
government's 5% pay norm. He then aggravated the tension by
assuming unilateral control over Labour's 1979 election
manifesto.

There had also been long-standing dissatisfaction about the
behaviour and attitude of some Labour MPs in safe seats. This
came to a head with the Prentice affair. The effect of these
events was to crystallise a three part constitutional reform
package: the mandatory reselection of MPs once in every
parliament; the party's National Executive to have ultimate
control over the election manifesto; and an electoral college
composed of all sections of the party to elect the party leader.
The Campaign for Labour Party Democracy (CLPD) gained an
enormous groundswell of support for these reform proposals.
They gave expression to the deep resentment of many party
members at the callous disregard for their views and hard work
by many Labour MPs and past Labour governments. The
reform package threatened the apparatus of right-wing
domination, enshrined in the sovereignty of the PLP, which the
Webbs had so carefully engineered. Hence the ferocity with
which the struggle was – and continues to be – fought.

At the 1979 conference mandatory reselection of MPs and national executive control over the manifesto were passed, while the proposal for an electoral college was defeated. The significance of these decisions was diminished because the conference set up a commission of inquiry to investigate all aspects of the party's internal life, including constitutional affairs. The idea of a far-reaching commission had been spawned by David Basnett in the Trade Unions for a Labour Victory. Whatever the genuine union concern about the party's depleted organisation and finances, objectively the commission was a device by which Callaghan, supported by Michael Foot, sought to stall the left's advance and halt the reforms.

The right organised a concerted political attack, making extensive use of their supporters in Fleet Street and the media. Callaghan had assumed the mantle of Gaitskell at the 1979 conference when he declared, 'I affirm the independence of the parliamentary party and of the Labour government ... at the end of the day they must take the decisions'. He paid detailed attention to swinging union leaderships to his side, placing high hopes of the AUEW. The Shadow Cabinet and the majority of the PLP pressed for changes in the compositions of the Commission of Inquiry. The right started to accuse the left of totalitarian intentions. Callaghan issued lurid warning of East European dictatorships.[4]

The vehemence and breadth of this onslaught placed the left on the defensive. The wrangle over the composition of the Commission created the impression that what was at stake was primarily a factional inner-party battle not a dispute over democratic reform. The right, readily aided by the media, re-raised the issue of Militant's role in the Labour Party to smear the left's democratic credentials. Reg Underhill, a veteran right-winger in the party bureaucracy, played the issue to full effect asking for his collection of documents to be published. The reality of Militant, its strategy and organisation, as a Trotksyist entryist organisation is widely known. A clear political statement by the National Executive while opposing any moves for expulsion could have defused the issue. Yet by ducking the problem the Executive cast doubt on its own leadership, while it stored up difficulties for the future, as the right exploited the genuine unease felt by many party members at the activities of entryist groups. The left was to pay heavily for this opportunism in 1982 as the revived right-wing again exploited the issue for a general attack on the left.

Although on the defensive, the momentum of the reform movement was not to be halted, even though support among the unions was uneven. Overall, the unions seemed divided on the reforms with the CLPs heavily in favour. The submissions to the Commission indicate this:[5]

	NEC Control of Manifesto		Mandatory Reselection		Electoral college	
	Yes	No	Yes	No	Yes	No
CLPs	190	7	133	4	124	13
Trade Unions	7	7	4	4	4	5

Despite their onslaught, the supporters of the status quo had gravely miscalculated. They underestimated the depth and strength of the reform movement and the momentum it had built up. The centre-rights response was to manoeuvre and resist. Only Basnett with his suggestion of a new institution – a Council of Labour – to elect the leader and supervise the manifesto, offered a specific, even if conservative, proposal for reform. The rest offered no change, while Callaghan directed his energies to swinging union leaderships. His pragmatism came unstuck. Jim failed to fix it. At Blackpool the chickens came home to roost in a classic lesson for those who place organisation above politics.

Despite shifting the AUEW vote, mandatory reselection was carried by 3,798,000 to 3,341,000. As expected the 1979 decision for national executive control of the manifesto was reversed, but by a narrower margin than anticipated with 3,508,000 for and 3,625,000 against. The major change came in the decision to alter the method of electing the party leader. The principle of an electoral college was agreed by 3,609,000 to 3,511,000. In January 1981, at the subsequent Wembley conference convened specially to decide on the college's format, a division of 40% to the trade unions and 30% each to the CLPs and PLP was narrowly agreed.

The structure of Labour's constitution had been dented. For

the first time in over six decades the division of labour and responsibility enshrined in the Webbs' constitution had been undermined. Mandatory reselection gives those who run the party more leverage over MPs. The electoral college opens up the possibility of collective class involvement in the parliamentary process. Despite the shortcomings evident in the deputy leadership contest between Benn and Healey, it was a much more democratic election than that in which Labour MPs alone elected Foot in preference to Healey. Even on the manifesto it is most unlikely that any future Labour leader will be able to operate a unilateral veto in the manner of his or her predecessors. Above all, there is likely to be a closer correspondence between what the party agrees and what it actually does in office. The reforms are an attempt to revitalise parliamentary democracy and to counter the widespread public cynicism about politicians by making Labour's actions in government square up to its electoral promises. This is not to deny that a new arrangement insulating the PLP under the centre-right's hegemony may yet be worked out. Indeed, the left's own parliamentarianism has led it to make exaggerated claims for the reforms, presuming that socialist policies will be enacted once there is 'an accountable leadership'.[6] The task of constructing an electoral and political majority for such policies remains daunting. It is here that we find the Labour left at its weakest.

Winning the People

Even in its heyday the Labour Party has never been a mobiliser of the working class. With the reforms and promise of the 1945 government it did achieve a mass membership peaking at over a million in 1952. As the reforming spirit of Labour waned and as the character of politics altered with the advent of electioneering by television, so the membership and activity of the party went into long term decline. *Labour Weekly* estimated individual membership for 1981 to be just over 300,000, while Labour's share of the vote in the 1979 election at 36.9% was its lowest since 1931. Its consistently poor, and occasionally appalling showing at subsequent by-elections has served to confirm the party's serious plight. The defection of over a score of Labour MPs to form the SDP has cast further doubt over Labour's electoral prospects. The precise character and scope of the SDP's challenge to Labour is still uncertain.

In its initial euphoria it seemed to appeal to a large section of that middle strata which had traditionally voted Labour since 1945, as well as to parts of the skilled and younger working class. However, Labour's vigorous opposition to an escalation of the nuclear arms race may have reduced these defections. While predictions in this area are rash it is evident that the SDP's emergence has made Labour's task of reversing its decline and recreating a wide base of popular support both more difficult and ever more urgent.

For the centre and right the remedy is straightforward. Halt the internal debate — or 'bickering' as it is pejoratively termed — rally round the leadership and project 'common sense' policies to revive the economy and public services. By avoiding any whiff of 'extremism' Labour would squeeze the SDP from the much-vaunted 'middle ground' and benefit from a natural revulsion at Tory monetarist policies.

To the left the woeful inadequacy of this scenario is very clear. What remains less evident is the character of the left's own response to Labour's plight. Some sections of the fundamentalist left, along with the Trotskyist groups, want the removal of all non-socialists from the Labour Party. In effect, they want the break up of Labour's broad church, and its transformation into a genuine socialist party, no matter what the cost in electoral terms or potential loss of trade union affiliation.[7] Other sections of the left associated with Tribunite figures like Neil Kinnock and Joan Lestor wish to preserve the gains which have been achieved and are fearful of the electoral and political consequences of further internal debate. They overestimate both the progress which the left has achieved and their ability to influence Michael Foot.

A one-sided interpretation of Eric Hobsbawm's seminal article *The Forward March of Labour Halted?*[8] has been used to justify their cautious approach. However, a more balanced interpretation leads to the third and most fruitful option open to the left. This approach recognises that left-wing alternatives to social democratic solutions will only dominate the Labour Party to the degree to which they have support within the working class and its allies as a whole. Labour cannot be transformed in isolation from the people. This makes the generation of class and popular struggles in alliance with other political, national and democratic movements the Labour left's primary task. The extent to which this is effectively achieved by socialists inside and outside the Labour Party will determine where the new centre of political gravity will lie within the Labour Party. This option offers a strategy of struggle and transformation which gives the left the possibility of achieving hegemony within a broadly-based party, with trade union affiliations and some electoral potential. There are some indications that this is the path which many of Labour's left intend to pursue. To succeed they will have to challenge some of the suffocating practices of Labourism.

The Weaknesses of Labourism

The first of these is the electoralism of ward branches and constituency parties. The task of electoral foot-soldiers ascribed to the CLPs in the Webbs' constitution remains the predominant characteristic of Labour Party life. The month-by-month existence of ward and constituency parties revolves around elections, formulating policy for elections and passing resolutions which place demands on parliamentary or council representatives. This kind of politics is debilitating and breeds passivity. While a minority of CLPs are encouraging involvement and campaigning with extra-parliamentary struggles, this break from electoralism is still very limited.

This is clearly related to a second debilitating Labourist characteristic, that of an opportunist and predatory attitude to popular movements. The Labour left is unable to comprehend the role of these movements, their broad non-party political character and their autonomy. The only relationship they have so far suggested is the organisational one of affiliation, an ill-thought out attempt to repeat the historically specific relationship between the trade unions and the Labour Party. The traditional Labour left response to these movements is to argue that the problems they are concerned with can only be solved by the election of a Labour council/government. The role of building popular movements and struggles is relegated behind vote-catching, yet a serious and sustained commitment to such movements is essential if the Labour left wishes to gain extensive grassroots support and build a solid, socialist base amongst the people.

In turn this requires a willingness to work with other parties in these movements on an equal footing and with no special privileges. This the Labour Party refuses to do, not just with the Communist Party but with larger parties as well. For example in Scotland they would not join in an anti-EEC campaign with the Scottish Nationalists in 1975 and were reluctant to work with the SNP and Liberals for devolution. On the progressive issues which it supports, the Labour Party seeks a party political monopoly. To help sustain this the left is willing to support a palpably undemocratic electoral system. Arthur Scargill is a rare notable Labour left proponent of proportional representation. The bulk of the Labour left collude in the dangerous fallacy that a Labour government elected by a minority of the people could undertake a radical, socialist programme. It needs to be stated unequivocally that the success of a new type of Labour government requires an electoral and political majority in the country. There are no short-cuts.

A mass membership activist-oriented Labour Party will play a major part in achieving this. A popular socialist movement depends on hundreds of thousands willing to engage in political activity and join political parties. Individual members who attend meetings, read literature, collect dues, support workers in dispute, go on demonstrations, hand out leaflets and go canvassing: these are a party's life-blood. As elsewhere it is these people who make the Labour Party tick. They ensure its survival and are its main hope for the future.

Revitalising Labour's base not only requires shedding its electoralist practices but also transforming the role of the individual member in decision-making. The Webbs' constitution deliberately excluded the constituency member and his/her local party from any influence. At present, at the annual conference, trade union votes outnumber the CLPs by nearly 10-1. The TGWU, AUEW and GMWU each cast more votes than all the CLPs. A mass active membership can only be built up if the members and the CLPs have a *direct* and substantial say in policy formulation and decision-making at all levels. This confronts the left with the trade union question.

The Labour Party and the Trade Unions

The unions affiliate to the Labour Party on the basis of the number of members who pay the political levy. This was a source of controversy within the party until 1946, and promises to become so again. A reversal to 'contracting in' is one of the punitive suggestions recently aired by the SDP. It has been taken up avidly by Mr Tebbit as one of a series of measures by which he hopes to nullify the organising, campaigning and political influence of the trade unions. After the General Strike the Tory government passed the Trades Disputes Act which forced trade unionists to 'contract in' if they wished to pay the political levy. As a result affiliated membership dropped by 3/8ths. In 1946 the Labour government reversed the position. The levy was paid automatically unless unionists declared they wanted to 'contract out'. After the passage of the Act affiliated membership rose from 2,635,346 to 4,386,074. In the engineering union the percentage paying the levy jumped from 24.6% to 82.1%. These figures indicate that a considerable proportion of the affiliated membership was dependent on relatively passive rather than active political commitment.

The same is still true. Seven major unions record over 90% of their members pay the levy. The TGWU figure is over 96%.[9] At the last election large chunks of the unionised working class voted Tory, Liberal or did not vote at all. It is impossible for these not to have included unionists paying the political levy to the Labour Party.

The limited political commitment represented by affiliation is further reflected by the low level of branch affiliations to CLPs and poor representation on their management committees. The official Commission of Inquiry confirmed that this weakness of affiliated involvement is a common feature.[10] The contradiction between trade union predominance at the top levels of the party and its relative weakness at the grassroots has rarely been sharper. It expresses both the depth of Labour's crisis and a more general and serious decline in working class politics.

A reversal of Labour's decline requires a reinvigoration of the affiliated membership. That won't be easy. Fundamental differences exist between the affiliated and individual membership. Taken at large, the latter have greater political understanding and commitment, assume more party responsibilities and pay a lot more cash. The reinvigoration of the affiliated membership is primarily dependent upon a popular, socialist renewal inside the Labour Party and outside its ranks as well. A broader politicisation of the working class would create the atmosphere and framework for renewed affiliated involvement.

The trade unions' role within the Labour Party is welcomed and valued by the vast majority of the left. The specific character of the party largely revolves around this institutional connection. It provides an organic relationship with the working class, whose interests Labour is meant to represent. Labour's future cannot be separated from its trade union connections.

It is precisely because they wish to cripple the Labour Party that both the SDP and the Conservatives have presented proposals to restrict and fracture this connection. What does require examination, as the LCC and others have suggested, is the specific internal form this relationship takes.

It is a serious weakness that the Labour left, especially in the trade unions, has not faced up squarely to the imbalance in voting strength within the party. They did when it came to an electoral college. Supporters of this reform proposed a variety of formulae giving different weight to unions, MPs and CLPs to ensure that each had a say in the election. None of the trade union supporters of the reform suggested direct election by a simple conference vote. The clear implication is that they oppose complete union domination of the leadership election. The same considerations logically apply to the conference. A shift in the relative voting strengths at the conference would be entirely consistent with the left's demands for all the rank and file, consituency as well as trade union, to have a significant say in policy formulation. Without this reform the resentment and aggravation already evident in the CLPs at their lack of power will persist along with the difficulty of building a mass membership.

*   *   *

Clearly a long haul lies ahead for the Labour left in transforming its party. The heavy stamp of Labourism permeates the party's structures and practices. This may slowly change in the next few years but there will be no overnight transformation; instead, it must be recognised that some of the problems are inherent in the very nature of the Labour Party. Its federal character inhibits its ability to generate mass movements. Even when it had a left NEC the Labour Party took no initiative comparable to that of the Communist Party in the fight against the Industrial Relations Act and the People's March for Jobs, or the Socialist Workers Party in the creation of the Anti-Nazi League. Its federal structure hinders its capacity to mobilise. Furthermore, this federalism inevitably spawns an endless variety of ideologies. This 'broad church' has drawbacks which are usually ignored by the left. It is often an unrealistic formula to evade issues or cover fundamental differences. It also affects the left's own thinking giving rise to the strategic shortcomings discussed previously. In recognising the strengths of a federal party, the complementary loss of ideological cohesion and direction must also be taken into account.

The Left Outside the Labour Party

It is precisely these limitations which raise the issue of the role of the left outside the Labour Party. Some argue that the key need is to develop an organisational relationship with the Labour Party forthwith. The options here are threefold. One can either maintain one's organisation secretly and affiliate individually in the manner of Militant – a course which the IMG has recently pursued. This is both dishonest and manipulative. Alternatively one can dissolve one's organisation and focus around a journal like *Tribune*. Eric Heffer declared that this is what the Communist Party should do.[11] For the Communist Party this would involve a serious loss of political cohesion, organisation and campaigning ability. Thirdly, one can try to affiliate openly as a socialist political party retaining one's own organisation but bound by the rules of the Labour Party. This suggestion is more honest but is both a political non-starter and a historical anachronism. The precise character of the Labour Party at its formation in 1900 cannot be recreated. The introduction of individual membership and CLPs after 1918 qualitatively altered the nature of the party. They took over the original function and role of the political societies, which now exercise minimal influence on Labour Party affairs. In these circumstances, with individual membership freely available, to ask for affiliation is to ask for special rights as a party within a party, and will inevitably be rejected.

More generally, this primacy which some place on an organisational relationship with the Labour Party is misguided. There are large and clear political spaces on the British left waiting to be filled. There are opportunities for the Communist Party and others to take. Briefly stated, the left urgently needs a party which sees its main priorities as the development of mass struggles on the issues of unemployment, peace, democratic rights, anti-racism and women's liberation, the encouragement of links and alliances between these struggles and movements in a non-opportunist manner, and the application of Marxist analysis and organisation to these struggles, along with the stimulation of extensive Marxist discussion and debate. A growing capacity for the Communist Party and other forces on the left to undertake this type of work is an indispensable complement to the positive developments within the Labour Party.

Conclusion

In the aftermath of its electoral defeat in May 1979 the battle to shift Labour to the left captured the imagination and enthusiasm of thousands of socialists both inside and outside the Labour Party. High hopes were expressed that this was the occasion to move the party irrevocably in a socialist direction. In the process there was a dangerous tendency to ignore the wider political trends moving against the labour movement and focus all attention and energy on the internal struggle.

A combination of external and internal factors from mid-1981 onwards brought this somewhat illusory period to an end. While the SDP showed its electoral threat, Labour's centre-right in the PLP and the trade unions declared its intention to stay and fight the left. They rallied round the Foot-Healey leadership to minimise their policy losses and hamper further left advance. Two things became clear. Under the impact of its threefold crisis labour had splintered but was not going to split. However, in the short term, neither was it going to shift dramatically to the left.

Yet it needs to recognise that its immediate priority is to defeat the present Conservative government whose monetarist, militarist and authoritarian policies threaten to undermine the achievements and institutions of the welfare state and Labourism. Thatcherite rule to the end of the decade would be a disaster for working people and for *all* sections of the labour movement. A protracted, arduous task lies before the entire left in swinging the people away from Thatcherism and onto a road of democratic, peaceful advance. It can be achieved, provided the left blends its socialist vision with realistic estimates of the present political situation and there is the utmost unity and co-operation among all the progressive forces and movements.

[1] R.H.S. Crossman, Introduction to W. Bagehot, *The English Constitution,* London 1963, pp.41-42.

[2] See, for example, Tony Benn, *Tribune*, 11 May 1979.

[3] For Hain, see his pamphlet *Refreshing the Parts*, Nottingham 1980; for Wise, see her speech in *The Debate of the Decade*, London 1980.

[4] At a National Executive meeting, July 1979.

[5] Reported in *Tribune*, 20 June 1980.

[6] Chris Mullin, *Tribune*, 11 May 1979; see also Ian Mikardo, *Tribune*, 28 September 1979.

[7] See, for example, Tariq Ali's interview, *New Statesman*, 11 December 1981 and Robin Blackburn, *Marxism Today*, January 1982.

[8] Reproduced in Eric Hobsbawm et al, *The Forward March of Labour Halted?*, London 1981.

[9] C. Maple, *Tribune*, 1 June 1979.

[10] Commission of Inquiry Report, point 11, section 2.

[11] *Labour Weekly*, 28 September 1979.

Notes on Contributors

Michael Bleaney, Lecturer in Economics at the University of Nottingham, is the author of *Underconsumption Theories* (1976).

Jon Bloomfield, author of *Passive Revolution: Politics and the Czechoslovak Working Class 1945-1948* (1979) teaches at the University of East Anglia.

David Currie is Professor of Economics at Queen Mary College, University of London, and a contributor to *Marxism Today* and specialist journals.

Andrew Gamble contributes regularly to *Marxism Today*; he is author of *The Conservative Nation* (1974) and *Britain in Decline* (1981), and is Reader in the Department of Political Theory and Institutions at the University of Sheffield.

Jean Gardiner, Lecturer in the Department of Adult Education at Leeds University, is a member of *Marxism Today*'s Editorial Board; she is also, with Sam Aaronovitch and Ron Smith, author of *The Political Economy of British Capitalism* (1981).

Ian Gough teaches in the Department of Social Administration at Manchester University, and is author of *The Political Economy of the Welfare State* (1979).

Robert Gray is Senior Lecturer in Social History at Portsmouth Polytechnic, and author of *The Labour Aristocracy in Victorian Edinburgh* (1976) and *The Aristocracy of Labour in 19th Century Britain* (1981).

Stuart Hall is Professor of Sociology at the Open University, and co-author of *Resistance Through Rituals* (1976) and *Policing the Crisis* (1978).

Eric Hobsbawm is Emeritus Professor at Birkbeck College, London University; amongst his books are *Bandits* (1969), *The Age of Revolution* (1962) and, with George Rudé, *Captain Swing* (1969).

Steve Iliffe is a Doctor in General Practice working for the NHS; a member of *Medicine in Society*'s Editorial Committee, he is author of *The NHS: A Picture of Health?* (1983).

Martin Jacques is Editor of *Marxism Today* and co-editor of *The Forward March of Labour Halted?* (1981).

Martin Kettle is a journalist; he is co-author, with Lucy Hodges, of a study of the 1981 urban riots, *Uprising!* (1982).

Tony Lane, author of *The Union Makes Us Strong* (1974), teaches in the Department of Sociology at the University of Liverpool.

Tom Nairn is a member of *New Left Review*'s Editorial Committee and an editor of *The Bulletin of Scottish Politics*; he is author of *The Break Up of Britain* (1977).

Bob Rowthorn won the Isaac Deutscher Memorial Prize for *Capitalism, Conflict and Inflation* (1980); Lecturer in Economics at the University of Cambridge, he is on the Editorial Boards of *Marxism Today* and *New Left Review*.

Lynne Segal teaches psychology at Middlesex Polytechnic; she is a co-author of *Beyond the Fragments* (1979) and editor of *What is to be Done About the Family?* (1983).

Index